AI is going to change the sales and marketing landscape immeasurably. This well-researched and clearly written book makes sure you don't get left behind.
Tabitha Goldstaub, Chair, Government AI Council

Katie King gives a lucid and engaging account that is ideal for non-technical professionals working in this field, setting out how AI has rapidly developed into an essential component of effective marketing and communications.
Roger Taylor, Chair, Centre for Data Ethics and Innovation

AI is disrupting markets globally and raising critical questions about values and ethics in business. This book provides an incredibly useful and comprehensive survey of the current best thinking on the progress and application of artificial intelligence, especially within marcomms but more widely too. Katie King has created an invaluable reference work for anyone who wants to find out about AI's global progress in a single volume.
Dr Jeremy Silver, Chair, Catapult Network, CEO, Digital Catapult

AI poses the most fundamental structural challenges of our era. Many changes will be highly positive and will constitute a revolution in how the world works. This book by the world's leading sales and marketing AI thinker, Katie King, sets out the opportunities and the pitfalls in the most comprehensive analysis I have ever seen. If you're thinking about the future, read this book.
Francis Ingham, Director General, PRCA, Chief Executive, ICCO

AI Strategy for Sales and Marketing captures today's world of data science and the essential skills for marketers to embrace new technologies. I recommend that marketers and influencers get a copy of this book and explore new ways to connect with consumers through AI. Think about creating new-age, augmented reality experiences with apps, curating numerous content with the power of AI, and so much more.
Loth Makuza, Co-Founder and President, Public Relations Society of Tanzania (PRST)

This book contains practical and actionable checklists for sales and marketing executives to align AI strategies with real business outcomes. Katie King has an engaging style that helps readers build a business case and roadmap for AI for all industries.
Peggy Tsai, Chief Data Officer, BigID

We have now entered the AI era with almost all industries expected to be impacted by AI – 'marketing' included – but the reality is only a handful really understand what it means, how it works or how it can be applied. Is a must-read if you want to stay at the forefront of marketing technology.
Alvin Foo, Co-Founder, NASDEX

A fascinating read on the application of AI in business with two critical business functions. It's also interesting to read about creating responsible AI for future applications of the technology. An excellent and well-thought-out book well worth a solid read.
James Rees, Managing Director, Razorthorn

In this exhaustive book, Katie King captures trends of AI and their impact on automotive, retail, finance and other sectors. She explains how to not be threatened by AI but how to use it to your advantage. Anyone interested in the impact of AI should read this book.
Martin Musiol, Data Science Manager, IBM

The book binds how the sales and marketing teams can leverage the AI products being built. It covers how the economics of building these solutions look and how the personas can focus on the business impact. It gives a good overview of different industries working on their AI solutions and how they drive customer experience. One of my favourite sections in the book is driving AI success with trustworthy methods. A must-read for technical and business leaders in the AI space.
Aishwarya Srinivasan, AI and ML Innovation Leader, IBM

AI Strategy for Sales and Marketing

Connecting marketing,
sales and customer experience

Katie King

Valeria

So great to meet you
in Toronto at
the Banking summit.
Enjoy the
book.

Katie

KoganPage

Sep 18 23

First published in Great Britain and the United States in 2022 by Kogan Page Limited

2nd Floor, 45 Gee Street
London
EC1V 3RS
United Kingdom
www.koganpage.com

8 W 38th Street, Suite 902
New York, NY 10018
USA

4737/23 Ansari Road
Daryaganj
New Delhi 110002
India

Kogan Page books are printed on paper from sustainable forests.

ISBNs

Hardback   978 1 3986 0202 1
Paperback 978 1 3986 0200 7
Ebook   978 1 3986 0201 4

British Library Cataloguing-in-Publication Data

A CIP record for this book is available from the British Library.

Library of Congress Cataloging-in-Publication Data

Names: King, Katie, 1967-author.
Title: AI strategy for sales and marketing: connecting marketing, sales
    and customer experience / Katie King.
Description: London; New York, NY: Kogan Page Inc, 2022. | Includes
    bibliographical references and index.
Identifiers: LCCN 2021049071 (print) | LCCN 2021049072 (ebook) | ISBN
    9781398602007 (paperback) | ISBN 9781398602021 (hardback) | ISBN
    9781398602014 (ebook)
Subjects: LCSH: Marketing–Technological innovations. |
    Selling–Technological innovations. | Artificial intelligence. |
    Customer relations.
Classification: LCC HF5415 .K521995 2022 (print) | LCC HF5415 (ebook) |
    DDC 658.800285/63–dc23/eng/20211018
LC record available at https://lccn.loc.gov/2021049071
LC ebook record available at https://lccn.loc.gov/2021049072

Typeset by Integra Software Services, Pondicherry
Print production managed by Jellyfish
Printed and bound by CPI Group (UK) Ltd, Croydon, CR0 4YY

CONTENTS

03 How AI is reshaping the world of retail and hospitality 71

04 Driving change in the automotive and manufacturing sectors 97

05 Optimizing AI data insights in finance, law and insurance 113

06 Revolutionizing customer support in the telecoms sector 145

07 New economic model for the robot revolution 173

ABOUT THE AUTHOR

Katie King is a leading business transformation consultant, with a consultancy career spanning 30 years. Katie is an accomplished keynote speaker and coach. She is a frequent commentator on BBC television and radio, and has delivered two TEDx presentations.

During her career, Katie has advised many of the world's leading global brands including Virgin, NatWest, BT, Accenture, Huawei and many more. Katie is CEO of AI in Business, and founder of digital marketing agency Zoodikers.

She has an MBA and a degree in languages, as well as a Diploma in Marketing. Katie is married with two daughters, Scarlett and Chrissy, and now lives with her husband, Terry, in East Sussex.

Katie's first book was published by Kogan Page in 2019: *Using Artificial Intelligence in Marketing – How to Harness AI and Maintain the Competitive Edge*.

ACKNOWLEDGEMENTS

To my incredible, indispensable colleague Ashley Przybyla, who has worked tirelessly to help bring this book to life during a difficult year of lockdown.

To Kogan Page, for believing in me for a second time.

To the wonderful contributors to this book whose sage advice and necessary words of warning lend further credibility and global interest in my work.

To my English A level teachers, Mr Anthony McNamara and Mrs Mary Jeniec, who inspired me beyond words and gave me the confidence to write.

01

AI and the future of work and society

New business imperatives for tomorrow's leaders

Optimism for innovation that benefits society and business

In this opening chapter, we will explore the much-anticipated dawn of a new era of technological optimism and innovation. We will reflect pragmatically on consumer need and desire for artificial intelligence (AI) services and products, as opposed to pure tech innovation. We will learn how, worldwide, the steady marathon pace has quickened into a sprint, encouraged by the rapid adoption of digital technology during the world-changing COVID-19 pandemic. We will compare different global AI strategies, reviewing progress across patents filed, and the funding available to business. We will also consider the impact of AI on the core business functions of marketing, sales and customer experience (CX) – an analysis that will be carried through across all of the subsequent chapters.

In 2021, we witnessed and wondered at the dramatic role played by AI in accelerating life-saving COVID-19 vaccine development, and spawning widespread business improvements across digital payments and telemedicine. Up until that point, it was growing increasingly difficult for many to grasp the business impact of AI, given how underwhelming the hyped pace of innovation had actually been. This oft-cited adage seems more pertinent than ever: 'Most people overestimate what they can achieve in a year and underestimate what they can achieve in ten years' (Farnam Street, 2019).

Driverless vehicle technology had promised much, but failed to deliver, while the malign impacts of social media, bound in data privacy and consent issues, severely damaged public opinion. Hailed by Amazon founder Jeff Bezos, AI had remained in the realm of science fiction for longer than many expected. Now in existence for over 75 years, it is yet to see true mainstream adoption. Over this period, AI has gloried in various cycles of excessive hype. Each of these phases was immediately followed by extended periods of disillusionment at enterprises worldwide: the so-called AI winters. However, a bright AI summer may be finally upon us, proving, as philosopher Plato taught us, that necessity is indeed the mother of invention. A number of crucial societal advancements, borne out of pandemic adversity, are clear indicators that the golden age of AI is finally beginning to surface. It is fascinating to note that innovation has always flourished during times of deep economic turmoil or prolonged world conflicts. A deep dive into the patents filed in the past 250 years reveals that the biggest surge in inventions came during the Great Depression.

Roaring twenties

Echoing this trend, it is now becoming clear that AI's impact on society and on business will be transformative, as befitting a fourth industrial revolution. *The Economist* predicts a 'roaring Twenties' but cautions that predictions of a technological Utopia could be overblown (The Economist Leaders, 2021). In the last decade, AI bounced back into prominence and has seen remarkable advances in techniques such as deep learning. It is now firmly back in vogue, with billions of venture capital dollars spurning AI start-ups globally. However, questions still remain as to whether it will be adopted mainstream this time or if it will slip into hibernation yet again. We will explore why, despite sizable business investment and giddy expectations, it has not yet been fully commercialized.

What is undisputed is that COVID-19 broke through cultural and technological barriers that had previously prevented remote work, setting in motion a structural shift in the location of work, at least for some people. The subsequent digital acceleration turned the tide for AI, making data more freely available and forcing leadership teams to plan for continued disruption.

Some uses of AI were more necessary than others. The Apple Watch takes advantage of AI to detect when users are washing their hands. The feature can detect handwashing motions and sounds, using a 20-second countdown timer to ensure that hands are cleansed effectively. It can also notify users who have not washed their hands within minutes of returning home.

Business value from AI will continue to increase in the coming years. The pandemic has created the right conditions for businesses to realize the importance of AI, prioritize efforts to move AI to production, and ensure organization-wide adoption. McKinsey's '2020 State of AI' survey (Balakrishnan *et al*, 2020) found that over 50 per cent of companies have adopted AI in at least one business function. Many companies reported that AI was creating an impact by generating revenue and reducing costs for those functions. Over the coming chapters we will explore, in great detail, how AI is reshaping business functions such as marketing, sales and customer experience (CX), and how sectors as diverse as telecommunications, education, retail, manufacturing, shipping, banking and professional services are faring.

The impact of machine learning

Let's turn now to one of the most exciting subsets of AI – machine learning (ML), which has been gaining traction because of its widespread applications that range from self-driving cars and fraud detection, to image recognition. One in ten enterprises uses multiple ML applications, proving that its algorithms and techniques are efficiently solving complex real-world problems. As IDC's research indicates, ML will transform every sector of industry, as worldwide spending on AI doubles to $110 billion in 2024 (IDC, 2020). It appears to be a realistic estimate, when you take into account the fact that 88 per cent of US organizations scaled up their use of AI during the 2020 pandemic.

Similar positive forecasts can be found in PwC's annual 'AI Predictions' survey (Likens *et al*, 2021), which explores the activities and attitudes of US business and technology executives involved in their organization's AI strategies. Predictions for 2021 and beyond revealed that a quarter of the companies participating reported widespread adoption of AI, up from 18 per cent in the previous year. Another 54 per cent were predicted to be heading there fast. It is encouraging to learn that organizations were no longer just laying foundations. Many were reaping actual rewards from AI, in part because AI proved to be a highly effective response to the challenges brought about by the pandemic.

Customer focus: smart marketing

Thanks to Korean giant Samsung Electronics, we are moving closer to the world I envisaged in my first TEDx talk, delivered in my home town of Tottenham, North London, in January 2015. It is a world featuring innovative new home appliances that can help automate daily tasks. At CES 2021, Las Vegas – a show renowned for being the global stage for innovation – Samsung unveiled its JetBot 90 AI+, which boasts smart technologies that optimize its cleaning route and respond to its environment. The company's Smart Dial Front Load washing machines and dryers also use AI to learn user preferences and recommend optimal washing and drying cycles. As I predicted – and still yearn for – such AI-infused home appliance innovations are intended to make life easier by reducing chores and giving families back cherished time.

In order for AI to move mainstream, meeting such customer needs must remain top of the agenda. This is expressed by Patrick Bangert, VP of AI at Samsung SDS America:

> Many business verticals will increasingly depend upon AI both to meet the ever-evolving expectations of the consumer as well as driving their own bottom line by lowering cost with automation – which is what a lot of AI practically amounts to. For late adopters, the next few years will be the last chance to adopt AI and remain competitive. For early adopters who have reaped the low-hanging fruits, AI will continue to drive their business through new business models, more direct consumer relationships and generating new insights.

Smart home devices have taken off over the past few years, with exciting products coming to the market. For example, many utilities providers have started to offer smart solutions that use AI and ML to monitor energy use and optimize supply. These devices monitor the way your household uses these resources and help tailor billing to ensure you are not overpaying. Smart thermostats such as those offered by Ecobee or Nest boast advanced temperature, humidity, ambient light and activity sensors, while others take it a step further and learn from your use habits to create a schedule by which the device will automatically control the climate settings in the home. Robot vacuum cleaners are no new feat, but over the years these devices have been upgraded with smart technology that allows them to learn the layout of your home over time for smarter navigation. 'Smart plug' devices also allow you to control your lights, television, or other electronics with just the sound of your voice. When you are away from home, you can entrust its security to the wide range of intelligent home security solutions available on the market, ranging from smart door locks to whole-home solutions that actively monitor the property for threats.

The personalized experience

Even if you have not yet invested in smart home devices, there is undoubtedly more AI in your home than you may realize. This might comprise Amazon Echo, Apple HomePod, or Google Home devices. Or if you are subscribed to a streaming service, such as Netflix, its algorithms analyse the content you watch or add to your watchlist in order to recommend other films or shows you may enjoy. Similarly, music streaming services like Spotify or Apple Music monitor your listening habits and inform the creation of tailored playlists or stations. All of this is made possible by ML applications that get smarter the more we interact with them, resulting in a hyper-personalized experience. These amazing gadgets and applications have made our home lives more comfortable, efficient, safe and enjoyable, but what about when we venture outside the home?

Driving change

Autonomous driving technology continued to mature in 2020, with the industry's leading companies testing driverless cars and opening up robotaxi services to the public in various cities. Fully automated driving, which enables rides without a human safety driver on board, will be necessary for the scalability and commercialization of autonomous driving. In 2020, China's Baidu became the first company in China to start robotaxi trial operations in multiple cities as it launched the Apollo Go Robotaxi service.

Grocery delivery robots have also been rolled out on the UK's streets, following a partnership between the Co-op and Starship Technologies – which was launched by two Skype co-founders. Co-op is the first convenience retailer to offer same-day robot deliveries in the UK, and has ambitious plans to deploy 300 of the robots by the end of 2021.

Commenting in *The Herald*, Scotland, Chris Conway, Co-op head of ecommerce, said: 'We continue to look for new ways to innovate and expand access to our products and services to deliver a truly compelling offer for consumers. Our partnership with Starship enables Co-op to offer further availability, flexibility and choice to meet community shopping needs for on-demand convenience.' (Press Association, 2020)

Residents use the Starship app to shop for a range of 1,000 items, the most popular being milk, eggs, bread, bananas and cucumber. Staff pick the order and place it in the robot. Users drop a 'pin' where they want their delivery to be sent and can watch in real time as the robot makes its journey via an interactive map. When the robot arrives, the customer receives an alert, and then can unlock the robot through the app, giving them access to their shopping.

A small window of opportunity

If you have ever flown long haul, the plane you were on was probably powered by Rolls-Royce engines. Sitting quietly behind the success of each engine's operation is a fabric of sensors, data and then AI, working silently on trillions of data points each year to keep each unit in tip-top shape. This Engine Health Monitoring was unique and disruptive in the marketplace, differentiating Rolls-Royce products and allowing them to provide new data-driven services and value to customers.

In recent years, Rolls-Royce has deepened its focus on AI and developed a framework that governs AI adoption in manufacturing functions, which we will explore in more depth in Chapter 4. Another area of expertise for Rolls-Royce is differentiation. The company's engines are found in vehicles that now occupy a prestigious corner of the automotive market and have earned a reputation for their quality and luxury. Many innovators in the AI space face the same challenge. In a market cluttered with new solutions and shiny tools, and with more competitors entering each day, it is becoming increasingly difficult for companies to gain a foothold.

Caroline Gorski is Group Director for Rolls-Royce's tech-focused arm – R2 Data Labs. Here she provides insight into how to achieve differentiation in the AI goldrush:

> Every business wants to be able to have a degree of commercial differentiation. They want a bigger market. They want to be able to attract new customers. They want to be able to produce goods or services that command a better price, or they want to be able to operate more efficiently. A key question to ask is: 'Where can I derive commercial differentiation from AI?' To understand this, you have to consider the structure of the AI market. The reality is that quite

a lot of things in the AI market are unlikely to remain differentiating for very long because almost all of the modelling is either open source or comes from the academic domain. So it's broadly shared. There are lots of interesting novel things, but for an industrial player like Rolls-Royce, there is very little to wrap your arms around and define as exclusively yours. This is either because the algorithms and the techniques are better when they are built in collaboration and therefore aren't uniquely owned, or because you are applying them in such a way that you would uniquely marry them to such a tight domain.

You only have a relatively short window of opportunity so if you can either invest to get access to the best compute, or have relationships with academic institutions or national governments to give you access to the best compute, then you can move a bit faster. But frankly, it's a fairly short-term window of opportunity to get that differentiation because prices come down so fast. In 10 years' time, there will be cheaper chips. So there's a short-term opportunity in having deep pockets and being able to buy access to high-performance computing, but it's not going to last for a very long time.

Is AI worthy of global attention?

Is AI really worth all of the attention, investment and effort that is going into it around the world? The clear answer is a definitive yes, and the *raison d'être* of this book is to provide unparalleled insights into why that is the case. Clearly the venture capital community believes in AI's potential, and it is their funding that is creating the explosion of tools that Chapter 2 will unveil. Christopher Schroeder is Co-Founder of Next Billion Ventures; Network Partner Village Global, and he explains:

AI is already having a massive impact on business across every spectra and sector and I expect only greater acceleration in both tech advances and innovation. There is no business over time that will not be an 'AI' business in some form, in that great understanding rendered from unique data sets is essential to any core operation, and will unleash new opportunities but also competitive threats. We will see in our daily lives more and more repetitive and mundane tasks rendered more effectively – especially in health care, finance, robotics and more. I believe we will attain a greater sense of 'mass customization', meaning that to businesses we were once viewed as a demographic or geography, now products and services can be ever more relevant to me as an individual. It will open significant opportunity, but also will have bumps and stir very strong debates on privacy and data security globally among other core issues.

We have already explored the ways AI might benefit society at large, become an integral part of our children or grandchildren's education and assist us at home. However, we will feel the effects most strongly in our professional lives as AI reshapes and redefines what it will one day mean for us to 'work'.

Let's turn the clock back to 2005 to understand what we are dealing with here. Back then, you had to flip open your mobile phone to make a call. Faxes were still being sent. Microsoft's idea of a 'smart assistant' was a cartoon paper clip. To check email out of hours, you used a PalmPilot or Blackberry. A 'lightning fast' download speed was a dizzy minute. Facebook was just for students, Twitter was a year from launch, Instagram was still five years from inception, and the first Snapchat was but a twinkle in its founder's eye. Few – if any of us – held job titles such as Big Data analyst, cloud services manager, UX designer, app developer or influencer because these capabilities were not yet in high demand, or simply did not exist yet.

By reflecting on how much has changed in our working lives in less than two decades, it is no longer unfathomable to consider the deep impacts that AI will have on our lives. A combination of media hype, science fiction and popular myth have resulted in unnecessary and often unfounded scaremongering. Change seeps into our lives; it does not bulldoze its way in. And, as we did before, we will gradually adapt once again. In fact, we are further along in the process than we may even realize. AI has slowly begun infiltrating our lives over the past few years; it does so in ways so subtle that we may not notice or recognize them as AI. Once again, consider Alexa, your Netflix queue, the smart reader on your gas meter and your favourite Spotify playlist. Gradually and unwittingly, we have been coming to terms with AI for a long time now. Even as adoption picks up steam and innovation continues to accelerate, our relationship with AI is still more likely to be more of a slow build than a rapid robot revolution.

AI's benefits to professionals in marketing, sales and CX are far-reaching and will often vary based on how the technology is used by a specific business. But over the early years of its adoption, several recurring benefits have emerged across various industries and organization types. These include:

1 **Better customer insights**: How well do you really know your customers? Keeping track of changes in trends, attitudes, needs and behaviours is difficult and time-consuming. AI can identify shifts, patterns and changes in sentiment quicker and often more accurately than a human worker could. This frees up human staff time, allowing them to focus on translating AI's insights into strategy.

2 **Less trial-and-error**: Having an AI-based predictive modelling system is a lot like gazing into a crystal ball. AI's algorithms make use of a wealth of data sources in order to predict which approaches, campaigns, messaging, strategies or processes would be most effective for achieving a goal. This saves on the time, resources and risks associated with trialling potentially unsuccessful methods.

3 **Smarter targeting**: Casting a wide net is often not the best strategy for businesses, and targeting the wrong audience segments is just as ineffective. AI is able to analyse existing customer data to identify exactly who your customers are. Its algorithms can also pinpoint new audiences or subsets of existing groups to target. Once these opportunities have been identified, tools can also be deployed to recommend the most effective tactics for reaching and influencing them.

4 **Increased efficiency**: Apart from the time-saving capabilities already mentioned, AI will enable businesses to optimize and automate their processes. Think of how much time you would save by letting technology handle all the mundane tasks in your day such as monitoring stats, searching for sales leads, following up, or drafting copy. The time gained can then be deployed to focus on higher-value and more creatively enriching activities.

5 **Sense and structure**: In our digitally driven age, businesses have access to more data than ever before. However, many of the benefits associated with this abundance are nullified by an inability to make sense of it. AI can provide structure to unstructured data and derive valuable insights that humans would take much longer to accomplish or overlook altogether. Furthermore, natural language processing allows data to be processed from a wider variety of sources and can even detect sentiment.

6 **Human-like communication**: One of the most common uses and earliest adopted functions of AI is chatbots. However, as the technology has become more intelligent, the conversations have become even more human. In fact, most of us would not even realize that we are conversing

with a bot. This capability has been extremely beneficial in customer service settings, but is now expanding into various functions of sales, marketing and HR.

7 **Personalization at scale:** Creating unique, memorable and tailored experiences has become a core priority and challenge for marketing and sales teams. AI is able to maximize available data, adapt in real time and present users with a website, sales experience, or even product that is completely tailored to them. So far, applications of this function have proved massively successful in retail, which we will explore further in Chapter 3.

As you work your way through the nine chapters, you may note the recurrence of these benefits in the various industry sectors, geographies and job functions that we address. These core benefits provide a simplistic overview of what you can expect to gain from adopting this technology, and should be kept front of mind as you read the rest of this book and begin to consider the potential impacts, benefits and use cases for your own AI adoption.

A global duty to raise living standards

While a busy marketplace poses challenges to companies looking to throw their hats into the AI ring, the rush for innovation and the introduction of a vast range of value-led solutions also impacts consumers and society at large. The new era of AI innovation has the power to raise living standards globally, if governments invest and allow it to flourish. This is one of the most pressing duties of global governments today. This, and other crucial macro issues, will be explored more deeply in Chapter 9. What is clear is that the competition for the AI prize will be fought fiercely. As McKinsey reports, the COVID-19 crisis has created an imperative for companies to reconfigure their operations, and an opportunity to transform them. To the extent that they do so, greater productivity will follow.

We must therefore turn our attention now to the global developments in AI. Numerous nations now appreciate AI's ability to provide competitive advantage and change work for the better. While some stagnate and live in fear of being left behind, others have developed AI strategies through investment, grants, tax incentives and talent development. Timing is critical, because the window for competitive differentiation will close more quickly as AI becomes even easier to consume, as Rolls-Royce illustrated.

Asia is dominant when it comes to AI. An important indicator of a country's AI lead is the number of AI patents it files. In these stakes, Europe lags behind. According to OxFirst (a specialist in IP law and economics, and a spin out of Oxford University), Samsung, IBM and Tencent have dominated the global AI patent race over the past decade (HPC Staff, 2020).

The data in Table 1.1 illustrates that Korea's Samsung dominates, with more than 5,000 patents worldwide.

TABLE 1.1   Company patent count

Samsung Electronics	5,073
IBM	2,062
Tencent	2,062
LG Electronics	1,541
Microsoft Technology	1,388
Baidu	1,221
State Grid Corp., China	1,027
AT&T	941
Ping An Tech, Shenzen	802
Intel	746

Market share

When assessing the patents by country, we see a clear picture emerge of the fight for market share in AI. China, the US and the Republic of Korea report most patent filings. The Chinese Patent Office records over 100,000 compared to the comparatively negligible 5,000 patents filed with the European Patent Office. In fact, no European company was to be found among the top 20 patent owners (HPC Staff, 2020).

TABLE 1.2   Countries' patent count

China (SIPO)	1,06,650
United States (USPTO)	60,003
World Intellectual Property Organization (WIPO)	20,407
Republic of Korea (KIPO)	12,897
Japan (JPO)	9,682
European Patent Office (EPO)	5,201
Australia (AU)	3,715
Canada (CA)	2,702
Taiwan (TW)	682
Great Britain (GB)	535

Featured in New Electronics (Tyler, 2020), Dr Roya Ghafele, executive director of OxFirst, comments:

> This data suggests that companies are recognising the economic potential of patents. The analysis helps assess how different patent owners perform in comparison to each other and how the patent space is distributed among them. Match this against a patent licensing rate of 15 per cent, which can be caught across the sector, and it becomes evident that even a small fraction of the patents in this space could offer attractive financial returns. This can be achieved by either trading the patents directly or indirectly.

Investment in AI is a different story. In 2019 the UK invested £1.3 billion. AI has been deployed in the UK in a range of fields, from agriculture and healthcare, to financial services, through to customer service, retail and logistics. It was extensively used to help tackle the COVID-19 pandemic, but is also being used to underpin facial recognition technology, deep fakes and other ethically challenging uses.

The AI race: the US and China

This race to invest has caused competition between nations and, in some cases, hostility. In December 2020, the United States came a step closer to setting a national strategy to maintain its lead in AI technologies. The US

House of Representatives approved a bipartisan nonbinding resolution to create an AI national strategy. It identified workforce development, national security, research and development and ethical use as key to an AI strategy. In a statement, Will Hurd likened dominance in emerging technologies such as AI to a 'new cold war' (Rockwell, 2020):

> If we don't take advantage of AI, Mandarin and the yuan – not English and the dollar – could dominate the global economy. Vladimir Putin once said that whoever masters AI will master the world. That is why America – not Russia and not China – must be at the helm.

According to the protagonists, the approval of the measure will allow America to take advantage of AI technology 'before it takes advantage of us' by setting a path for the next several decades.

Reporting in the *Financial Times* (FT) in January 2021, Yuan Yang, the FT's deputy Beijing bureau chief, remarks:

> The problem for Biden is twofold: first, the US has lost its dominance in many aspects of global technology. Second, the Trump administration's offensive on Chinese tech is easily read as a protectionist attempt to claw back that dominance. That is no way of reassuring allies in Europe or Asia. The US cannot be self-sufficient in technology, much as any other country cannot. Reaching out to allies would be a start.

> (Yang, 2021)

Russia also has a firm eye on the potential of AI. Yandex – the Russian equivalent of Google – and social networks have long used ML to identify potential customers for their advertisers. It is based on the analysis of personal information of users: their interests, demographic characteristics and other aspects. This kind of targeting works by processing a huge amount of data.

Professor Dr Sc. Marina G. Shilina of the Plekhanov Russian University of Economics explains:

> In recent years Russia has adopted its state Program of the digital economy (2017) and a national AI road map (2020). AI is now a widespread technology across marketing and advertising, for example programmatic. In marketing, the main task of new AI technologies is to get to know customers better and sell them relevant products and services. AI creates personalized offers in real time. For example, even in the mid-2010s, X5 Retail Group used AI-driven marketing

proposals, tailored to hundreds of factors, which increased the effectiveness of targeted marketing by 5 per cent and reduced communication costs by 40 per cent, thereby improving loyalty programmes.

AI not only generates personalized offers for customers such as the next best offer, but it can also suggest the likelihood of converting a lead into a deal and recommend further best actions. According to the researchers of TAdviser, Huawei and Technoserv (2020), 68 per cent of companies adopted AI and ML. They believe that in the future the use of artificial intelligence will become a competitive advantage. In 2020, Sberbank, one of the biggest banks in Russia and an 'AI native' and pioneer in this field, exceeded $1 billion in part due to its AI system implementation. In 2021, the board of Sberbank approved the principles of ethics for the development and application of artificial intelligence technologies in the Sberbank Group, proving that this field is becoming even more mature.

Predictive analytics becomes an assistant of a company's call centre. So, for example, the Russian *Predict* algorithm automatically reads the gender of the subscriber, the purpose of the call and the time of the call. Furthermore, the entire array of information is presented in the form of organized data. This information allows them to more accurately customize marketing campaigns and adjust the work of the call centre operators.

Russian start-up Malivar is one of the first in the country to create a digital avatar. Its CGI, Aliona Paul, is one of Russia's most popular virtual influencers. She writes long texts, encourages wearing masks so as not to get sick with COVID-19, and in October 2020, she 'visited' the Open Innovations forum.

Real citizens also created their CGI. For example, the first Russian virtual influencer was the digital twin of Sasha Panika's model from St. Petersburg, named Asya Strike. Now Asya 'works' with great brands like Adidas.

AI in the Middle East and South Asia

UAE boasts the world's first dedicated AI research university

Next we move across to the Arabic-speaking world, which may be a late-comer, but with a 500-million-strong population that is young, ambitious and wealthy, it is likely to thrive in the 2020s. According to data shared by MAGNiTT (Radcliffe, 2020), capital invested in the region's start-ups increased from $657m in 2017 to $803m in 2020 despite the pandemic. Dr Eric Xing, the world-renowned computer science professor, was appointed president of Mohamed bin Zayed University of Artificial Intelligence (MBZUAI) in 2020. Commenting on the Office of Public and Cultural Diplomacy website (2021), he shares his bold vision and target of putting the UAE 'on the map of AI superpowers':

> My vision is to really use this opportunity to turn MBZUAI into one of the major players, and use this as a platform to train talent and the workforce for the local economy and for the community ... I don't want to be the one who bought the ocean by doing everything, and end up mediocre in all dimensions. We're in a stage of AI development where there is still a lot of fear. It's like when the automobile was invented. People were scared and they wanted to keep using a horse and buggy.

UAE AI Strategy 2031 and Saudi Arabia's Vision 2030

Both the UAE and Saudi Arabia have placed AI as a top priority through the UAE Artificial Intelligence Strategy 2031 and Saudi Arabia's Vision 2030. The two countries have committed to using 'smart' solutions to transform businesses, government and schools. During the 2020 lockdown, the UAE's Dubai Police integrated AI solutions to distinguish vehicles belonging to those working in the vital sectors and those who had breached lockdown rules. AI is also being used across airports and by airlines in the region. Etihad Airways uses AI and automation to screen passengers for any visible symptoms of coronavirus in a bid to prevent any potential transmission. Additionally, the UAE has also launched the first AI university, named after His Highness Sheikh Mohamed Bin Zayed. The university can serve as a strong platform to foster and nurture students who aspire to become prominent members of the AI industry.

Dr Vikas Nand Kumar Batheja, co-founder and director – Capital University College in UAE, explains:

> Although it has been identified that AI and machine learning have numerous limitations, it has transformed to become an integral part of business. One of the most notable limitations is its inability to understand context, especially in the case of languages. I strongly believe that they are unlikely to replace humans at least in the near future; however they will remain a valuable tool to streamline and support many human activities. This is possible mainly due to AI's neutral technology and ability to accurately collect and analyze data.

While there are many employment opportunities that are created by AI, there are going to be many job roles which will be dominated by AI instead of human capacity. Hence, this will require humans to prepare and train themselves for a better transition which not only creates opportunities but also has the right balance of replacing human capabilities. In all, AI must only be a supporting tool for human needs and there shouldn't be an opportunity where it could completely replace us.

AI has taken care of many menial tasks, which has allowed human beings to complete some tasks in less time. Hence, we have some extra freedom that will bring in a sense of joy at first glance, but we must be aware of how to channel this newfound freedom in doing something more productive and efficient.

There is little doubt that AI will shape the future of the Middle East. Speaking to ZDnet, Khalid Al Rumaihi, chair of the Bahrain Development Bank, comments:

> Our region has its challenges, including legacy issues such as difficulties in registering businesses, job protectionism and low investment in research and development... On the other hand, we have a significant advantage thanks to our youthful demographic profile. The region's median age is under 30, and strong population growth continues. There is no country in the GCC where people under 25 make up less than 30 per cent of the population.

(Radcliffe, 2020)

The potential is huge, and there have already been notable successes such as the acquisition of Souq.com by Amazon and Careem by Uber.

R&D and free zones

In the United Arab Emirates, free zones, such as Dubai Internet City (DIC), were successfully deployed to help stimulate new businesses. DIC was launched in October 2000, and has rapidly expanded to 1,600 business partners and 24,000 professionals, spanning technologies including AI, cloud and robotics.

Another nation thriving in this region is Israel, which boasts the world's second-highest R&D expenditure as a percentage of GDP at 4.58 per cent, compared with an OECD average of 2 per cent. By comparison, its neighbour Iraq invests a mere 0.04 per cent, according to UNESCO data (Radcliffe, 2020). According to Deloitte, Israel has become the world leader for number of start-ups per capita – with 2,000 start-ups founded in the past decade, another 3,000 small- and medium-sized start-up and high-tech companies, 30 growth companies, 50 large technology companies and 300 multinational corporations R&D centres.

Google invests heavily in India

Situated midway between the heavily investing Middle East and the global AI superpowers in eastern Asia sits a country whose potential many tech companies are beginning to take note of: India. In the summer of 2020, Sundar Pichai, CEO of tech giant Google, announced a $10 billion investment in India over the next five to seven years. Its focus is to digitize the Indian economy and build India-first products and services. Drawing on this India Digitization Fund, Google announced in the same year its investment in two Indian start-ups, Glance and DailyHunt.

Former head of Facebook India, Umang Bedi, is the co-founder of DailyHunt, which features the Josh app. According to Techcrunch (Singh, 2020), 'Josh and Roposo are among over a dozen apps in India that are attempting to fill the void New Delhi created after banning TikTok in late June in the country. TikTok identified India as its biggest overseas market prior to the ban.' Clearly the region is highly attractive based on its impressive tally of unicorns.

Glance is an AI-first company, part of Inmobi – one of the largest advertising exchanges in the world, and the first unicorn in India. Manish Gupta is Senior Vice President and GM at Glance. He explains:

> Today, we use AI for content creation and content moderation. The true power of AI is about personalising what kind of content feed you should show. In a similar manner to Tik Tok, we use the true power of AI. The interaction that happens on Glance feeds the recommendation we give to users.
>
> There are very few companies like Glance who are truly harnessing the power of AI. In the next few years, I see business interest in AI increasing as they realise that there is real value in a couple of areas. One is about hyper-personalization of products and services that are there. The second is in terms of streamlining all the processes, or automation of many of these processes.

Also based in India, Dr Mona N Shah is founder and Director of Vayati Systems and Research Inc. She comments:

> From being the bogeyman threatening liberty and privacy to almost acquiring the status of a 'board member' in organisations and institutions, AI and related

technology has gained acceptance at all levels – strategic, functional and operational. AI too has undergone a sea change from the early times of the Turing Test and McCarthy's work of the mid-twentieth century to the expert systems that are in use around the world today. In between these two points lay the advancements and disappointments that experiments with AI in machine translation (Alpac Report, US), the Lighthill Report (Cambridge, UK) and the Fifth Generation Computer System Project (Japan) have undergone.

The progress in AI research and advancement witnessed growth spurts and pauses by way of funding. There wasn't, however, a complete shift to non-AI *per se,* and advanced computing and data storage systems spurred the push towards Big Data analytics. The human and machine interface of IBM's Deep Blue was first highlighted in the game of chess against Gary Kasparov from the 1980s onwards into the nineties. While codes were being written to replicate the human mind, a parallel Big Data computing challenge was being addressed in molecular modelling to map the dynamics of molecules in continuous motion. What we see today is a culmination of advanced computing by machines from other machine data sources and the other, which interacts with human beings, using past and programmable data.

The next couple of years and up to 2030 would be the years of rapid consolidation of existing AI tech that is available as a result of greater acceptance of AI among the masses. The catalyst to this has been the decisive year of COVID-19, which has resulted in causal and resultant drivers to adopt AI. In India, with its massive powerhouse of software professionals and specialists, a considerable mushrooming of AI start-ups is emerging. AI is based on several basic models on which successive individual solutions are based: Data as a Service (DaaS), Analytics as a Service (AaaS), Infrastructure as a Service (IaaS), Platform as a Service (PlaaS) and many other models in which AI solutions exist. Their work ranges from providing enterprise digital transformation, blockchain, business excellence models, AR/VR, IoT, mobility and cloud solutions to game development, mobile apps, product solutions, chatbots, voice apps and start-up agility, to name a few.

The notable firms in India in AI are Third Eye Data, Talentica Software, Wow Labz, F(x) Data Labs, Accubits Technologies Inc, Algoscale Technologies Inc, Day One Technologies, Valiance Solutions, Cartesian DataSciences, CronJ AI, Botosynthesis, Cognitive Machines, Beneath Analytics, Knoldus Inc, Cedex Technologies, Katpro Technologies, Affle Enterprise, Fusion Technologies, Maruti Techlabs, Zignite Solutions, NeenOpal Inc, Ideas2IT Technologies and hundreds of other specialized firms.

Another Indian success story is gnani.ai, a conversational AI company with products and solutions for omnichannel automation and analytics. Ganesh Gopalan, CEO and co-founder at gnani.ai, comments:

In the coming years, conversational AI will sit beside humans as their assistants and strengtheners or enhancers. AI will enable all sorts of functions to perform more efficiently by bringing automation across every department. While simplifying decision-making by analyzing mountains of data, AI-based solutions will help businesses respond to customer queries, complaints and concerns more effectively, both online and offline. Implementing AI into your core CX strategy and allowing conversational bots to take up work in contact centres will bring down costs involved in supporting customers with improved FCRs, NPS and CSAT. On the other hand, AI-driven speech-recognition solutions will get huge traction in the coming years. We will witness massive voice biometrics adoption as an authentication medium across banking, health care, HR and telecom industries.

A top loan provider sought an AI-based end-to-end solution to automate the collections process due to the substantial costs involved in loan recovery and payments across an extensive product portfolio. The client was looking to replace 'human agents' with voice bots to achieve scalability while ensuring a human-like CX.

To help them scale and automate, we implemented ASR and NLP-based conversational AI-based virtual assistant solutions that freed up agents' time and boosted their productivity. Within six weeks from the deployment date, the custom-built bots scaled linearly from 10K calls/day to 1 million in multiple languages, with an 80 per cent drop in the collections costs. There was a significant reduction in payment delinquency rate, with 43 per cent of collections achieved in just six months with the help of persistent calling via bots.

Also, robotic process automation (RPA) bots automate repetitive tasks across contact centres, address customer queries, study user sentiment, book appointments, fill in paperwork, process payments and offer personalized suggestions as and when required. Conversational AI further enhances these capabilities with natural language processing as a core element needed to drive human-like and natural conversations.

By 2030, many will prefer next-door technologies to blend invisibly into various business functions and backgrounds. Some businesses and customers may choose technology with human-like interfaces, and some may like conversational engagement with technology in their language. Connectivity will propel the demand for smarter and intelligent communications between machines, businesses and humans. Also, there will be rapid and significant digital investments and business process innovation. Automation will no longer be considered as labour displacing, but more like labour-share reduction. Cashless payments, speech-recognition technology, contactless biometrics solutions and AI-enabled Bots will potentially make their way into every sector and department, thereby improving organizational efficiency and customer experience.

AI in Europe

Attractiveness to AI start-ups

Let's switch our attention now to Europe, starting with Germany. In December 2020, the German government published an important update to its first AI strategy released in November 2018. In the intervening two years, Germany established a national research consortium for AI, and improved the framework conditions for start-ups. One key finding of the updated AI strategy is the country's recognition that in order to stay internationally competitive in the field of AI, Europe, and particularly Germany, must become a more attractive location for companies to establish their businesses. The five focus areas are: professional expertise; research; transfer and application; the regulatory framework; and society. The German report highlights a number of ethical issues that are as yet unresolved, given that the laws and frameworks are in their infancy. While we await firm guidance in Europe and beyond, it is incumbent on those developing and implementing AI to do so ethically. We will explore such issues in Chapter 9.

This applies to Germany's close neighbours in Europe, for example Spain.

Spain's national AI strategy

In 2020, we also witnessed Spanish Prime Minister, Pedro Sanchez, announce a 600 million euros (around 725 million US dollars) investment between 2021 and 2023 in a National AI Strategy. 'If things are done well', he added that this could increase by a further 3,300 million euros of private investment (Xinhuanet.com, 2020). The investment will focus on promotion of AI research and new national multidisciplinary technological development centres, as well as the creation of aid programme for companies to develop AI solutions. High on the agenda also is university and professional training, and the promotion of Spanish as a working language in AI.

Investment in AI for marketing

For marketing professionals, this is a turning point and a major opportunity to derive real insights on behaviours and trends. Isabelle Quevilly is Head of Creative Shop UK at one of the world's leading technology companies, Facebook. She explains:

> The strategic implementation of AI tools in your marketing operations starts with a clear understanding of the problem you wish to solve to deliver growth. How to know what fashion styles are trending in real time? How to deliver better-performing creative across multiple markets? How to anticipate product demand at a hyper local level?
>
> AI is a tool, and its power lies in the unprecedented level of scale and complexity it can tackle. However, understanding how AI technologies can build your competitive advantage needs a strong starting point that only human creativity can address, by asking the right questions for AI to solve. Implementation will require cross-functional collaborations and a focus on small, incremental and measurable pilots that will add up to the broader marketing transformation you want to realise.

As Facebook's community grew to more than two billion people, it became increasingly clear to the company that it should not be making so many decisions about speech and online safety on its own. The Oversight Board was created to help Facebook answer some of the most difficult questions around freedom of expression online: what to take down, what to leave up, and why.

AI for improved collaboration

The Oversight Board at Facebook uses its independent judgement to support people's right to free expression and ensure that those rights are being adequately respected. The board's decisions to uphold or reverse Facebook's content decisions will be binding, meaning that Facebook will have to implement them, unless doing so could violate the law. Dex Hunter-Torricke is Head of Communications at the Facebook Oversight Board. He comments:

> AI is already creating huge value for businesses, helping them sift through the mountains of data being produced each day, and also automating a lot of internal and external functions. In a post-COVID world, I think the immediate focus for many organizations will be on how to adapt AI tools to fit with the new ways of working. In a world where many workers will continue to operate remotely, through increasingly global and decentralized teams, AI services that can help improve collaboration and decrease cross-border, cross-team frictions will have transformational value.
>
> In spite of all the innovations in targeted advertising, most marketing strategies are still pretty imprecise. How much time and money goes into pitching the wrong products to the wrong customers? AI that is responsive to customer needs and informed by their preferences has the potential to offer much more personalized service, and to help inform development of better products. Look at how companies like Netflix and Amazon have trained their recommendation engines over the years, and have been able to optimize new products to fit the market needs identified through all the data they've learned about consumers.

Assessing the human need

Dex Hunter-Torricke continues:

> The most important criteria for a successful AI strategy is recognizing that AI, like any technology, won't magically solve all your problems. Technology is only one side of the coin for businesses. The other is the people component. What kind of organizational processes, leadership and culture are you connecting with the tools on offer? Too often, organizations embrace a flashy piece of technology that they think will lead to greater productivity or sales, but they don't do anything to innovate in the way they hire, develop and manage people.
>
> You have to start by understanding what the human needs of your organization are, and then to shape your technology strategy around that, not the other way round. Having leadership as well as employee buy-in is critical too and having a realistic cross-organizational consensus about expectations for the new technology. Studying carefully the potential side effects of AI, particularly on external stakeholders and employees from underrepresented

backgrounds, is also really important. The ethical dimension of technology needs to be a core part of the strategy, or it can lead to chaos.

There are many issues which anyone working in the AI field should be deeply concerned about. The biggest is probably around the values and biases that go into shaping AI products. All technology, including AI, is shaped by human emotions, values, biases and judgements. We need to be really careful about what kind of assumptions are made by the creators of AI and that can have huge and unforeseen impacts on people and communities. We've already seen the impact of biased AI in hiring algorithms and offensive facial recognition tools. In general, technological innovation is advancing faster than the social and ethical agenda we need to ensure that technology is developed and applied in a responsible way.

As the pandemic has shown us, we are living in a new era of greater global uncertainty. We can safely say that by 2030, emerging technologies will have matured further and will be having a greater economic and societal impact than at present. But we're also heading into a decade with increased geopolitical competition, the breakdown of old social structures in many advanced economies, and also the massive uncontained threat of catastrophic climate change. Leaders and businesses have to be wide-eyed about the challenges of the next decade, not just looking at the future with rose-tinted specs.

Another major tech vendor in the world of AI is IBM Waston. Featured in *Forbes* (Talbot, 2020), Randi Stipes, Chief Marketing Officer of IBM Watson Media and Weather, comments:

> Over the last decade, more than 30,000 businesses across industries have leveraged IBM Watson to make more accurate predictions, automate decisions and processes and optimize employees' time to focus on higher-value work. Yet less than 25 per cent of global companies leverage AI to its full potential, illustrating the increased opportunity to harness this technology across media and marketing.

IBM Watson wants to help marketers to move beyond simply automating action. Its plan is to augment human thinking. AI-enabled advertising algorithms can recognize patterns, make predictions and learn over time. The marketing team benefit from speed and accuracy, with decisions based on consumer intent. IBM Watson believes that AI is the answer to the problems faced by marketers such as IDFA, GDPR and regulatory compliance, as it enables the necessarily agility required by companies to stay ahead.

AI in Australia

Let's now consider the impact of AI in Australia as we hear from Karen Khaw – a senior consultant of The Tantalus Group, a global consultancy, and founder of V-Engage Australia. She comments:

> There's never been a more significant time for AI to play a major role in society with the enormous data to make sense of. After all, AI thrives on data. Furthermore, the expectations of 'faster speed to market' due to a relatively more digitised world compared to pre-COVID and rapidly declining average attention span of humans will be the perfect environment for AI to thrive in. Technologies such as virtual reality, augmented reality and mixed reality (VAMR) that offer immersive experience will complement AI to deliver more targeted, efficient and precise training programmes that will nurture future-forward talents. Imagine your sales representatives utilising a virtual reality simulation of the three most likely services generated by AI for your customer and experiencing the reactions before the real follow-up calls to the customer.
>
> Another impact of AI on businesses will be the continuation in the rising popularity of virtual influencers such as Lil Miquela and Imma. Fictional computer-generated 'people' who have the realistic characteristics, features and personalities of humans will likely be a part of our daily lives, so businesses will need to familiarise with how to manage virtual influencers as part of the workforce. It will be near impossible to not have an AI strategy over the next two years and AI should be a criteria knowledge of all employees, regardless of size of business.

Beyond the pretty shiny objects

As PwC's annual AI Predictions survey states: 'AI is hard. Too many AI investments end up as "pretty shiny objects" that don't pay off. Most companies have yet to adapt talent strategies, organizational structures, business strategies, development methodologies and risk mitigation for a world that moves at AI speed' (Likens *et al*, 2021).

The focus of this book is to provide organizations worldwide with the factual evidence, the case studies of successes and failures, and the essential data on vendors that will enable them to plan for and execute an effective AI strategy. What has become evident is that digitization – and the volume of data it creates – is an essential prerequisite for AI adoption. In recent years, our daily lives have become increasingly digital, transforming the way we shop, learn, find a partner and exercise.

This is echoed by Jan Chan, Associate Partner, Business Modelling and Analytics, Ernst & Young LLP:

> We have to balance out the optimism about future change versus the reality of business and the cost of doing business in this way. The companies that are currently investing in their system improvement will find the most benefit, obviously, because they have the best data to feed into systems that operate around AI. Others don't have access to that quality of data; if they don't spend money building up their own data fabric and/or relationships with data providers, then they won't see noticeable benefits in AI.
>
> Then, over five to ten years, they will struggle to compete without making that investment. If you don't get into the habit of adapting to change, you won't be prepared for disruption, and you are unfit. As a company, that means you will struggle going forward, to try to maintain the competitive edge in business.
>
> Over the coming years businesses are going to be seeing 'co-opertition', a portmanteau of cooperation and competition. It is both a mechanism and an environment whereby companies can work with their competitors to create a better standard of information for the ecosystem that they operate in and, as a result, create a better environment for everybody involved, from citizens to consumers and companies.

AI is not a silver bullet for comms

As we will explore in-depth in Chapter 2, AI looks set to make its mark on the world of marketing, comms and advertising, as Richard Bagnall, Co-Managing Partner and CEO of Europe and Americas, CARMA, and Chairman, AMEC, explains:

> There's a lot of confusion in the PR and comms industry about what AI can, and cannot, do. It's no surprise – a recent USC Annenberg School for Communication and Journalism report cited that when asked what matters for their future, 80 per cent of PRs see tech as important, 18 per cent see AI as critical and yet only 3 per cent claim to be knowledgeable about the topic. Into this melting pot of enthusiasm and desire, it is easy to be seduced by the hype of various SaaS platform vendors and their overenthusiastic sales teams making big claims.

When it comes to the measurement and evaluation of communication effectiveness, AI is not a silver bullet that can do the thinking for you. PR and comms professionals still need to do the hard work and lean in to ensure that their measurement is meaningful. This means linking activity-driven output metrics to what target audiences and key stakeholders think, and most importantly do, as a result of the comms activity. And why this matters to their organization.

We live in an era of uncertainty – and accountability. CFOs all around the world are under pressure to rein in spending and preserve cash. Any activity without benefit is just a cost. If PR and communication professionals only measure activity this is how they will be seen – as only a cost-centre. They need instead to go beyond counting the automated vanity metrics that Big Data too often throws up, and look instead to demonstrate the benefits of the work they do for their organization.

Meaningful evaluation of comms and genuine insight require context, relevance, critical thinking and experience – skills which humans add to Big Data, not things that AI can replace.

From a measurement of comms perspective, AI throws up some interesting challenges. Is the content selected for measurement relevant? Has it been cleaned properly? Was it created by a human or a bot? Was it read/seen/heard by humans? How accurate is the coding matrix and implementation of the evaluation? Has bias been written in – or out – of any AI claiming to make an accurate assessment of what is being communicated? Steve Jobs' words ring as true today as ever – 'computers don't make mistakes, humans do'.

Digital twins

Digital twin technology is becoming more widespread, with Deloitte predicting that the global market for digital twins is expected to reach $16 billion by 2023. In simple terms, a digital twin is a virtual or digital replica of a physical entity such as devices, people, processes or systems. It is used to help businesses make model-driven decisions, and marketing teams are starting to take advantage of it. Dr Anand S. Rao is a partner at PwC, and the Global AI Lead, based in Boston in the USA. He explains:

> There's a lot happening on the marketing and sales side. On the pro side, AI is getting very sophisticated and is able to do very much at an individual level of personalization. Everyone has talked about segmentation for at least a couple

of decades, but it is far more practical now with the amount of data that is available on each and every individual. The downside is how much of that data is collected, and potential data privacy violations. The next stage is taking this data and essentially creating digital twins. Now we are doing it at scale, with millions of digital twins, which are essentially like consumers. Consumers make purchasing decisions: what, why, when, how, talking to whom, or messaging with whom. All of that data is there and then you suck that into the digital world. Now we have created a digital equivalent. Then you go to the next stage, and begin to understand the behaviour and project it into the future. So what would this customer be doing? When are they likely to buy this product? When does the repeat purchase happen? Are they likely to buy this product or the other given all the other customers who look like them or their own preferences in the past?

Now, this is where it gets interesting. Of course, marketing has always prided in gently nudging customers to do what they want them to do. That's why it's more around behaviour modification, not just understanding behaviour or projecting behaviour, but modifying that behaviour. In some cases, it is by benefiting the customers. In some cases, it is benefiting the company. In some cases, it is benefiting both of them. That's where it gets into a tricky situation, when it is to the detriment of the consumer but to the betterment of the company. Is that ethical to do? Should you just nudge them only if it is truly useful for the customer? Also, is the customer aware that they are being nudged, or even been asked for their permission?

PRACTICAL TAKEAWAYS CHECKLIST: TOP 10 TIPS

1 AI's impact on society and on business will be transformative, as befitting a fourth industrial revolution.

2 The COVID-19 pandemic broke through cultural and technological barriers. The subsequent digital acceleration turned the tide for AI, making data more freely available, and forcing leadership teams to plan for continued disruption.

3 One in ten enterprises uses multiple ML applications, proving that its algorithms and techniques are efficiently solving complex real-world problems.

4 For marketing professionals, this is a turning point and a major opportunity to derive real insights on behaviours and trends.

5 In order for AI to move mainstream, meeting customer needs must remain top of the agenda.

6 There is only a relatively short window of opportunity to differentiate using AI.

7 We will see in our daily lives more and more repetitive and mundane tasks rendered more effectively – especially in health care and finance.

8 AI will help marketers achieve a greater sense of 'mass customization'. Its algorithms can pinpoint new audiences or subsets of existing groups to target.

9 As we move closer to 2030, automation will no longer be considered as labour-displacing but more like labour-share reduction. Cashless payments, speech-recognition technology, contactless biometrics solution and AI-enabled bots will potentially make their way into every sector and department, thereby improving organizational efficiency and customer experience.

10 The most important criteria for a successful AI strategy is recognizing that AI, like any technology, won't magically solve all your problems.

Bibliography

Baidu (2021) These Five AI Developments Will Shape 2021 and Beyond, *MIT Technology Review*, www.technologyreview.com/2021/01/14/1016122/these-five-ai-developments-will-shape-2021-and-beyond/ (archived at https://perma.cc/FTD6-W6ZD)

Balakrishnan, T, Chui, M, Hall, B and Henke, N (2020) The State of AI in 2020, McKinsey & Company, www.mckinsey.com/business-functions/mckinsey-analytics/our-insights/global-survey-the-state-of-ai-in-2020 (archived at https://perma.cc/BF5K-DKW5)

Farnam Street (2019) Gates' Law: How progress compounds and why it matters, www.fs.blog/2019/05/gates-law/#:~:text=The%20most%20probable%20source%20is,often%20known%20as%20Amara's%20Law (archived at https://perma.cc/RRT6-BZCL)

Gerner, M (2020) Is the UK Still an AI leader?, *Raconteur*, www.raconteur.net/global-business/uk/uk-ai-leader/ (archived at https://perma.cc/6SB2-YTF6)

Ghoshal, A (2020) Samsung Is Working on Lifelike AI-Powered Avatars to Fill in for Humans, *TNW*, www.thenextweb.com/news/samsung-is-working-on-lifelike-ai-powered-avatars-to-fill-in-for-humans (archived at https://perma.cc/ZK2X-7UZT)

House of Lords (2020) AI in the UK: No room for complacency, *London: House of Lords Liaison Committee*, Chapter 2: Living with artificial intelligence, www.publications.parliament.uk/pa/ld5801/ldselect/ldliaison/196/19604.htm#_idTextAnchor007 (archived at https://perma.cc/A3HU-525J)

HPC Staff (2020) Samsung, IBM, Tencent Lead AI Patent Race, Europe Lags, *insideHPC*, www.insidehpc.com/2020/07/samsung-ibm-tencent-lead-ai-patent-race-europe-lagging/ (archived at https://perma.cc/K2MU-3DBW)

IDC (2020) Worldwide Spending on Artificial Intelligence Is Expected to Double in Four Years, Reaching $110 Billion in 2024, According to New IDC Spending Guide, www.idc.com/getdoc.jsp?containerId=prUS46794720 (archived at https:// perma.cc/8N35-MSJ3)

Kesari, G (2020) Why Covid Will Make AI Go Mainstream in 2021: Top 3 trends for enterprises, *Forbes*, www.forbes.com/sites/ganeskesari/2020/12/21/why-covid-will-make-ai-go-mainstream-in-2021-top-3-trends-for-enterprises/?sh=19c4648a797a (archived at https://perma.cc/ZFQ2-3KLS)

Likens, S, Shehab, M, Rao, A and Lendler, J (2021) AI Predictions 2021, *pwc*, www.pwc.com/us/en/tech-effect/ai-analytics/ai-predictions.html?blaid=1766210 (archived at https://perma.cc/KYG7-C9F2)

Loh, D (2020) Asean Faces Wide AI Gap as Vietnam and Philippines Lag Behind, *Financial Times*, www.ft.com/content/e99fcb64-2a26-4fa89911-03942fbf4493 (archived at https://perma.cc/WY9Z-RUAV)

Lund, S, Madgavkar, A, Manyika, J and Smit, S (2020) What's Next for Remote Work: An analysis of 2,000 tasks, 800 jobs, and nine countries, McKinsey & Company, www.mckinsey.com/featured-insights/future-of-work/whats-next-for-remote-work-an-analysis-of-2000-tasks-800-jobs-and-nine-countries (archived at https://perma.cc/CYD8-H53K)

McLean, S (2020) House of Lords Committee Publishes New Report 'AI in the UK: No room for complacency', *Lexology*, www.lexology.com/library/detail.aspx?g=824a5ef8-9e0b-44d9-98f4-6ade65ebb2e5 (archived at https://perma.cc/6D3Q-WWBL)

Office of Public and Cultural Diplomacy (2021) MBZUAI President lays out bold vision to put UAE 'on map of AI 'superpowers', www.opcd.ae/mbzuai-president-vision-to-put-uae-as-ai-superpowers/ (archived at https://perma.cc/3VX8-B7MB)

Press Association (2020) Co-op Expanding Use of Robots to Deliver Goods, *The Herald*, www.heraldscotland.com/news/national-news/18896712.co-op-expanding-use-robots-deliver-goods/ (archived at https://perma.cc/MP7K-GFPF)

Radcliffe, D (2020) Middle East Tech: Nine proven ways to unlock the region's startup scene, *ZDNet*, www.zdnet.com/article/middle-east-technology-nine-proven-ways-to-unlock-the-regions-startup-scene/ (archived at https://perma.cc/4JLQ-3NQ8)

Rockwell, M (2020) House Approves Plan to Create AI Strategy, *FCW*, https://fcw.com/articles/2020/12/09/national-ai-strategy-resolution.aspx?m=1 (archived at https://perma.cc/2YX5-MAES)

Samsung USA (2021) Samsung's New AI-Powered Robotic Vacuum and Laundry Products Automate Home Cleaning, *Samsung Newsroom*, www.news.samsung.com/global/samsungs-new-ai-powered-robotic-vacuum-and-laundry-products-automate-home-cleaning (archived at https://perma.cc/3GRD-K26N)

Singh, M (2020) Google Invests in Indian Startups Glance and DailyHunt, *TechCrunch+*, www.techcrunch.com/2020/12/22/google-leads-145-million-investment-in-indias-glance/?guccounter=1https://techcrunch.com/2020/12/22/google-leads-145-million-investment-in-indias-glance/?guccounter=1 (archived at https://perma.cc/H9ZL-CASS)

Sneader, K and Singhal, S (2021) The Next Normal Arrives: Trends that will define 2021 – and beyond, McKinsey & Company, www.mckinsey.com/featured-insights/leadership/the-next-normal-arrives-trends-that-will-define-2021-and-beyond (archived at https://perma.cc/ZQ8Z-3CY2)

Talbot, P (2020) Inside the World of AI at IBM Watson Advertising, *Forbes*, www.forbes.com/sites/paultalbot/2020/11/17/inside-the-world-of-ai-at-ibm-watson-advertising/?sh=7b3ed2573f70 (archived at https://perma.cc/CZH9-Q5AK)

The Economist (2021) Why a Dawn of Technological Optimism Is Breaking, *Leaders*, www.economist.com/leaders/2021/01/16/why-a-dawn-of-technological-optimism-is-breaking (archived at https://perma.cc/2QVK-AS8X)

Thought Leadership (2020) Where Will the Next Wave of Innovation Come From?, *Wamda*, www.wamda.com/2020/12/wave-innovation-come (archived at https://perma.cc/WXL4-WLJR)

Tyler, N (2020) Europe Lagging on AI development, *Newelectronics*, www.newelectronics.co.uk/electronics-news/europe-lagging-on-ai-development/228518/ (archived at https://perma.cc/D99Q-LKWM)

Vincent, J (2019) Jeff Bezos Is Launching a New Conference Dedicated to AI, Optimism, and Amazon, *The Verge*, www.theverge.com/2019/1/17/18186481/amazon-remars-jeff-bezos-conference-ai-machine-learning-robotics-space (archived at https://perma.cc/V5UL-MB4J)

Warner, K (2021) MBZUAI President Lays Out Bold Vision to Put UAE 'on Map of AI Superpowers', *The National*, www.thenationalnews.com/uae/education/mbzuai-president-lays-out-bold-vision-to-put-uae-on-map-of-ai-superpowers-1.1152633 (archived at https://perma.cc/B4NE-T9ZL)

wiseguyreports (2021) Artificial Intelligence (AI) in Marketing Market Analysis by Size, Share, Growth, Trends up to 2023, *Murphy's Hockey Law,* www.murphyshockeylaw.net/uncategorized/1014828/artificial-intelligence-ai-in-marketing-market-analysis-by-size-share-growth-trends-up-to-2023/ (archived at https://perma.cc/6GS6-5BHM)

Xinhuanet (2020) Spain to Invest 600 Mln Euros in National AI Strategy, www.xinhuanet.com/english/2020-12/03/c_139559155.htm (archived at https://perma.cc/6QRD-PZ99)

Yang, Y (2021) Joe Biden's New Year Resolution? A fresh approach to China tech, *Financial Times*, www.ft.com/content/ea9c3d83-a8ab-48ad-bcb8-01a5bed3ec2f (archived at https://perma.cc/46EC-9TN7)

02

Strategic AI tools for marketing, sales and CX

In 1993, American speculative fiction author William Gibson famously stated: 'The future is already here – it's just not very evenly distributed'. This still rings true today, insofar as there are certain parts of our lives that, although we may not even really understand it yet, are being completely transformed by the deployment of varying degrees of AI. Examples include recommendation engines that underpin what you view on TV, or what you purchase online, particularly in the wake of the COVID pandemic. An increasing amount of our disposable income, as well as people and things we are advised to follow and communicate with, and even what we actually think, is being mediated and dominated through artificial intelligence (AI).

> In this chapter we explore some of the key vendors who are disrupting and reshaping the business landscape. We discuss the ways in which these tools are providing benefits to professionals in various functions including customer service, sales, HR, marketing and communications. Additionally, we delve into the relationship dynamics that human staff and disruptive technology may develop over time, and the importance of this partnership.

A 2020 survey by International Data Corporation (IDC) revealed that adoption of AI is growing worldwide. The most promising finding is the direct correlation between AI adoption and superior business outcomes. Ritu Jyoti is Program Vice President, Artificial Intelligence (AI) Research, with IDC's software market research and advisory practice. Commenting in the IDC report, she said:

> Early adopters report an improvement of almost 25 per cent in customer experience, accelerated rates of innovation, higher competitiveness, higher margins and better employee experience with the roll out of AI solutions. Organizations worldwide are adopting AI in their business transformation journey, not just because they can but because they must, in order to be agile, resilient, innovative and be able to scale.
>
> (International Data Corporation, 2020)

There is no question that this decade has disrupted business life irreparably and set us on a course for workplace technology that we are unlikely to ever turn back on. The impact of the 2020 COVID pandemic on business accelerated digital transformation and sent businesses around the world on a race to adopt new technology in order to stay afloat and maintain their edge

Once a business identifies the problem that needs to be solved, the natural next step is to begin looking for solutions. AI adoption will only be as effective as the tools invested in, and technology should never be introduced simply for the sake of it. Over the past several years we have been spoilt for choice when it comes to AI vendors and software. There are thousands of sales, marketing and communications-focused tools already available, with new vendors entering the market regularly. The upside is that irrespective of your needs and problems to solve, there is likely a tool readily available for use. The drawback is that it can at times be difficult to know who to turn to or where to begin, a veritable 'Wild West' according to many CEOs that I consult with.

Which tools are available?

For many organizations considering using AI in their marketing, sales and CX, there is still uncertainty as to how best to move forward. Once again, we are forced to confront the Wild West scenario of AI disruptors on the market, and turn for guidance to third-party endorsements of vendors. In spring 2021, Forbes partnered with two venture capital firms, Sequoia Capital and Meritech Capital, to compile its AI 50 list of US companies using AI. Here are a few of the relevant vendors.

Clari for efficient CRM

One of the companies featured is Clari, which tackles the issue of inefficient customer resource management (CRM) systems. Clari streamlines CRM updates, alleviating the data entry burden for sales teams, while managing sales and forecasting with predictive insights.

Cresta to handle effective customer queries

Cresta deploys AI to learn the most effective replies to customer questions from the best agents. It then provides real-time prompts to less effective call centre agents, on what could be the 'best', or most effective, replies to customer queries.

Gong to shorten sales cycles

Gong's natural language processing capabilities enable busy sales teams to close deals and shorten sales cycles. CEO Amit Bendov explains, '99 per cent of the information shared by customers never makes it to the CRM and the 1 per cent that does is heavily filtered.' (Ohnsman *et al*, 2021) 'Gong translates the information into "higher-order insights". First, it transcribes customer emails, phone and video calls, then it employs machine learning to analyze everything from when a customer is ready to be pitched for a product refresh to which deals are at risk of being lost.'

Replicate human reasoning

There are tools now available that help avoid poor, costly decisions being made. Rainbird allows companies to build visual models of their smartest employees' thought processes, then uses these models to automate decision-making at rates typically 100 times faster and 25 per cent more accurate, with full explainability (see Figure 2.1). James Duez, CEO of Rainbird, comments:

> For me AI is a singularly unhelpful term. It's such a broad church of technologies. Ultimately, when most people hear the term AI, they think about Big Data and machine learning. It's almost become synonymous with that. Whilst of course machine learning and all of its different guises – deep learning and so on – is absolutely AI, not all AI is machine learning. Rainbird has a slightly different

take on it. Rainbird is actually more human down than it is data up. We're in the low code/no code realm of enabling typically subject matter experts, or certainly the business, to be intrinsic to the process of building tools that benefit the business. We would describe ourselves as an automation business more than we actually would an AI business. We're very much focused on helping organizations. It's about how you action what you know.

We represent a new category. We're partnered with five out of the big six global accounting firms, who use Rainbird for automating tax decisions. We work with quite a lot of the big banks and financial service organizations around fraud, financial crime, credit decisioning, KYC and all these different things. Since COVID, we've been doing quite a bit in healthcare. What all our use cases have in common is that they are all typically processes that today have to be done by people. They cannot be reached by other forms of AI. What Rainbird does is it replicates human reasoning.

FIGURE 2.1 Rainbird assists sales teams by building visual models of employees' thought processes

Email   Phone   Event tracking   Automation

SOURCE Rainbird Technologies (2021)

We actually can reason over data in a very similar way to how people reason. When we make a decision, we have all these rules in our head that are the results of our formal education, our careers, the rules that we operate our business by, the experiences of others, and we mix that together with data that we see around us. We might ask questions to get more data if we don't have enough, and eventually we make an inference. We make a judgement. People make between 15 and 20,000 decisions a day, and we're pretty terrible at it. There is a tremendous hidden cost of inconsistent decision-making, which sits latent in organisations because people just make routine errors. What we do is synthesise that process, so we can take logic from your head and we can build that into Rainbird as a Knowledge Graph-based technology. So Rainbird is a rules engine, it's just a very different type of rules engine that can synthesise a process of human reasoning and make decisions at a speed that is of tremendous scale. But, critically, it can make decisions that outperform the expert that built the model. There's no magic. There's no machine learning in Rainbird. The reason why this is important is when Rainbird makes a decision, it can explain itself.

Marketing is going to continue to be significantly enhanced by AI, and machine learning in particular. I think sales is an intrinsically human process, so I think that they are different, but I would say marketing is going to be enhanced by improved development of algorithms that enable you to figure out who to target, how to target them, when to target them and what language based on the large corpus of data that is out there. And that's a perfect machine learning problem because you've got large amounts of data and it doesn't need to be explainable, because if you get it wrong, you pay a commercial price but it's not a question of life and death.

AI and events

Harry Chapman is Global Digital, Portfolio and Content Director at Clarion Events, the company responsible for events such as the Digital Transformation EXPO.

He explains:

The biggest impact AI will make is in areas like automation, where companies are keen to automate basic tasks using technologies such as robotic process automation (RPA). In the longer term my personal view is that digital assistants will have a significant impact, making our working life more productive and supporting us by taking notes in Zoom calls, for example.

AI, for my role, will significantly improve our market research with our audience. We're already able to use tools like Bombora that scrape the web to discover trends in what people are interested in, meaning we can better design our events around our audience's needs. It has also allowed us to automate some content provision functions to ensure our audience stays engaged with our products. Once physical events return, AI will make the onsite meeting experience more productive with improved matching for 1–1 meetings and more efficient encounters between attendees.

There are many ethical questions around AI and I think ethical frameworks are critical for any business long term. Ultimately there needs to be a gold standard on this which is either set down by national governments or the United Nations to ensure AI tools are developed in a way that not only supports humans but also protects them and, in particular, does not disadvantage certain groups such as minorities. Looking ahead to 2030, I think there will be many different tools available to make our working life more efficient. Ultimately, having enhanced AI tools will help improve the way that business leaders can often feel overwhelmed with information and contact points. It should allow them to be more focused on goals, while not missing something which could be business critical.

Emotionally intelligent chatbots

Taking advantage of AI and machine learning (ML) to improve customer service is a big focus in Google's work, as Toju Duke, Responsible AI Program Manager at Google, explains:

> AI is currently being utilized by various organisations to enhance the customer experience. For example, we now have emotionally intelligent chatbots where nearly half of consumers prefer communicating with chatbots for customer service enquiries. Organisations such as Sephora, Asos, Nitro Cafe, Duolingo, Starbucks and so many other businesses, particularly in retail, are adopting the use of chatbots which are driven by AI in handling their customer service programmes. For marketing and sales, the likes of GPT-3, which is a recently launched Natural Language Processing model that uses deep learning to produce human-like text and has the ability to create anything that has a language structure such as websites, blogposts, translate various languages, take memos and even write code; might be the next AI system to carry out marketing tasks, further automating the marketing sector.

As the founder of *The AI Journal*, a free open-source information hub on everything to do with AI and emerging technologies, Tom Allen has his finger on the pulse of the impact AI is having on the business world, and on customer service. He comments:

> Over the next few years, AI will allow businesses to understand their customers in ways never before thought possible. It will also change internal processes that include HR, sales and marketing. It's important to note that not all of this impact will be good. I expect we will see a number of companies attempt to implement AI into their processes without having properly thought out the deployment strategy; this might actually do more damage than good.
>
> Analytics is going to be huge. Everyone will want data visualisation on every device. I'm confident companies like Tableau (Salesforce) will have a great decade ahead of them in terms of revenue. From the analytics, we're going to see AI implemented in customer journeys to make it feel like you're buying from someone who knows as much about you as your best mate, drastically improving the conversion (sales) rates of businesses who utilise AI while lowering acquisition costs. AI will also affect the advertising market massively; consider companies such as Adverity who are making great tools. AI will make the business cost per acquisition when running an advertising/marketing campaign so much more efficient by almost knowing your customer and where to find them without the need of what can be lengthy A/B testing.
>
> There are a number of issues which are troubling, such as how data is used. The fact that the cyber security market is expected to hit close to $100bn by 2023 keeps me awake at night. Another worrying factor is how much businesses will know about someone on their first introduction. At times it will feel great, but at other times it will just feel weird, like speaking to a random stranger on the street who, with no reason at all, knows what food I bought two weeks ago and where I ate out for dinner two months ago.

Let's now take a further look at the AI tools available to the marketing, HR and CX teams.

Start with what you know

Over the past few years, popular software companies have integrated AI tools into their platforms to create 'one-stop shops' for sales, marketing, CX and even HR. Salesforce is one example of this, as its products span multiple business areas, with the company's 'Einstein' AI deeply integrated and providing insights, process automation and assistance.

Salesforce's competitor HubSpot is a popular and intelligent CRM platform. It has seamlessly integrated marketing, sales, customer service and content management into one platform that boasts impressive AI in the back end. Some of these capabilities include: easy importing and management of contacts including duplicate prevention; automatic call recording and transcription; SEO suggestions; webpage optimization and management tools to provide optimal online experiences to customers; insights and research into key contacts; detailed and in-depth insights into customers; predictive lead scoring; and automated customer service offerings.

Accessible for smaller budgets

Tried and trusted platforms are using AI assets to diversify their offering, stay current, and better serve their users. For example, MailChimp has been one of the go-to platforms for newsletters and email marketing for over 20 years. In recent years, it has added a range of AI-powered capabilities to its platform to allow smaller businesses to access some of the same advantages as their larger competitors. This includes personalized product recommendations, forecasting tools for behavioural targeting and tools for writing better email subject lines. Strategic acquisitions have only strengthened the company's offering. Acquiring Sawa led to MailChimp being able to offer its customers a tool to design their own visual assets, while its acquisition of B2B messaging start-up Chatitive allowed MailChimp to move into the territory of conversational automated SMS marketing.

Investing in one strong platform is a wise move for organizations looking to solve problems in multiple areas of their business, but in most cases a specialist tool can create the most impact when tackling a specific problem area.

Minimizing daily minutiae in customer service, sales, HR and marketing

Customer service

One of the major benefits of employing AI is that it is able to take on many of the routine, mundane, time-consuming yet essential tasks that staff must perform every day. In customer service, the day typically involves answering the same customer queries over and over again. Chatbot software is able to alleviate much of the pressure agents face by handling these queries and engaging customers in a dialogue so interactive that they will have no idea they are conversing with a bot. IPSoft's 'Amelia' chatbot is astoundingly human-like. Her 'brain' uses episodic memory, process memory, intent recognition and emotional intelligence to respond to complex queries, process transactions and deliver personalized customer service that adapts according to context. Amelia can analyse 50,000 conversations in less than one second, and highlight to the agent the top five best responses based on semantic analysis.

While many bots can handle queries and converse in multiple languages, some start-ups are developing bots with local and cultural considerations front of mind. Arabot is the first chatbot to use an Arabic NLP engine to understand and analyse Arabic content and conversation in an accurate and efficient way. The bot can understand and communicate in a wide range of Arabic dialects, as well as in English.

Sales

For sales, most of the daily minutiae comes from prospecting, research and following up. Chorus helps make this simpler by automatically transcribing and analysing calls, identifying agreed-upon next steps and collating conversation histories and insights for all of your contacts. ZoomInfo helps find the right new prospects by assisting with territory planning, lead scoring, sales prospecting, conducting targeted outreach and more.

Speaking of one such tool, Nikolas Kairinos says:

> Prospex is one example of a leading start-up that is making great strides in the
> AI sales and marketing space. Prospex's sophisticated AI engine gets to know
> businesses, their marketing objectives and their ideal client. It offers firms a cost-
> effective way to target promising leads and provides increasingly tailored results
> as the engine learns more about the business and its requirements.

The more the sales rep uses Prospex, the more the algorithm learns about their ideal target. Prospex describes its AI tool as 'single-minded', allowing it to focus solely on studying leads and identifying targets. This way, the rep is able to waste less time in hunting down the right leads or casting their net to a wide but potentially disinterested audience.

However, finding new leads is only half of the battle for sales professionals. Aviso helps sales reps stay ahead of the game with deal forecasting and statistical modelling to predict the probability of various opportunities in the sales pipeline. Outreach's AI-powered dashboard allows you to see which prospects are engaged, when contact was last made and what opportunities exist based on data insights. Tools like these enable members of the sales team to spend their time closing the right deals instead of chasing dead ends.

Given the positive influences on efficiency, productivity and effectiveness, there is usually implicit cost savings when adopting AI tools. However, one tool in particular is designed to help sales teams actively generate ROI. People.ai's sales solution analyses years of activity and contact history in order to anticipate risk and make recommendations for a path forward. The platform generates some amazingly detailed insights about prospects and boasts some excellent tracking features to help the sales and marketing teams keep up to date with the status of their efforts and the impacts they are generating. But what's arguably most impressive about the platform is the namesake portion of People.ai: its sales rep-focused capabilities. The People.ai sales solution analyses team performance to track individual performance against targets and identify who is on track to meet their goals and who needs assistance or intervention. People.ai helps companies generate ROI by investing in the skills of their teams. As the platform monitors individual performance, it is able to offer the rep relevant coaching in order to help them overcome hurdles and keep pushing the deal forward.

HR

Building successful teams is a challenging and time-consuming process, as many HR professionals can attest. AI is helping to streamline recruitment and alleviate the burden on the hiring team by handling the first steps of the process.

Textio helps recruiters write job descriptions that will resonate most with potential applicants and can even help to remove language that might imply underlying biases. Platforms such as Mya are being used by some of the world's top companies to build candidate databases, help identify best-fit candidates and applicants, engage them through the process, answer queries, conduct screenings and successfully schedule interviews. Pymetrics helps employers create culture matches by vetting new candidates based on insights from current staff. Current employees take a series of video game-like tests that allow the algorithm to build a persona for the ideal candidate who might fit into specific roles or teams. Candidates take similar tests and are scored based on how well they match. The interview process itself is also benefiting from automation. CV and Impress are some of the leaders in this space, offering capabilities such as bot-conducted text and phone interviews.

Hiring candidates with the right skills and future-ready mindsets is one avenue businesses can take in their digital transformation journey. However, many will choose to invest in the people they already have via training opportunities and professional development initiatives. Much of this can be facilitated by AI. Soffos.ai uses conversational AI in order to offer hyper-personalized workplace learning. Tutoring occurs as a 'Socratic method'-style dialogue between the employee and an AI avatar. Soffos can provide step-by-step guides to complex processes, allowing the trainee to ask for further detail whenever required or prompting actions to avoid mistakes. The platform provides insight into which teams or individuals have gaps in their understanding and can also identify highly competent members of staff. The insights Soffos provides to managers allows them to intervene where necessary and gain an understanding of where their people need the most support. This ultimately helps to save time and valuable resources down the road.

Marketing and communications

However, it is marketing and communications professionals who will see the most relief in their daily workload thanks to AI. So much of the marketer's job has become focused on monitoring and reporting rather than on actual creative strategy. AI tools have been massively beneficial for freeing up time for marketing teams while delivering high-quality insights and outputs.

Reducing the dull tasks that fill marketers' days was the mission of Mark Simpson, founder and former CEO of Acoustic, an independent marketing cloud that has been designed to solve the problems marketers face. The integrated platform allows customers to access all aspects of their marketing in one place, with a simple user interface that makes it easy to craft even the most complex and personalized user experiences. Simpson is optimistic about the future impacts on business given the availability of insight-rich data. He explains:

> AI is already having a significant impact on business today and this will continue to accelerate in both the short and long term… Either way, looking forward there won't be many areas that AI doesn't touch. Over the next two years, as AI gets smarter and more data gets understood, AI will be applied to more and more help those people make better decisions. AI will make business processes more efficient; it will understand more and more complex data and give further insight into our comprehension about individuals.

Acoustic's suite of AI-powered tools put this data to good use in order to help marketers perform a range of their most time-consuming tasks with ease. Its analytics tool helps turn raw, complex data into detailed and in-depth insights about customers and their journey. The personalization tool uses these insights to help deliver a consistent brand experience across all touch-points, as well as providing the individualized experiences today's customers have begun to expect. Acoustic Campaign uses behavioural and profile data to create relevant campaigns across email, web, mobile, SMS, social media and offline channels including telesales and print. The company offers products that span every step of the customer journey and boast unique capabilities that allow marketers to automate the most time-consuming steps in the process.

In addition to Acoustic, there are many other available tools designed to save marketers, PR practitioners and communications professionals precious time while producing valuable outcomes. Signal AI is one such platform. Its 'brain', named AIQ, can read and interpret over 5 million pieces of content a day in over 100 languages and across millions of sources to spot trends and potential crises, interpret customer data and relevant news, and make recommendations to the marketing, PR or comms team. Genus AI's Growth platform helps segment audiences by adding thousands of data points to existing customer data and assigning communication archetypes. From here, the marketer can test out various predictive models to assess the potential effectiveness of content or even the draw specific influencers may have with that audience. Quantcast is another great analytics platform, which helps marketers to drill down into their audiences. The platform helps marketers save time and effort casting a wide net by precisely targeting smaller audience targets with the biggest reach. Its 'Q' AI tool leverages optimal reach and frequency metrics to provide a slow and steady drumbeat of ads, which helps grow brand perception and loyalty in the mind of consumers and draw customers into the sales pipeline before they are even in-market.

Cortex and Unmetric's Xia both ease the burden of conducting competitive analysis and will make campaign and content recommendations based on what these competitors are doing or what will work well with audiences. Acrolinx is another tool that can help businesses develop optimal content strategies and provide scalable solutions for content creation. Conversion.ai's Jarvis AI copywriting assistant is a popular choice for agencies and individuals alike, and is highly effective for generating website, social media, newsletter, advert, email and headline copy. The generated copy boasts perfect grammar, and can automatically be translated into over 11 different languages. You might assume that any copy written by a bot would be staid and formal. Jarvis allows you to select a tone for your copy, such as intelligent or funny, so that your content reflects your brand image effectively.

For companies who are just starting out or considering a rebrand, ZeBrand uses algorithmic logic to create complete brand strategies and generate a brand blueprint. Users are guided by the platform as they refine their thinking about their target customer, their vision, brand story and messaging. The platform's algorithms then use this information to recommend the optimum combination of all visual brand elements including logos, typography, imagery, colours and so on.

Ensuring relevance and brand appropriateness can be a challenge for digital advertisers. How can you absolutely ensure that your ads are ending up where your customers are most likely to see them? Gumgum's advertising platform boasts Verity™, a contextual intelligence engine that uses computer vision and natural language processing to identify and score online content such as images, videos and text to find opportune placements for your adverts that are always brand relevant. Even more impressive though is Verity™'s ability to analyse context in order to steer clear of placements that may be detrimental, insensitive or inappropriate. Before any of your adverts are ever served, Verity™ scans the content for offensive text and imagery, and filters based on your brand's unique safety concerns. That way, your content only ever ends up in the right places at the right time.

Smarter social listening

Social media has become a massively important tool for customer engagement and has revolutionized the way most brands connect with their key audiences in the digital age, which has placed a heavy burden on comms teams. Social media is fast moving, which requires near-constant monitoring for changes in trends or conversation. It is an open forum built on word of mouth, which helps with the success of influencer strategy but also allows negative sentiments to spread like wildfire. There have been loads of advancements in social media-focused AI tools in recent years, which has really allowed marketers to get a strong grip within this ever-changing landscape.

One brand that does this well is Coca-Cola, which produces 3 per cent of all the drinks consumed worldwide. 'AI is the foundation for everything' that Coca-Cola Company does, according to Greg Chambers, Global Director of Digital Innovation at Coca-Cola, as featured in *Analytics India Magazine* (Chaturvedi, 2021). The company harnesses the power of AI and social listening to better understand its consumers. Through Salesforce, Coca-Cola has set up over 40 'social centres' that collect data from social media and analyse it for insights into how the company's products are discussed and shared via social platforms. The company also uses image recognition technology to target potential new customers online. For example, Coca-Cola-owned iced tea brand Gold Peak targets its ads by looking through users' posted images that suggest they like iced tea, or by having algorithms recognise images with logos of competing brands. This is both an efficient way to maximise their ad spend, and also an efficient way to keep up with fast-paced online conversations.

Capabilities such as these can bring massive value to businesses, and we are seeing a rise in tools to make these functions more accessible. As one of the top-ranked social listening tools on the market today, Brandwatch combines the capabilities of various different platforms in order to provide users with unparalleled consumer insights. The Brandwatch Consumer Research platform searches through millions of posts, comments and online conversations to generate insights into audience attitudes around any topic or brand, identify potential trends and spot negative discourse. Brandwatch allows users to sort these conversations into categories such as feedback, comments, opinions and more in order to allow the user to quickly contextualize how and where their brand is being discussed (see Figure 2.2 A and B).

However, the platform's built-in AI assistant, called Iris, is the true star of the show. Iris can track spikes in conversation for you, saving you a lot of time, so that you can then gain insight into why these increases in conversation may have occurred. Brandwatch's AI can also analyse sentiment within these online conversations to gauge customers' attitudes surrounding any brand and identify potential problems before they have a chance to escalate. The platform can analyse 1.5 trillion historical conversations dating back to 2010, as well as monitoring conversations in real time from 105 million unique sites and billions of sources. In fact, 500 million new conversations are added every day.

AI is a fundamental element of the Brandwatch platform. Mercedes Bull, Product Marketing Manager at Brandwatch, explains:

> AI is baked into our products in lots of different ways. We've touched on Iris, our AI assistant, and that helps you surface peaks and spikes within your data. But we've got other features like image analysis, which is also powered by AI. To give you an example of how AI image analysis works, if you're a large brand with a recognisable brand logo, the image analysis will show you locations where your logo has appeared online. Now, that just wouldn't be possible for a human to find. You couldn't possibly look at every single picture online to see if someone's wearing a T-shirt with your logo on it in the background of a photo. It's just not viable. So AI is very much essential and present in lots of different areas of our products. It comes up in lots of different places including Brandwatch Search. This feature launched at the end of last year, and it's an AI-powered search function that automatically knows what you're looking for. So now, if I type the word 'dove' into Brandwatch Search, it's going to know that I mean Dove, the toiletries brand, and not the bird. And again, this is an example of how AI saves time for analysts who are used to typing out these very long, complex boolean queries. In the past, they'd have to type out 'Dove NOT wings NOT bird NOT animal' but now, you don't have to do that. It's just a click of a button, so AI really is embedded into every aspect of our products.

The Brandwatch team has been very strategic in their use of AI, ensuring that it is used to provide maximum benefit rather than providing gimmicky features designed for flash rather than function. Vic Miller, Brandwatch's VP of Global Comms, says:

> One thing that we're mindful of is not to say, 'Oh, look at this shiny new AI thing...' So as a company, we have to be really careful to always be customer first. What challenges are they trying to overcome, and what's their day-to-day workflow? Where can we build in features and clever little additions that are going to really smooth out those workflows? And that's where I think AI will be used well and purposefully and in a meaningful way rather than a gimmicky way. That's really critical.

Since its introduction in 2007, and after various strategic acquisitions and enhancements, the Brandwatch platform and its capabilities have created

FIGURE 2.2 A and B Brandwatch is able to show you where your brand is being talked about online, how often, in what languages and more

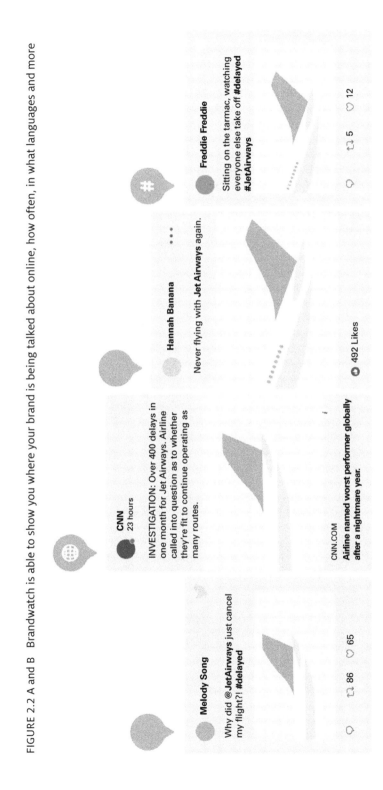

FIGURE 2.2 B

Comments Over Time | All Languages | Last 91 days

Mention volume for Days broken down by Languages

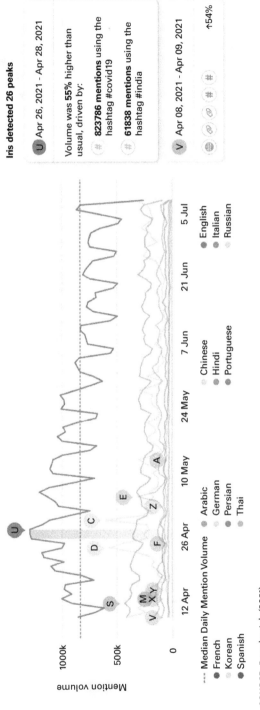

Iris detected 26 peaks

U Apr 26, 2021 - Apr 28, 2021

Volume was **55%** higher than usual, driven by:

823786 mentions using the hashtag #covid19

61838 mentions using the hashtag #india

V Apr 08, 2021 - Apr 09, 2021

@ ⌗ ⌗ ↑54%

--- Median Daily Mention Volume
● French ● Korean ● Spanish ● Arabic ● German ● Persian ● Thai ● Chinese ● Hindi ● Portuguese ● English ● Italian ● Russian

Mention volume

1000k 500k 0

12 Apr   26 Apr   10 May   24 May   7 Jun   21 Jun   5 Jul

SOURCE Brandwatch (2021)

massive benefits for some of the world's biggest and most-beloved brands. Miller says:

> I think the biggest impact we're seeing and we expect to see in the coming years is around two key areas, one being speed and the other being accuracy and depth of insight, and breadth of insights as well. But often it's speeding up the process, so it's doing the work that analysts have to spend a lot of time doing. For example, going through millions of mentions around a big topic. It's finding things that human analysts would struggle to or would never find. It would either take too long or it would be missed just because, again, humans don't have the capacity to go through millions of mentions in extreme detail. So those are probably the most fundamental things that we're seeing, and I think that's why we're seeing a lot of analysts using the platform. They're keen to leverage AI in the right way.

Similarly to Brandwatch, Talkwalker keeps marketing and PR pros in the know with real-time social media monitoring and insights into what's happening on all online media across 187 languages. Digimind and Synthesio both also monitor online conversations about brands and offer in-depth recommendations. But when it comes to social media, content is key. Persado helps generate content that will earn the maximum engagement from users by suggesting the most effective words, images or calls to action for brands to use. Sprout Social's automated technology can help generate tweets replying to fans, customers or followers. BuzzSumo allows users to input specific topics and keywords to receive a breakdown of popular trending posts in those categories, which can then inform content creation. When content needs to be used to drive sales leads, Uberflip makes it possible for brands to personalize experiences by aggregating all of their content into a resource centre based on buyer personas, target accounts or industry verticals.

Examples from hospitality

Many of the major global hotel chains work directly with top vendors including IBM, Google and Amazon to develop their own white-labelled tools that offer guests one-of-a-kind experiences. But while some of these top vendors supply the hardware for in-room AI, the software powering these devices usually comes from elsewhere. There are many hospitality-focused vendors and start-ups shaking up the space and offering massively beneficial tools for improving guest experience.

SONIFI is the largest in-room technology provider in hospitality and is used by top global hotel chains including Hilton, Marriott International, IHG, Hyatt, Wyndham and Radisson. Its interactive solutions and smart room integration technology is what powers many of the Alexa and Google devices guests interact with in their room to control their environment, receive recommendations and make in-room purchases. Other hoteliers, hospitality groups, entertainment venues and airports use Volara's voice-based engagement software to power their guest experiences and answer queries, interpret and translate 29 languages in real time, control room functionality and provide recommendations. India's DigiValet also offers in-room automation with a focus on creating unique experiences tailored to the properties it works with. Meanwhile, in China, start-up Xie Zhu Technology is enhancing the in-room experience by utilizing artificial intelligence of things (AIoT) to power guest-room systems such as smart door locks, smart lighting and smart air-conditioning in over 8,000 hotels across the country.

Dining out is arguably the one area of hospitality where an experience tailored to each guest's exact requests is most essential. When customers order a meal, they expect quality, accuracy and speed. Nala Robotics is changing the game in this space and ensuring customers' specifications are met with its technology, which powers the world's first AI-based robotic restaurant, opened in the US in April 2021. The proprietary AI chef hardware and software can adapt and create dishes precisely as customers request them, ensuring their food is customized to their preferences and dietary requirements. True to its name, India's Fastor Future AI-enabled self-checkout technology platform gets your food to you faster by expediting the takeaway and dine-in process.

In the hospitality industry, guest experience starts before they ever reach their room or sit down at their table. There are loads of amazing tools available to help drive the sales journey to completion and make a strong first impression. One of these is allora.ai, which encourages guests to book direct, helps with upselling or cross selling and reduces cancellations by offering guests specialized targeted offers, discounts, upgrades or incentives. InnSpire's GuestMagic.AI customizes each guest's experience by presenting personalized discounts and event or experience offers, and targeted messaging throughout their journey. Guests can even check into the hotel in a tech-forward way using the platform's facial recognition software. The Hotels Network's Oraculo uses predictive personalization to tailor the website experience at every touchpoint and allow for behavioural and intent-based targeting.

Many hospitality venues are turning to AI-powered robots to provide top-quality service to guests. While some innovative hoteliers have been using robotics at their properties for years, we saw a wider uptake of the technology as a result of the coronavirus pandemic as guests put a greater emphasis on safety. To assist with enhanced cleaning and sanitation measures, hospitality hubs including Heathrow Airport, St Pancras International, various convention centres and hotels around the world are now employing the UV-sanitizing robots offered by companies such as Savioke, Xenex and Denmark's UVD Robots. As guests began to prefer contactless experiences, two of China's biggest hotel chains introduced robots created by ExcelLand to deliver room service to their guests. To deliver contactless food service, many restaurants around the world are adding Pulu Robotics' BellaBots to their waitstaff. Given the impacts of the pandemic, it is likely that we will continue to see more vendors entering the marketplace offering tools that reflect the changes in priorities that COVID-19 left in its wake.

The human side of AI

Despite the friendly demeanours of voice assistants and bots, or the deep levels of personalization that seem to know us better than we know ourselves, we tend not to think of technology as something that is warm, personable or emotional. AI is data driven, so we view it as being straightforward and facts focused, concerned only with hard metrics and concrete figures. Surprisingly, some of the most remarkable use cases for AI in areas such as sales, marketing, HR and CX are those that deal with human complexity and emotion. AI may not be human, but it can provide some incredible insight into a key area that separates man from machine: sentiment.

In sales, it can sometimes be difficult to read whether or not a prospect is interested or to gauge a customer's mood based on their interactions. Cogito uses real-time conversation analysis to detect human signals in customers' speech and offers recommendations for the reaction the sales and support teams should provide. According to Miller, the sales teams at Brandwatch use a tool called Drift in their sales cycle to improve how they interact with buyers. The sales team is able to personalize conversations at an early buyer stage and bring prospects through the process smoother by answering questions rather than continuously offering a demo. Drift allows the team to identify if the prospect needs a bit more human interaction, some content, or more information.

There are various benefits to marketing as well. Affectiva uses novel 'Emotion AI' to analyse consumers' unfiltered and unbiased emotional and cognitive responses to videos, adverts and other content pieces. Talkwalker, the social media monitoring tool mentioned previously, also has built-in sentiment analysis to help assess the tone of online conversations, and the negative or positive feelings that may be attached to a brand or campaign.

In HR, HireVue can assess the candidate's body language, tone, work ethic and more in real time during a video interview. But once a candidate is part of the team, how can the organization encourage them to stay? There has been an emergence of tools focused on improving company culture and employee experience, which in turn helps to avoid costly turnover and low morale. Culture Amp is a popular tool in this space. It can assess underlying issues within the organization and alert leadership before these problems grow bigger. Other use cases include conducting more developmental and positive performance reviews, providing a continuous constructive feedback loop and gaining insight into employee engagement.

Replacement versus reshaping

Given the enhanced capabilities and outputs these tools can provide, one of the biggest concerns that staff have when their company is adopting AI is whether or not their job will be replaced by technology. The truth is that some roles will be replaced by automation, but in terms of functions such as sales, marketing, HR, comms and PR, it is much more likely that AI will reshape rather than replace.

While many of these tools boast multiple beneficial capabilities, the fact of the matter is that AI is a specialist technology. It can often perform these functions better than a human can, but AI lacks the versatility that humans have. Technology has not yet reached the point of superintelligence or general intelligence, and some experts are doubtful if it ever will. AI tools can provide insight, but humans are still needed to make sense of that information and translate it into contextual and business-relevant actions. While AI can help to inform or roll out a strategy, we are not at a point where it can actually create the strategy for the business. Human workers and technology need to work in tandem to ensure that the tools being employed are getting the right results and helping the organization achieve its goals.

CASE STUDY
Phrasee and Dixons

Parry Malm, CEO of Phrasee, comments:

> A great example of how Phrasee has been used to accelerate a digital
> transformation is that of Dixons Carphone. We've worked with the brand for well
> over a year now, and were helping the team increase reach and effectiveness of
> its online business. And it was all well and good and so forth. Then Coronavirus
> hit, and suddenly these traditional bricks-and-mortar retailers had to supercharge
> their digital transformation because it was no longer a matter of doing it across
> the next five years. It was a matter of doing it across the next five minutes. So
> what Dixons Carphone did was to double down its investment in Phrasee and
> started really embracing the concept that online was the way forward. Off the
> back of that, Dixons Carphone reports back to us that it gets a 29-to-1 ROI from its
> investment in Phrasee, which I mean, is great. Ultimately what it's meant is if you
> look through the sort of overarching results that the Dixons Carphone group
> released to the city, it's had an absolutely storming time in its online business.
> That's because it was an early adopter of advanced technology like Phrasee and
> others (See Figure 2.3 A, B and C). And what that meant is that it was set up to
> really expedite that transformation. Other companies, sadly, are not so fortunate,
> because they had been resting on their laurels assuming that the good times
> would never end.
>
> The people who will survive and thrive – in whatever the future landscape
> might look like – need to be able to deal with ambiguous situations. They need to
> be able to synthesize many different sources of disparate information and they
> need to be able to take risks when risks are needed. It will be those beholden to
> the status who will suffer and those who can adapt to change will succeed, no
> matter what the landscape looks like in ten years.

Predicting customer needs at scale

Glint is an emerging leader in employee engagement and survey technology,
which was acquired by LinkedIn in November 2018. Mary Poppen is Chief
Customer Officer. She explains:

> I believe AI will be more widely applied across industries and allow organizations
> to innovate at an even further accelerated pace as well as more closely target
> specific customers' needs. Currently it takes organizations a significant amount
> of time to combine data points across systems and then run analyses looking for

FIGURE 2.3 A, B and C Three examples of the Phrasee platform's interface

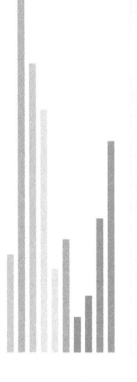

Dashboard

Campaigns

Hey there,
you look awesome
today!

Welcome to the Phrasee Dashboard.

Create new campaign

Open rate leaderboard

Don't you forget about me   Control

Psst! I'm still waiting...

Don't leave your cart behind (ready to return to shopping?)

Don't you forget about your cart? Click to come back

I'm still here!

Find out what's inside this message 😊

One click and I'm yours!

Your cart is lonely without you 👀

Check this out: the items you were looking at are still available

Your items are waiting... Have another look at THESE

FIGURE 2.3 B

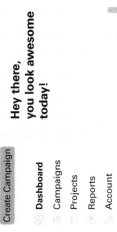

Create Campaign

Dashboard
Campaigns
Projects
Reports
Account

Hey there,
you look awesome
today!

FIGURE 2.3 C

Dashboard
Campaigns

Hey there,
you look awesome
today!

Welcome to the Phrasee **Dashboard**.

Here are your campaign results form
your weekly promotional email campaign.

Create new campaign

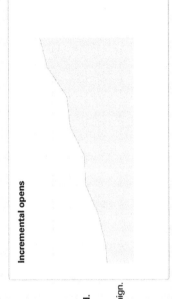

Incremental opens

Incremental clicks

Total Avg. open uplift

Total Avg. click uplift

SOURCE Phrasee (2021)

interesting insights. Also, if you don't know what questions to ask, you aren't likely to find insights that will help you innovate or differentiate the customer experience. AI will proactively point companies toward what is important for customers vs. companies having to struggle to find it.

Ideally, AI will help companies predict customer needs at scale while also helping shape what customers want. This will allow companies to be more proactive than ever before in addressing customer needs. In addition, it will allow companies to continue to innovate and differentiate their service as a customer needs change. AI takes time to build correctly and to ensure the insights are valid and accurate; my concern is around relying on AI too soon and making high-impact decisions before validation is determined. Like humans, AI isn't perfect, therefore a caution should be to rely on additional validation techniques before making significant decisions.

By 2030, companies will be able to deliver a much more personalized customer experience to each and every customer based on dynamic insights gained from multiple seamlessly integrated data sources! And much of the tactical customer experience will be automated, leaving more time for live interactions to be strategic and transformational.

AI-enabled marketing automation

Dynamic market forces such as fast-changing consumer behaviour puts added pressure on marketing professionals. In order to address these shifting customer needs, they require reliable insights. AI-enabled marketing automation solutions enable them to remain agile and surface deeper insights. This allows them to take a more strategic approach to their email marketing programs. AI-enabled marketing views customers in real time, taking account of their changing behaviour and preferences, and improving customer segmentation accordingly.

Centralized customer data enables marketers to use AI-powered email marketing to make smart predictions and to segment and market to their customers according to lifecycle stages.

Connecting marketing, sales and CX for long-term advantage

Guy Gadney is founder and CEO of Charisma AI, which powers interactive narrative experiences for broadcasters, games companies and immersive media. It uses natural language processing (NLP) to create strongly character-focused entertainment, bringing these characters to life for audiences who want to deepen their experiences of the stories they love. Gadney explains:

> Above-the-line marketing will change substantially through good use of NLP to power voice-driven characters for campaigns, brand representation and discovery. A significant percentage of press releases and company updates are already being written by AI, and ironically read by AI to be summarized and categorized. As regards CX, we will see AI-powered hyper-personalization of content, where the customer's profile details are used as a prompt to generate original content. GPT-3 is well-capable of this. Indeed, CX and marketing could easily overlap as content for campaigns becomes colourized and scripted uniquely to you, with a soundtrack created for you, and offers presented using 'trigger sentiment' to make you purchase!

Another company worthy of our attention is Behavioral Signal Technologies, Inc. (Behavioral Signals), which is bridging the communication gap between humans and machines by introducing emotional intelligence, from speech, into conversations with AI (see Figure 2.4).

The company has created an evolving and robust emotion AI, enabling users to add emotion and behavioural recognition to their own software solutions, through the Oliver API. Whether it's for a virtual assistant on a mobile phone, on the web, in a car, on a smart speaker, or for a social robot, an interactive child's toy or a robotic carer, companies, developers or DIY enthusiasts can now design and build engaging interactions. The company's CEO, Rana Gujral, explains:

> As more companies start to use AI, the way they understand their own business will evolve. You'll see your basic AI analytics where a decision-maker garners insights and makes better decisions. You'll also see more sophisticated solutions like the one we provide, AI-Mediated Conversations, that influence the conversational dynamic and aim for improved employee performance. The possibilities of AI are endless. Anything that can be improved by automation and data insights will have an impact. Even if it's just a simple insight of knowing if one's consumer is actually engaged with one's brand or products.
>
> AI applications, and more specifically Emotion AI, have the potential to impact every aspect of our lives, from e-commerce, media and entertainment to health care and advertising. Marketing, sales and CX are all important aspects of these industries.

In marketing, emotions are memory markers. They influence brand awareness and drive purchase decisions. Major brands will use emotion AI to quantify consumer emotion engagement with their content and brands. In media and entertainment, a movie studio can use emotion analytics to determine viewers' engagement during a trailer and tweak it to make it more impactful. An automotive company can leverage emotion AI to provide the best in-car experience with emotional awareness and a driver's personalized profile. Emotion AI can help control the operation of the vehicle or to determine when to introduce hints to counter the emotional stress of the driver.

FIGURE 2.4 Behavioral Signals infuses emotion into customer communications by analysing speech

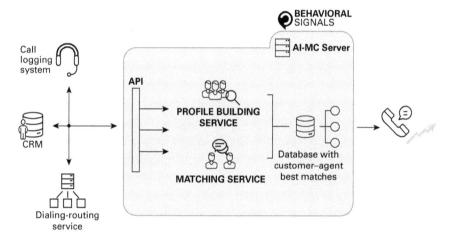

SOURCE Courtesy of Behavioral Signals (2021)

Over the coming years we will see more industries using AI, but the solution will include a human element. AI can take the redundant, process-related work, so that humans can focus on what they do best. AI is most accurate when there is a human on the back end training and optimizing the models. It is relatively easy to automate manual tasks but finding the insights that are actually valuable has proven difficult for companies. There is an incredible opportunity for marketing teams to better use those insights to understand what it means for consistent messaging across the organization.

In this buyer-centric world, companies need to connect with customers on their terms. Drift helps companies engage in real-time, personalized conversations with the right customers at the right time, so they can build trust and accelerate revenue. Their Revenue Acceleration Platform helps them to achieve this. Maggie Crowley, Senior Director of Product at Drift, explains:

> Over the next two years we'll likely see a better understanding of what AI actually means and how you can apply it. We'll also get a better understanding about what data sets are available for companies to use because AI ultimately depends on your ability to have a good set of training data. We'll hopefully not just see innovation in how we get access to training data, but on how that training data is fair and combats biases.
>
> Marketers now have to squeeze every last drop out of the activities they're investing in. With AI automating more redundant tasks, it should allow marketers to focus on the hard questions, like what is the right story? Who are we as a brand? What do our customers care about? That's what people want to think about and AI should allow marketers to be more efficient and give them time to think about the more complex tasks.

CASE STUDY
Drift and Smartling

Adrian Cohn is Head of Marketing at New York-based firm Smartling, a leader in translation management software and translation services. When he joined the marketing team, his priority was to fix product messaging and brand experience. It was also painfully obvious that their challenge was beyond messaging. The buyer experience was fundamentally out of date.

As Cohn explains on the Drift blog: 'Our website was stuck in 2010 and was too old school. Hard to navigate. Forms everywhere. Complicated buying process. We spent a lot of time developing the website with very little return.'

He turned to conversational AI tool Drift Automation, which engages every customer on a client's site in seconds using automated chatbots, gently steering them in the right direction. The Drift insights provide valuable and unexpected guidance for marketing strategy:

> Drift was the key technology on our new website to connect with our buyers – and it became a competitive advantage for Smartling. Instead of the complex forms of the past, we asked three simple questions through Drift, 'Do you want to know about our translators, do you want to know about our technology, or do you want to book a meeting right now?'.
>
> By engaging people immediately and eliminating forms, Smartling made it more likely for interested people to share their contact information. As a result, Smartling doubled conversion of leads engaged on their website. At a later stage,

Smartling saw an opportunity to maximize every business opportunity by connecting in the moment with qualified buyers, irrespective of the time of day or team availability. Creating this seamless experience offered a competitive advantage at every touchpoint in the customer lifecycle. It has paid dividends.

You learn an incredible amount about what your prospects and customers are looking for in the conversation data from Drift Automation. We didn't have a 'plans page' on Smartling's website and we wanted to have better conversations with our buyers about pricing upfront. After reviewing the conversation data, we realized that 150+ people each month were asking about pricing and packaging, and withholding this information at the entry point to our brand was not simplifying the buyer's journey.

With this insight, Adrian redesigned the pricing page in a way that directly addressed what he now knew potential buyers were asking. 'This became part of our top-level navigation, and a key converting page for our website' (Drift, n.d.).

The new AI sales landscape

In this digital world, buyers are inundated with content from multiple vendors via a plethora of channels from an assortment of vendors. In turn, sellers can lose sight of what is important and where best to focus their time. AI and machine learning simplify this by transforming data from content analytics into intelligent insights that enable go-to-market teams to maximize revenue and improve conversion. A seller can now take advantage of AI to provide tailored, timely recommendations in order to maximize sales.

Seismic drives growth through storytelling

Seismic is the global leader in sales enablement, which enterprises such as IBM and American Express use to deliver engaging buyer experiences that drive growth. Its Storytelling Platform allows marketers to orchestrate content delivery across all channels, and for sellers to engage with prospective buyers in a tailored way at each step of the buyer journey. Eve Alexander, Senior Director, Product Marketing at Seismic, comments:

At the top of sales-related job descriptions, modern salespeople are expected to spend time with clients and customers, build relationships and share relevant information to help buyers make decisions. But then reality strikes, and the actual day-to-day work of a salesperson becomes a juggling act of priorities, such as training, irrelevant meetings and more. This leads to information overload and decision fatigue on what to do next. AI can help sellers share the most useful content that leads to a better buying experience, while getting salespeople back to spending time with customers and closing deals.

Seismic's vision for AI-guided selling is to make sellers more efficient and effective by using data to offer focused, real-time recommendations, and empowering the seller to execute those recommendations. AI will give sellers a competitive edge and more time back in their day to engage with buyers.

Seismic's vision of AI-guided selling falls into four main opportunities:

1 **Provide relevant reminders.** For example, the last time you spoke to this prospect, you sent this piece of content. Seismic's technology shows that they have not read it yet, prompting you to consider following up with a related piece of content.

2 **Share broader context.** For example, this prospect has been active in online discussion groups about how your product compares. Here is relevant content you can share with them to move the conversation along.

3 **Identify gaps and opportunities.** For example, this meeting includes Ken, who is very technical. Seismic has your presentation to include relevant slides for Ken.

4 **Recommend the next best action.** For example, based on the questions the client had in this meeting, here are a few ways to follow up.

At the centre of this new era of AI selling is content, for example blogs and web copy. Measuring such content actually allows the organization to assess the impact of marketing effectiveness, seller performance and buyer engagement. Equipping marketing and sales teams with the right tech tools allows them to build up an essential picture of content use, performance and value, which hugely impacts revenue optimization. It unearths crucial analytics such as content performance internally, externally and across multiple platforms. It provides the essential science needed to assess the efficiency of content production with regards to resource and budget.

Bluecat uses Gong to understand its sales pipeline

Bluecat works the world's biggest enterprises, helping them to overcome the compounding complexity in their networks so they can focus on bigger things.

BlueCat found pipeline management very challenging, and forecasts were often inaccurate. Data was not available to understand why results in different regions were inconsistent.

Gong allows BlueCat to understand customer sentiment, and whether engagement is going up or down. The company also knows which staff to deploy in a deal to ensure success. Coaching has improved, and teams have easy access to product feedback.

Quoted on the Gong website, Jason van Ravenswaay, Head of Global Sales Operations at BlueCat, explains:

> I think I'm most proud of the fact that we've increased communication across departments. We had a sales organization that was going and doing what they were supposed to do. We had a product organization that was going and developing what they thought customers want. Gong has really allowed us to understand the value that customers see in our product and where our product could potentially go in the future.
>
> (Gong, n.d.)

Replicant scales human-like customer service calls

Replicant features an AI bot with a humanlike voice that can hold a conversation with people calling with customer service questions. It eliminates wait times and can autonomously resolve basic issues, routing more complex queries that require greater empathy to a human agent.

In the insurance sector for example, Replicant seamlessly interacts with new and existing policy holders to improve conversion of new policy sales. If a potential client starts the insurance process, but doesn't complete it, Replicant advises them to call or send a text to schedule a call-back. The insights allow firms to offer complementary insurance coverage to existing policy holders to increase up-sell by automatically scheduling outbound calls for follow up.

Narrativ helps brands acquire customers through trusted creators

Voted by Fast Company as one of the most innovative enterprise companies of 2021, Narrativ enables brands and retailers to acquire new customers. Its platform automatically identifies independently produced online reviews and links them to the relevant e-commerce sites. Reviewers can opt in to earn a percentage of any sales driven by their link.

Comm tech and decision augmentation

Comm tech is a new term being applied to the impact that tools such as AI are having on the world of communications. The challenges for comms professionals are varied and crucial – for example, the eye-watering volume and velocity of data available and the imperative to dynamically understand the perception, reputation and risk of your brand. AI technology now has the power to transform these challenges into opportunities.

Commenting in the company blog, David Benigson, founder and CEO of Signal AI, comments:

> I believe that we are at the dawn of the age of augmented intelligence, where machines can be trained to learn and enhance human thought and knowledge. This possibility of augmenting decision-making means platforms like Signal AI will be used as an extension to the decision-making capabilities of business and comms leaders. This empowers leaders to surface insights in the moment. Before you have to ask, the system has served up nuggets of intelligence, warnings of risk and emerging opportunities for you.
>
> There is of course no substitute for exceptional and specialized industry knowledge. But given the volume and velocity of information available in the world, AI is an enabler of higher-quality and differentiated work that simply builds on and enhances existing knowledge.
>
> (Benigson, n.d.)

Move up the food chain to strategy

For decades, PR professionals have focused activity on tactical, albeit important, tasks such as news monitoring and creating coverage reports. The CIPR's State of the Profession report illustrates this clearly: 'Despite calls for public relations professionals to shift away from tactics towards strategic influence, practitioners are still overwhelmingly engaged in tactical delivery.'

But AI is now changing the game, offering valuable data insights that enable teams to create effective communications strategies and improved reputation-based decisions for the company, as opposed to basing decisions on scientifically flawed metrics such as Advertising Value Equivalency (AVE).

As Signal AI states, comms teams are now expected to be able to ask and answer strategic questions to make these better decisions, such as:

- What do we want our company to be famous for?
- What are the key drivers of trust in our brand?
- What threats and issues are emerging in my supply chain?
- How do we measure the impact of our work and relate the impact back to business performance metrics?

Reporting on Joe Biden's first three months as US President

Media reporter Sara Fischer, from Axios, used Signal AI's data-powering tool to report the topics most associated with US President Joe Biden's first three months' presidency as featured in the US top-tier media.

In his blog on the company website, Signal AI's CEO Benigson explains how this was possible:

> A human can't monitor all of this in real time, with potentially thousands of media in hundreds of languages, or make these connections or unknown unknowns that our knowledge graph serves up. Traditionally this would have taken 100s of hours for a team of analysts to achieve, so it is the symbiosis of the knowledge with the power, trainability and scale of the AI.
>
> Our platform scans the world's information, analysing it on behalf of the user and checking it for hidden risks and opportunities. The change can be seen as moving from a passive system, where you tell the tool the brand you are interested in, to an interactive system where the user and the tool are working with each other.
>
> We need new tools and capabilities to answer those questions in a sophisticated way. This is not to say that cuttings or monitoring is redundant, but it now needs to be combined with sophisticated insight and data gathering. For example, the Signal AI platform ingests over 5 million documents a day and can be trained to understand emerging risks and opportunities in real time, with the ability to create bespoke perception and reputation indexes. It can surface themes a brand, person or product may be most associated with, and track how that changes in real time, providing crucial in-the-moment insight into emerging risks and opportunities.
>
> (Benigson, n.d.)

AI-powered reputation-based decision-making

Global banks are using Signal AI for key reputation-based decision-making through a bespoke trust and reputation index.

Deloitte uses Signal AI to track and monitor global data to spot pertinent changes in regulations for their clients, surfacing hyper-relevant updates on trending topics related to compliance and providing sentiment signals for where regulatory change might be occurring.

EY, one of the world's largest professional services firms, uses Signal AI to co-create a 'trust' score to identify the trustworthiness and perception of organisations. This enables better decisions by creating custom machine learning models on critical pillars of trust, such as ethics, financial scandal, brand perception, allowing the model to reflect the client's criteria. EY saved hundreds of hours of analysis by dynamically monitoring trust, but more importantly the partnership has led to a different process in key decision-making altogether.

Jennifer Prosek is founder of Prosek Partners, an international public relations and financial communications consultancy. At Signal AI Leadership Summit, she commented:

> It used to be 'it's not personal, it's business'. That has gone out of the window now, everything is personal, we're talking about a health crisis, we're talking about a race and inequality crisis, making the workplace a safe place while the rest of the world is falling apart. These are incredibly important and relatively new things for business leaders, who used to only have to think about the investors, and the bottom line.
>
> (Benigson, n.d.)

The successful comms leaders will adopt these tools and thereby gain a significant advantage over their peers, drive crucial trust in their own brand, and ultimately power business performance.

For our last interview of this chapter, we turn to Marc Woodhead, Founder and CEO of Holograph – a digital consultancy that helps businesses solve their problems using existing systems alongside its own software as a service platform. This enables brands and product owners to communicate better with their consumers and clients, from digital campaigns to automated communication and consumer care (see Figure 2.5). Woodhead comments:

> Machine learning is being used more and more effectively to do everything from manipulating the outcome of elections to enticing consumers into a purchase

funnel. The more data collected on each demographic, the more opportunity the new algorithms have to develop an understanding of each and provide a suitable matched output. For example, if you have a range of drinks from alcoholic to soft but you collect data across your entire consumer base in a modern CDP, the opportunity to enhance sales across each group increases. Using time, location, weather and learned interests as the basic programmatic markers, we can ensure the right advert, with dynamic messaging and imagery, is delivered at the right time to the right person to increase the chance of conversion in that moment.

In the future, with enhanced and generalised use of facial and biometric data, real-time advertising can target individuals without their knowledge, subconsciously increasing the chance of sale of that brand or product 'in the moment', as you come near the store or even on your journey to a shopping centre. Imagine each car seeing a different advert on their journey as they pass large outdoor signage.

Is the tech ready yet for this to happen at scale?

This tech is already being used at scale, with the subtle influences of remarketing, targeted advertising etc being highly effective methods to increase sales and entice consumers into advanced and personalised sales funnels. Examples range from Instagram and YouTube to search engines and programmatic advertising on outdoor signage. Holograph specialise in bringing all of this together and using a combination of our own tools and others to create an advanced CDP at a cost-effective level.

Is it affordable? How can CMOs get started?

Systems are becoming more ubiquitous and generally available. Most major consumer sales-oriented companies are investing heavily in this sector, but the basics are already available for free through good use of Facebook, Instagram, and Google advertising tools.

The most important thing is for a CMO to recognise the advantages and upskill or source skills to enable the opportunity for their business. After that, the tools range from the ones mentioned above to global powerhouses in this sector such as P&G all the way through to MailChimp communication automation services. There are tools and price points for any organisation, so it does not need to be costly to get started.

FIGURE 2.5   Holograph uses in-depth insight to deliver the right content at the right times

SOURCE Holograph (2021)

PRACTICAL TAKEAWAYS CHECKLIST: TOP 10 TIPS

1   As well as leading vendors such as AWS and IBM Watson, there are now multiple, affordable AI tools on the market for sales, CX and marketing.

2   Using AI, companies report improvements of almost 25 per cent in customer experience, as well as accelerated rates of innovation, higher competitiveness, higher margins and better employee experience.

3   AI can help teams to be agile, resilient, innovative and able to scale.

4   There are AI and ML tools now available that avoid poor, costly decisions being made.

5   Marketing will be enhanced by improved development of ML algorithms that enable professionals to figure out who to target, how to target them, when to target them and in what language, based on the large corpus of data that is out there.

6   Emotionally intelligent chatbots in sectors such as retail are increasingly handling customer service programmes.

7   The impact of analytics will be huge. Deep knowledge of the customer will drastically improve the conversion rates of businesses who utilize AI while lowering acquisition costs.

8   Investing in one strong platform is a wise move for organizations looking to solve problems in multiple areas of their business, but in most cases a specialist tool can create the most impact when tackling a specific problem area.

9   Marketing and communications professionals will see the most relief in their daily workload thanks to AI. It will free up time while delivering high-quality insights and outputs.

10 Some roles will be replaced by automation, but in functions such as sales, marketing, HR, comms and PR, it is much more likely that AI will reshape rather than replace.

Bibliography

Balakrishnan, T, Chui, M, Hall, B and Henke, N (2020) The State of AI in 2020, McKinsey & Company, www.mckinsey.com/business-functions/mckinsey-analytics/our-insights/global-survey-the-state-of-ai-in-2020 (archived at https://perma.cc/GQ5T-SARV)

Benigson, D (n.d.) Changing the Way Communicators Work, *Signal AI*, www.signal-ai.com/blog/changing-the-way-communicators-work (archived at https://perma.cc/42FC-YEZ5)

Chaturvedi, M (2021) How Coca-Cola and PepsiCo Use AI to Bubble Up Innovation, *Analytics India Magazine*, www.analyticsindiamag.com/how-coca-cola-and-pepsico-use-ai-to-bubble-up-innovation/ (archived at https://perma.cc/7465-6YXB)

Clement, J (2021) COVID-19 Impact on Global Retail E-commerce Site Traffic 2019–2020, *Statista*, www.statista.com/statistics/1112595/covid-19-impact-retail-e-commerce-site-traffic-global/ (archived at https://perma.cc/MVU7-PZS6)

Drift (n.d.) How Smartling Modernized Their Buyer Experience with Drift, *Drift*, www.drift.com/case-studies/smartling/ (archived at https://perma.cc/QVL8-3VDM)

Gong (n.d.) BlueCat Empowers Their Field Team to Understand Their Pipeline, www.gong.io/case-studies/bluecat-empowers-their-field-team-to-understand-their- pipeline/#:~:text=Jason%20van%20Ravenswaay%2C%20the%20 %E2%80% 8E,they%20were%20supposed%20to%20do. (archived at https://perma.cc/6G6S-L5X8)

International Data Corporation (2020) IDC Survey Finds Artificial Intelligence Adoption Being Driven by Improved Customer Experience, Greater Employee Efficiency, and Accelerated Innovation, *IDC*, www.idc.com/getdoc.jsp?containerId=prUS46534820 (archived at https://perma.cc/WW83-RYPN)

Lardinois, F (2020) Mailchimp Launches New AI Tools As It Continues Its Transformation to Marketing Platform, *TechCrunch*, www.techcrunch.com/2020/09/22/mailchimp-launches-new-ai-tools-as-it-continues-its-transformation-to-marketing-platform/ (archived at https://perma.cc/YE5T-H5GL)

McKinsey & Company (2021) The Next Normal Arrives: Trends that will define 2021 – And beyond, www.mckinsey.com/featured-insights/leadership/the-next-normal-arrives-trends-that-will-define-2021-and-beyond (archived at https://perma.cc/AD2Z-S76G)

Ohnsman, A, Cai, K, Popkin, H, Pratap, A and Wolpow, N (2021) AI 50 2021: America's most promising artificial intelligence companies, *Forbes*, www.forbes.com/sites/alanohnsman/2021/04/26/ai-50-americas-most-promising-artificial-intelligence-companies/?sh=4df39fec77cf (archived at https://perma.cc/E3KF-3LDW)

Soper, T (2021) Mailchimp Acquires Chatitive, A B2B Messaging Startup and Madrona Venture Labs Spinout, *GeekWire*, www.geekwire.com/2021/mailchimp-acquires-chatitive-b2b-messaging-startup-madrona-venture-labs-spinout/ (archived at https://perma.cc/MG8H-Y3ZR)

03

How AI is reshaping the world of retail and hospitality

In this chapter we investigate the important role that AI is playing in the retail and hospitality sectors, and review its precursor, the dot com wave. We explore the impact of the technology through case studies, and review many of the tools now available for the innovative retailers and hospitality companies. By now readers should be evolving beyond the stereotypical belief that AI equals machines replacing human employees. We uncover even more evidence of the power of AI to unleash innovation and expedite revenue growth across the sales, marketing and customer experience functions.

Fear of artificial intelligence (AI) has most certainly dissipated, and interest in AI/machine learning (ML) tools has been steadily growing. According to a 2021 Juniper Networks survey:

- 95 per cent of people who are directly involved with their company's AI plans believe that their organizations would benefit from embedding AI into their daily operations, products and services;

- 88 per cent would like to use AI as much as possible;

- 6 per cent of C-level executives have reported adoption of AI-powered solutions across their organization.

Really intelligent retail

The retail industry is in an interesting but difficult spot. Today's consumers are more digitally savvy than ever before. Thanks to smartphones, we have access to whatever we want, whenever we want it. If our local high-street shop does not have the exact item we desire, we can simply order it online and have it delivered to our home swiftly and cheaply. This move to the dot com world was a major hurdle for retailers to overcome. Sadly, many beloved and well-established brands closed their doors permanently after folding to the pressures of omnichannel and the increased global competition. Then, adding to the sector's woes, the pandemic hit.

When businesses were forced to shut their doors due to lockdown restrictions, their customers flocked to their websites. Data from Statista found that retail websites generated almost 22 billion visits in June 2020 at the height of the pandemic, up from 16.07 billion global visits in January 2020 when most countries had yet to take action and lock down (Clement, 2020).

As we move forward and rebuild, customers are no longer satisfied with distinctly digital or physical experiences, and instead want an experience that encompasses the best of both and transitions seamlessly between the two environments. Being able to easily navigate this space and effortlessly provide tailored, relevant and unique experiences is one of the key benefits of adopting AI for customer engagement. Retailers around the globe have begun successfully harnessing the power of this technology in order to boost their bottom lines and better serve their customers through improved website visits, memorable in-store experiences, smarter stocking and demand forecasting, theft prevention, increased convenience for customers and more personalization throughout the entire customer journey.

Expanding the lead

Many of the world's most prominent retailers are adopting AI tools in order to keep their competitive advantages or even deepen their stronghold. At present, Walmart is still managing to edge out Amazon as the world's biggest retailer, and it is hoping to use technology to maintain that edge. Walmart has managed to stay on the cutting edge for years and was even one of the earliest adopters of using RFID technology for inventory tracking. In 2020, Walmart began rolling out its AI-powered Express Delivery service in a number of its US stores. Once a customer takes their order to the checkout stage on the company's website or app, a logistics algorithm uses resource optimization and delivery routing to determine whether or not that order can be delivered in a given 'express time slot.' Once the Express Delivery order has been successfully placed, it is routed to yet another AI-powered system that handles fulfilment and coordinates picking, packing and delivery pickup. This step in the process can be completed in as little as 15 minutes. Soon, the last leg of this journey may be fully automated, as the company has announced various partnerships with companies offering self-driving vehicles.

But as many retailers turn to tech to compete in the e-commerce space, Walmart is focusing many of its efforts elsewhere. One key advantage the company has over online players such as Amazon is its own physical locations worldwide and those of its global subsidies such as Asda, Sam's Club, Seiyu and Massmart. In 2019, Walmart decided to devote energy into maximizing these assets by exploring AI's benefits in the physical retail environment with the launch of its Intelligent Retail Lab (IRL). The 'Lab' isn't a lab at all but rather one of Walmart's busiest stores located in New York. The 50,000 square foot retail space is equipped with a bevy of sensors, cameras and processors that assess conditions such as product availability, stock on shelves, quality of fresh food products and customer footfall. The AI working on the back end of these sensors and processors is then able to notify employees when stock needs to be refreshed or rotated, queues have grown too long, or the supply of shopping trolleys runs too low. The pilot has been a success for the company, helping improve inefficiencies and even leading the company to introduce and patent a new shelving design. Four other stores in other US locations have since been adapted into labs and, if successful, these IRLs will inform the company's future store designs.

Gains in grocery

Walmart is not the only food retailer leveraging technology to optimize its inventory, efficiency and customer experiences. Although disruptors such as Ocado have made fully-online food shopping a possibility, and many of the world's biggest grocery chains have begun integrating e-commerce elements into their businesses, the grocery game is still primarily bricks-and-mortar dominated. It is in this space that we see some of AI's biggest benefits in retail come to life.

Many grocers have adopted AI in recent years to help boost efficiency and reduce costly wastes within their businesses. Costco, a US-based warehouse store chain with outlets in various countries worldwide, uses ML to optimize its in-store bakery sections. Using historical sales data, the retailer worked with SAP to develop an algorithm that allows them to better predict customer demand to ensure they have the right amount of stock of each product on specific days and at certain times. The algorithm is informed by years of historical sales data, the experience of bakery staff, and even external elements such as current weather conditions, upcoming sports events and holidays when generating demand forecasts. The tool has helped Costco reduce waste by 30 per cent and increase efficiency by 10 per cent, and the application has since been rolled out to 500 of the company's warehouse stores.

Costco is not the only retailer feeling the benefits of better demand forecasting. In 2018, supermarket chain Carrefour released an outline of the strategic plans it planned to achieve by 2022. AI and other technologies have been a major element of these plans, with Carrefour allotting a €2 billion annual investment budget primarily for IT and digital technology projects. Among these initiatives is the deployment of Viya, an AI solution developed by SAS that collects and processes data from stores, warehouses and e-commerce sites to better predict demand and improve supply. When this solution was introduced in 2019, it made Carrefour the first retailer in France to use AI optimization in its supply chain. Since then, the company has kept up its investment in AI to work towards its strategic goals. Similar to what Walmart did with the IRL, Carrefour created the Carrefour-Google Lab to enable the creation of AI and ML solutions that are then tested within the company's retail outlets. One such solution, an assortment recommendation tool, has led some stores to see up to 40 per cent additional revenue on some single items.

Beyond providing customers with a better and more tailored range of products, some supermarket chains have set their sights on reducing other experiential pain points in-store. At the end of 2020, US supermarket giant Kroger announced that it would be rolling out Everseen's Visual AI tool in 2,500 of its stores to improve customers' self-checkout experiences. The tool uses AI and ML to analyse real-time video to spot common errors like improperly scanned items and automatically alert staff to provide assistance. This saves the time customers must wait to correct errors, and helps the retailer reduce lost profits from unscanned or incorrectly scanned items. This is just one of the company's recent AI adoptions in-store. In early 2021, the company began testing a 'smart' shopping trolley called the KroGo, which uses an AI- and ML-enabled in-built camera and scale to automatically scan items as customers place them into their carts.

The trolley also features a touch screen with an in-built payment system that makes it quick and easy for customers to pay for the items in their basket. At the time of writing, the cart has only been tested at one of the company's stores, but its success indicates a high probability of widespread rollout.

Kroger are not the only grocers to use smart trolleys like these. Amazon added its name to the supermarket roster with its Amazon Fresh grocery concept. On the surface, the store looks like any other supermarket, but the e-commerce giant designed these physical locations with loads of tech operating in the background to provide shoppers with a seamless experience. Like Kroger, Amazon offers customers smart trolleys called Dash Carts that use computer vision-enabled cameras to identify and scan the items customers add to their carts. To begin shopping with a Dash Cart, a customer scans a QR code that links their trolley to their Amazon account, which is automatically charged for whatever items the customer leaves the store with. But that's not the only smart tech powering the Amazon Fresh experience. Alexa-enabled kiosks can answer customer queries and provide directions for where to find certain items. Using their own Echo devices at home, customers can ask Alexa to add items to their shopping list. Once they arrive at their local Amazon Fresh store, the customer can pair their mobile phone with the Dash Cart, which will then display their list, direct them where to go to find the items, and automatically check items off the list as they are added to the trolley. This convenience for customers may seem subtle but is a massive game changer in terms of making omnichannel retail experiences more seamless.

Now, imagine the smart trolley's capabilities, but on a storewide scale. That concept became a reality when Amazon opened its Amazon Go convenience stores equipped with 'Just Walk Out' technology. Similar to the KroGo and Dash Carts, these shops are equipped with AI and ML cameras that are able to automatically identify and scan the items a customer picks up. They can put the items directly in their own bags, their pockets, or even just keep them in hand. The storewide sensors will still be able to identify and scan the products. Then, since the customer gains access to the shop by scanning their mobile phone, their Amazon account is automatically charged for the items they pick up and they are able to simply walk out of the store when they are finished. Amazon has a number of these store models already in operation with plans to open more soon, and its first UK location opened in London in early 2021. There are rumours that Amazon may expand this technology to its Whole Foods supermarkets, and competitors such as Aldi are supposedly exploring the option of introducing similar technology in their own stores. The introduction of this technology is rumoured to be part of a £1.3 billion digitalization initiative announced by the growing German supermarket chain in early 2021.

Tesco, a UK-based supermarket chain, is another such organization taking steps to implement cashierless payments in its stores. It has partnered with Israeli start-up Trigo to pilot this technology and is aiming to bring computer-vision checkouts to its shoppers soon. Once launched, this will help Tesco to further compete with its UK competitors who have also begun utilizing AI in their own stores. For example, Sainsbury's is successfully using AI to predict and prevent supply chain disruptions, and to halve the number of thefts from its stores. Meanwhile, Morrisons uses AI to reduce shelf gaps and decrease stockholding time.

The benefits of AI as demonstrated by the grocery retailers could easily be applied to other traditional bricks-and-mortar stores, and some (such as inventory management and loss prevention) already are. But it's not unfathomable that we could one day walk into a store pick up a shirt and walk out with it without ever visiting a till. It's no secret that the high street is struggling, and AI solutions may just be its saving grace.

That said, when it comes to retail, AI does some of its very best work in the e-commerce space.

Personalization in fashion

There is now a raft of companies using AI to personalize how people shop online. Julie Bornstein built the AI shopping app THE YES in 2020. It pulls items of clothing from brands and retailers' websites and shows them in a feed within the app. Using ML models, the like and dislikes inform each personalized feed of items that a user can buy.

Speaking to WIRED (Burgess, 2021), Bornstein explains:

> AI is simply the ability to understand consumer behaviour and act on it. The problem with e-commerce is that the infrastructure doesn't exist to do that today. You need to rebuild the tech stack. We factor in hundreds of data points. These include preferred brands, price range, size and item silhouettes.

Since it launched in May 2020, the company has added over seven million 'yes' and 'no' entries into its recommendation system, which is now in its tenth iteration of the algorithm.

The digital imperative

AI has become so integrated into the online shopping experience that you probably never even think twice about it. If you have ever used a customer chat service while shopping online, you have likely interacted with AI. If you've ever abandoned your basket only to receive email reminders with offers attached, you have been in contact with AI. If you have ever been recommended similar products you may be interested in while looking at a different item, AI has used your data to make that suggestion. It's convenient, it's tailored and, most of the time, it is seamless.

Retailers in all categories are adopting tools for thier e-commerce, but the technology thrives in fashion. Clothing retailers have had a hard time competing on the high street in recent years due to the convenience, efficiency and variety available via e-commerce. So, to compete, they shifted online. But many faced the challenge of how to create an engaging journey for customers online where they cannot touch or try the products.

Online fashion giant Asos combats this with its Fit Assistant tool. Customers answer questions about their height and weight, body shape and desired fit for the garment. The tool then uses AI to analyse the answers and compare the feedback to other customers' profiles to recommend a size. The tool has been successful at helping shoppers order garments that fit properly and helps to mitigate the costs of the company's free returns policy. Many other retailers have since adopted the tool in their own sites.

For H&M, the first step was to ensure that its customers could buy the products they want, when they want them. The retailer has integrated AI and predictive modelling into the business to better forecast trends to inform purchasing decisions, and to monitor inventory to ensure popular items are well-stocked. Not only is this allowing H&M to organize and reallocate masses of unsold stocks to stores with high demand to reduce the need for discounted sales, but it is also helping to reduce clothing waste.

British high-street mainstay Marks & Spencer is also leveraging customer data and ML to inform its inventory. The retailer uses an AI platform in its new product development process to get customer feedback on new products to inform decisions about style, features and even pricing.

The result of these initiatives is product offerings that customers actually want to buy. But that isn't the only way retailers are putting their customers at the forefront of the shopping experience.

The rise of me-commerce

Have you ever received a product suggestion that made you feel like your favourite store knew what you wanted better than you did? With AI, that phenomenon is becoming much more common.

According to McKinsey, a positive customer experience has the power to yield 20 per cent higher customer-satisfaction rates, a 10 to 15 per cent boost in sales-conversion rates, and an increase in employee engagement of 20 to 30 per cent (Lindecrantz, Tjon Pian Gi and Zerbi, 2020). Personalization at scale makes every customer journey feel one-of-a-kind and can reduce retailers' marketing and sales costs by around 10 to 20 per cent. Retailers obtain massive amounts of data from customers every day via browsing history, store visits, historical purchases and loyalty programmes. It is this data that feeds AI and enables retailers to offer their customers experiences that are almost scarily tailored to their needs, wants and habits.

American retail chain Target has long known the value of customer data and has employed it very successfully in its marketing and advertising functions. From their first interaction with the company, every customer is assigned a unique Guest ID that is used to track their future purchases, interactions with the company, and their habits and demographics. While it sounds invasive, this has allowed Target to provide its customers with highly relevant product recommendations and offerings and form deep-rooted loyalty with its shoppers. The company has adopted a strategy of right product, right place, right time that has allowed it to position itself as a one-stop-shop for whatever the customer needs whenever they need it.

Drugstore and pharmacy chain CVS also keeps a close eye on its customers to deliver timely and relevant offers or messaging. The company worked with Microsoft Azure to develop an ML programme that could learn the habits of its customers to identify the right time to send an offer, what that offer should entail and the right medium to send it. Its competitor, the Walgreens Boots Alliance, partnered with Microsoft and Adobe to enable mass personalization in its marketing and CX. The platform allows Walgreens to launch an individually tailored prescription experience for its pharmacy patients, while Boots offers a bespoke beauty experience and provides custom product recommendations.

These companies are just a small sample of the thousands of other companies in other retail categories delivering relevant messaging and offers directly to customers' phones, feeds and inboxes. But what if your favourite store showed you a relevant advert while you were shopping in-store? Swiss AI start-up Advertima uses computer vision and ML to interpret customers' demographic information and in-store actions to deliver targeted, real-time advertisements via smart signage. Its signage solutions are already in use by global grocery chain SPAR and Swiss pharmacy chain TopPharm, and other customers include Red Bull, Westside, Volvo, Porsche and Mercedes-Benz.

While it's nice to receive a special offer or a list of products picked just for us, there are certain products that feel almost too personal to buy online, or too risky to buy sight unseen. These are the types of products we tend to want to try before we buy, and often our experience of the product is what informs the purchasing decision. How can AI be leveraged here? Let's examine the issue further in one of the most challenging retail categories.

Exceptional experiences: the case of beauty retail

Beauty is one of the most traditionally experiential forms of retail. Typically, customers need to visit a store in order to find the right foundation for their skin tone, swatch lipstick shades, or sample a product. With AI and other disruptive technologies, this is no longer the case. Many beauty brands and retailers have begun harnessing the power of these tools in order to bring the in-store experience directly to their customers, a truly valuable capability in today's digital age.

The coronavirus pandemic proved an interesting time for retailers in the Beauty and Personal Care products space. There was a rising trend in 'self-care' as customers sought to look after their well-being while in lockdown. As salons and department stores shut their doors and pharmacies blocked off products deemed 'non-essential', customers flocked to e-commerce in order to satisfy their self-care needs. A survey fielded by Euromonitor in the height of lockdown found that 34 per cent of consumers could now be considered 'digital beauty' shoppers, meaning they purchased via e-commerce or were influenced by digital and online user- or expert-generated content when shopping for or using products. There was a massive shift in the skincare category, with one-fifth of shoppers (21 per cent) fitting this distinction. Retailers noticed this shift and responded to it with a greater focus on their digital experiences. By July 2020, 70 per cent of respondents in the Beauty and Personal Care industry had reported having intentions to reshape and implement digital strategies in their businesses (Euromonitor International, 2020).

While many retailers were steered towards digitization by this shift in consumer behaviour, some forward-thinking companies had already been experimenting with next-generation technologies such as AI and augmented reality (AR) for years. In the early years of the adoption of these applications, most were powered on the backend by two early innovators in the space: ModiFace and Perfect Corp.

Founded in 2006 by a University of Toronto professor and boasting over 30 patents, ModiFace has long been a leader in the beauty tech space. The company has developed a range of AR- and AI-powered solutions that allow customers to virtually try on a range of different cosmetics, hair colours and styles, and nail varnishes. Its revolutionary Skin AI application is an anti-ageing and skin care simulation that can detect and quantify changes in the skin, as well as predict changes in the skin condition after the use of a specific skin product. The user's phone camera scans their face and measures the severity of their skin conditions, then the software predicts the impact of a product on the consumer's skin after several applications. ModiFace's technology has been white-labelled by brands such as Unilever, Shiseido and LVMH, as well as beauty retail giant Sephora. The company was acquired by L'Oréal in 2018 in a huge step towards beauty tech leadership for the conglomerate. The company began its foray into the tech space in 2014 with its Makeup Genius app, which is largely considered to be the first 'mainstream' application of AR in beauty. Since the acquisition, ModiFace has become a massive part of L'Oréal's strategy.

ModiFace technology has powered many tech-focused innovations for L'Oréal's brands in recent years. Most of the beauty conglomerate's owned brands now offer virtual try-ons or skin assessments powered by ModiFace, both in store and online, and the brand has created a range of filters for Instagram and Snapchat. In an attempt to bring smart technology into consumers' homes, L'Oréal developed Perso, a smart skincare device that uses AI, location data and user preferences to formulate personalized moisturiser. The company released the first of its Perso-powered products to the consumer market at the start of 2021 with the Yves Saint Laurent Rouge Sur Mesure, which utilizes colour cartridge sets of YSL's Velvet Cream Matte Finish lipsticks to create thousands of bespoke shades with a single touch.

Many other companies have now begun offering solutions similar to ModiFace's products, but the company's biggest competition comes from Perfect Corp. Since its launch in 2015, Taiwan-based Perfect Corp. has been a major disruptor in the space, offering several services harnessing AR, facial recognition and colour-matching technologies. The company's most sought-after product is its Yocum application, which uses AR to allow users to virtually try on SKUs, diagnose skin conditions, get personalized recommendations and discover products. An offshoot product of the original Yocum, the Yocum SkinAI diagnostic tool allows brands to recommend customized skincare regimens to their customers by using AR, computer vision and AI to assess the skin for various conditions such as wrinkles, oiliness, dark circles, pore size and so on.

YouCam's technology has been used widely in online or mobile functions but has also been adopted in bricks-and-mortar retail to create unique and memorable customer experiences. Many brands and retailers have begun offering customers 'magic mirrors' in store that allow them to assess their skin conditions and try on products without a need for physical samples. In response to the coronavirus pandemic, Perfect Corp. added four contactless functions to enhance YouCam's in-store applications including gesture control, voice activation, face mask detection and the ability to virtually view multiple lipstick swatches on one's arm.

At the start of 2021, the company secured $50 million in series C funding in order to scale up operations, invest in more AI tech and support its plans for continued global expansion across all categories for e-commerce, stores, social channels, web and mobile. Unlike the L'Oréal-owned ModiFace, Perfect Corp. has never been acquired, allowing the company to offer its product suite to and forge meaningful partnerships with brands of all sizes and specialties. Some of these relationships include Target, Estée Lauder, Neutrogena, Ardell, Benefit Cosmetics, Kate Tokyo, e.l.f., Whole Foods Market and Aveda, as well as tech giants Google, YouTube, Douyin, WeChat, Snapchat and Alibaba. The company has also forged partnerships with retailers outside of the beauty space, expanding YouCam's capabilities to allow for the virtual try-on of eyeglasses and jewellery.

This type of technology has largely been utilized by the bigger companies who are better able to afford it, but in recent years it has become more accessible to a wider range of companies thanks to new disruptors in the space.

One such vendor is Beauty Matching Engine, a white-labelled AI solution for beauty-specific retailers, e-tailers, supermarkets, hairdressers and brands of all sizes. After users take a short quiz, an AI-based personalization engine predicts the product choices customers are more likely to buy and offers personalized recommendations, upsells and landing pages at all points of the customers' online journey. Some of the company's reported case studies have created impacts such as 400 per cent uplift in sales conversion rates and a 65 per cent increase in average order. Past customers include Harrods, Harvey Nichols, Liberty London, LookFantastic, Clarins, The French Pharmacy, BY TERRY and Bobbi Brown.

Many other brands have begun to develop their own tools, all with the aim of enhancing some element of their brand. Most often, the intention is to improve customer experience. For example, global haircare giant John Paul Mitchell Systems has begun offering its partner salons a 'Hair AI' device that works as a clip-on camera device for iPhones and uses AI and computer vision to analyse an undisclosed number of data points, such as scalp flaki-ness and hair-strand breakage, through an accompanying app. Using the insights provided, stylists are able to provide their clients with better results by tailoring their service and the products used to the customers' specific needs.

Coty understood that its customers would primarily use its cosmetics to get ready at home and began offering a 'Let's Get Ready' skill for Amazon's Echo devices that boast a screen. Upon activating the app on the device, it will ask the user for details about their hair, eye and skin colour, their look preferences and the event they are attending. After analysing the responses, the application will display curated looks, visual tutorials, beauty tips and recommended products from Coty's consumer beauty portfolios on the screen of the Echo device. If desired, users can attend makeup tutorial sessions, following along with Alexa's spoken instructions and on-screen visuals, and they can also ask Alexa to add the products used in the tutorials to their shopping list through the 'Shop the Look' feature.

Another popular application of AI in the beauty industry is to create better products. In fact, AI and NLP algorithms are incredibly skilled at analysing comments, reviews and feedback posted by customers on e-commerce websites, social media and other online platforms. Avon Cosmetics developed its own AI and ML tool for this purpose in order to determine the top features customers craved most in a mascara, and devel-oped the '5-in-1 Lash Genius' mascara based on the results. Similarly, Proven Skincare has customers take a quiz, and their responses are then analysed against a database of more than 8 million customer product reviews, 100,000 skincare products, 20,000 ingredients and information from scien-tific or peer-reviewed journal articles about skin and ingredients. Then, ML algorithms match the customer's unique skin profile and suggest a skin care regimen. The customer's data is then passed on to a cosmetic chemist in the company laboratory to create tailored products designed for each individual customer's needs.

Rather than sourcing information from online conversation or cross-referencing from third-party sources, some beauty companies are offering personalized products based on data provided solely by the customers themselves. Atolla is an MIT skincare start-up that offers truly personalized skincare products. Customers sign up for a monthly subscription online and answer a series of questions about their skin, environment, lifestyle, diet, allergies, preferences, daily routines and current product use. They are then sent a test kit to complete. The results are sent back to Atolla, whose algorithms analyse the data to develop a customized serum based on each customer's needs. As this process is repeated monthly, Atolla is able to learn from any changes in the customers' skin and adapt their formula accordingly, and can even adapt to fluctuating needs based on seasonal conditions or other environmental factors.

AI has made it possible to shift to virtual many elements of the very sensory-focused beauty commerce experience, even in the most olfactory-reliant product category. Fragrance is arguably the most subjective beauty category, with purchase decisions driven by individual taste, experience and preference more than in any other category. Though technology has not made it possible (yet) to sample fragrance products virtually, AI and ML are making massive strides in developing fragrances that the maximum number of customers will enjoy the scent of.

Symrise AG, a leading German producer of fragrances and flavours, and IBM Research partnered to develop Philyra, an AI-based system trained on formulas for 1.5 million existing fragrances and other scents that uses deep neural networks to create new fragrance combinations. These formulas were labelled with information about associated human perceptions, as well as 'success factors' such as sales figures or a client's initial approval or disapproval of a novel scent. Feeding this information into the algorithm allowed it to become more successful over time, resulting in the creation of several well-received fragrances.

In addition to aiming for mass appeal, AI is also being used to help customers create their own personalized signature scent. After customers visiting Netherlands-based ScenTronix's in-store laboratory answer questions such as 'How do you see your role in life?' and 'What kind of environment did you go grow up in?', an algorithm analyses the data to create unique perfumes for the customer within seven minutes. The entire process happens in person and in real time using a device similar to a 3D printer that is powered by AI and ML software.

These examples merely scratch the surface of AI's current applications in the beauty retail space and are simply a starting point for the potential applications we may one day see. We are solidly in the experience age, driven and backed by digital technologies. The major lesson to take away is that if an industry as heavily experientially focused as Beauty and Personal Care can harness the power of AI in the day-to-day, imagine the possibilities for other experience-based businesses and sectors such as entertainment or recreation. The options are truly endless, and very exciting.

CASE STUDY

L'Oréal and Facebook: scaling beauty adverts using AI

The L'Oréal Paris Casting Crème Gloss campaign was targeted at females under 35, the first-time hair-colourers discovering their first grey hairs. L'Oréal decided to launch a campaign with no TV budget for the first time in the UK and looked for a digital strategy that would achieve reach and scale in a digital-only campaign and reach new consumers through relevant and engaging creative. Working with Facebook and Instagram, the brand needed to gain traction with hair-colour communities.

Work out the best creative and scale it

Facebook used its 'Create For Growth' approach to optimize the creative before scaling the campaign using AI. This allowed the platform to determine which creative would generate the best results, enabling it to maximize the impact of L'Oréal Paris' investment.

PHASE 1
Facebook determined the best creative for the product, target audience and problem it was trying to solve. Having worked with L'Oréal Paris before, the platform knew what type of assets work well – but it hadn't had a chance to explore how these methods worked specifically for products within the hair-colour category.

PHASE 2
They worked together to determine the optimal message – by working out the best product message and combining with the strongest seasonality and lifestyle message.
    Facebook and L'Oréal Paris tested and iterated the assets.

PHASE 3

They needed to establish the best way to measure the impact of the campaign: video views or awareness. L'Oréal's ultimate KPI is to influence purchasing decisions and drive product sales – so it determined, with Facebook's help, that video views would be its best KPI for this campaign.

This approach helped L'Oréal Paris to optimize and scale its first digital-only campaign in the UK – ensuring the brand got the best possible return on its spend.

IMPRESSIVE RESULTS

- L'Oréal recorded a 12-point lift in ad recall from video views among 25–34-year-olds.

- The campaign drove a four-point lift in purchase intent.

- Ad recall for L'Oréal Paris Casting Crème Gloss increased significantly in the Video Views test group.

- An increase was seen in favourability towards L'Oréal Paris Casting Crème Gloss Hair Colour among 18–24-year-olds in an awareness test group.

Featured in *Campaign* (Simpson, 2020), Rich Kivell, Creative Strategist at Facebook, comments:

> Casting Crème Gloss was a really interesting challenge for us, in that it would be the first L'Oréal Paris campaign without TV. This meant we were able to move quickly and approach a large brand with a disruptor mindset. Through our iterative campaign, we were able to test, learn and ultimately find new audiences based on real insights from the hair-colour community.

In the same *Campaign* article (Simpson, 2020), Helena Osborne, Senior Social Brand Manager at L'Oréal Paris, said:

> Working alongside Facebook and the strategic approach in planning this campaign enabled us to identify clear insights and creative formats that best resonate with our consumers. These are valuable learnings that will help to plan and optimize our social strategy.

Elevating customer experiences

Beyond improving internal processes and enhancing staff's capabilities, many firms will adopt AI tools for external-facing functions essential for enhancing customer experience. In fact, in the previously mentioned 2020 IDC survey, delivering a better customer experience was identified as the leading driver for AI adoption by more than half the large companies surveyed.

Many companies have begun adopting AI tools in order to deliver the types of personalized, unique and memorable experiences today's customers are coming to expect. Whereas most of the marketing, sales and HR tools already discussed can be used in any industry or sector, when it comes to CX, many vendors are developing specialized tools for specific industries. Here we will explore how some of these tools are reshaping one of the most experience-heavy industries: hospitality.

Hospitality's helping hand

To explore this further, we begin by speaking to a leading brand in the leisure and hospitality sector: Hilton. Ben Bengougam is Senior Vice President Human Resources EMEA. He explains the ways AI will impact his sector:

> AI is likely to fundamentally change how information is processed and decisions are made by customers first of all. The ability to search at speed and depth linked to a customer's detailed preferences will soon be able to be done in seconds or milliseconds, transforming the search and book experience. Product aggregation (hotel, flight, transfers, car hire, experiences booking) will also be able to be managed seamlessly and incredibly fast and intuitively thanks to AI solutions.
>
> How we dynamically manage revenue/yield using super-bright and talented people today might also be transformed by AI solutions enabling faster, more accurate, and at the point of time and service, decisions on rates to be offered (or not as the case maybe).
>
> How we digitally take products to market and promote them might also be radically changed by AI solutions that will provide ultimate analysis, speed, channel and timing decision support as well as project ROI.
>
> The link between AI and VR products might also offer a new dimension of 'try and taste before you buy' through VR experiences.

Driving the future of work: intelligent marketing

AI is driving the future of work and becoming an essential tool for today's intelligent marketing, sales and CX professionals. They are now taking advantage of AI-driven tools and systems that can continuously model, simulate and recommend 'next best action'. AI is now a cost-effective way to automate the precise processing of the millions of data points, which are beyond our human scale. It can therefore reduce costs, speed decision cycles and create new opportunities for innovation and disruption. For AI to be truly effective, it needs to be absorbed into the organization's processes. Here are some examples of companies taking advantage of AI.

CASE STUDY
Personalization at scale

Nike's personalized online experiences

Using AI, Nike creates a personalized experience for customers who visit its website, making recommendations that are uniquely tailored to them. Customers can also search for products using conversational language and images without the need to interact with a person.

Amazon's personalized shopping recommendations

Amazon customers are guaranteed a personalized and effective shopping experience thanks to AI product recommendations, which track historic purchases and similar products of differing pricing points. AI also equips Amazon to seize a first-mover advantage with dynamic pricing, adjusting to market demand.

Hyatt is making room for the human touch

Hotel chain Hyatt uses a virtual assistant for parts of its reservations journey. This automates many of the dull, routine tasks (for example, authenticating customers or gathering their travel dates and destination) before transferring the call with all the relevant context to an agent who can focus on the more empathetic aspects of the sale.

Starbucks' reward programme/mobile app

Starbucks uses AI by capturing customer data to offer a unique rewards programme. Customers benefit from free coffee on their birthday, for example. Also, using the mobile app they can take advantage of voice assistance to order their drinks with the barista. Access to data insights such as customer buying history means that Starbucks can offer customers tastes it knows they will enjoy.

Alibaba and Mars

Offering a diverse and expanding portfolio of treats and snacks, food, and pet care products and services, Mars Incorporated has been around for more than a century, but the organization understands the power of technology to help it stay ahead.

Mars collaborated with Alibaba to use AI to ascertain which chocolates and candy Chinese consumers prefer. Alibaba continually gathers data from the habits of the millions of shoppers on its various platforms. It unearthed a surprising and counterintuitive finding that many Chinese shoppers of chocolates also purchase spicy snacks. As a result of these insights, Mars developed a sweet-and-spicy product: a candy bar containing Szechuan peppercorns, the source of China's spicy 'mala' flavour. Known as Spicy SNICKERS®, the product was really popular. AI therefore saved the brand time, shortening the typical two- to three-year timeframe to launch a product to less than 12 months.

In May 2021, Mars announced the expansion of its relationship with Microsoft, enhancing and accelerating digital transformation using Microsoft Azure platform. Sandeep Dadlani, Chief Digital Officer for Mars, explains:

> Our relationship with Microsoft is helping transform how data and technology are used to continue ensuring compliant customer solutions and build trusted brand and consumer experiences. It will change the relationship between our brands and consumers, deliver hyper-relevant consumer experiences that include content and media, and fulfil needs and expectations across every touchpoint in the consumer's journey.
>
> (Bradley, 2021)

Alibaba's FashionAI store

Alibaba also deploys AI to optimize the fashion retail experience in-store in Hong Kong. Products have special tracking tags containing radio-frequency identification (RFI), gyro-sensors and low-energy Bluetooth chips. The gyro-sensor allows the tag to decide which garments can be touched. Smart mirrors – with intelligent touch screens – display information about the garments and can recommend complementary purchases. Technology is also enhancing the fitting experience, by providing the sales assistants with the information they need to proactively suggest fashion items and accessories that complement an outfit. This extends to the 'Virtual Wardrobe' mobile Taobao app, thereby creating a true omnichannel capability for customers.

Just Eat uses data insights to meet evolving customer needs

In an interview with Econsultancy (Sentance, 2020), Matthew Bushby, UK Marketing Director at Just Eat, commented on how lockdown altered customer behaviour, in particular the timing of meals. The 'dinner peak', which normally took place between 6.30 and 7 pm, moved forward to around 5.00 pm, most likely due to the lack of an evening commute. The company also saw an increase in the amount of food ordered for lunch, and an increase in breakfast ordering, which Bushby dubbed 'The emergence of breakfast'. 'We're taking on more than a million data points every day. The challenge is then how do you use them effectively to improve the experience of customers, of restaurants and couriers? For consumers, it was all about, "How do we personalise the experience?" Your experience needs to be relevant when you arrive at lunchtime – there's no point showing you a dinner menu at lunchtime.' (Sentance, 2020)

The company had to adjust accordingly, making necessary changes to call-centre staffing to meet the demand of these changing peak times.

Reshaping digital marketing

The advanced power of data collection and processing, fuelled by ML algorithms, will revolutionize the future of digital marketing. Growth is likely to be exponential, as social media, websites and the Internet of Things (IoT) devices collect vast volumes of data. According to Statista, ad spend worldwide is estimated at around $649 billion (Statista Research Department, 2021). Despite the global pandemic, this spend will increase dramatically as more organizations deploy AI as part of their advertising strategy. AI allows them to uncover – and sometimes predict – micro trends, reducing waste and improving overall ROI.

The ability of marketers to process this data better will pave the way for super-personalization of marketing messages. The four main ways in which the discipline of digital marketing will evolve are as follows.

Improved marketing content

The behaviour of target customers can be analysed by AI tools, allowing the marketers to deploy the most effective content swiftly and easily. Optimal results can be secured, without the huge investment in time and resources on tests and surveys.

Cost-effective AI tools mean that AI is accessible to companies of all sizes, even those with small budgets or those with junior teams, and can assist across the content creation process with:

- writing data-driven blogs that rank well for SEO;
- drafting optimized social media posts that drive engagement;
- personalizing emails and web copy for improved conversions;
- effective keyword research to match user intent.

Content can now be generated efficiently and easily. Email content, personalized reports/messages and social media content can be automated using tools such as Rocco.

There are numerous AI tools on the market that can help a digital marketing team to create social media posts, blog synopses and slogans, for example Nichesss, Writesonic and CopyAI. One issue that they must grapple with is algorithmic bias, especially important when dealing with sensitive projects such as the NHS's recent drive to encourage BAME people to seek vaccinations. They were able to take advantage of IBM Watson's language system to finetune campaigns, using real-time data about article engagement to help inform their strategy.

Conversational marketing: improved CX with chatbots

Chatbots are evolving and now range from basic customer service to those that can drive sales conversions through fast, real-time conversations. A major benefit of this conversational marketing is the ability to offer effective localized customer service.

This can be delivered in the customer's chosen language, around the clock, and across different time zones simultaneously.

According to the Drum, over 50 per cent of customer queries may be managed today via AI Chatbots. Lidl developed a wine bot called Margot that advises on the different types of grapes used, offering customers wine pairings based on their choice of food.

Relevant, cost-effective advertising

The advertising industry looks set to benefit dramatically from AI tools. Historically, a brand would be required to shoot a commercial multiple times using different colours or brand names. Synthesia worked with marketing and ad agency Craftww on a campaign for JustEat. Following the successful Snoop Dogg advert, JustEat's Australian subsidiary – known as MenuLog – used AI to leverage the successful campaign in all the markets in which it operates. Synthesia used its synthetic media and deep learning capability to transcreate the ad, altering Snoop Dogg's lip movements and thereby saving the brand huge sums.

Elsewhere, brands are taking full advantage of a new generation of content creation tools to allow digital advertisers on platforms such as Google,

Facebook and Instagram to provide optimum experiences. Relevant ads can be shown to users based on their demographic data, e.g. gender and age, as well as their interests. The organization benefits because the ad performs better and improves the return on investment of the spend.

Safe, fast and accurate voice search

The growth of mobile, combined with the popularity of Alexa, Siri and similar virtual assistants, is leading to a rise in voice search, which is far quicker and safer than typing.

ML algorithms can now understand human speech, allowing for far more accurate speech-to-text conversion. Google's algorithms have an accuracy of 95 per cent, which equals that of a real human. As a result, marketers are having to alter their search engine optimization (SEO) and content marketing strategies in order to cater for and take advantage of voice search.

How can AI support sales?

AI-guided selling looks set to revolutionize this crucial business function, removing the guesswork and making sales a much more scientific discipline. Below is a breakdown of the multiple impacts AI is having:

- **Demand forecasting**
  - Forecasts are automatable despite their complexity. AI allows automatic and accurate sales forecasts based on all customer contacts and previous sales outcomes.
- **Enabling sales reps**
  - AI allows sales teams to prioritize their time more effectively, focusing them on prospects that are most likely to convert. It does this by leveraging huge quantities of data on factors that can increase a prospect's likelihood to make a purchase.
- **Lead generation**
  - AI arms the sales reps with the leads they need, allowing them to focus their time on closing deals.

- **Predictive sales/lead scoring**
  - AI can score customers' likelihood of converting based on third-party and company data, allowing sales reps to prioritize effectively.
- **Sales content personalization and analytics**
  - Once prioritized, the customer can be served with content that is personalized to their needs and preferences.
- **Sales rep next action suggestions**
  - AI will analyse your sales reps' actions and leads will be analysed to suggest the next best action. No one wants to waste time on email setting up a demo, when they could be closing another deal.
- **Automate sales activities**
  - AI can automate the simple tasks that do not require a sales relationship.
- **Sales data input automation**
  - AI can sync data from various sources effortlessly and intelligently into a company's CRM platform.
- **Sales rep response suggestions**
  - During live conversations or written messages with leads, AI can provide invaluable prompts.
- **Meeting setup automation (digital assistant)**
  - Tools such as Calendy free up sales time by coordinating conversations to a calendar. Another tool such as Clara can respond to emails and schedule meetings.
- **Sales rep chat/email bot**
  - AI sales chatbots can improve success rates with personalized messages. Customized emails can be crafted, saving the sales team valuable time.
- **In-store sales robots**
  - Home-improvement chain Lowe's has introduced 'LoweBot' in its San Francisco store. It is capable of answering simple questions, such as where to find items, and can assist with inventory monitoring. However, one of the main benefits is capturing detailed data about the products on the shelves and customer buying patterns, which can increase efficiency and accuracy in inventory management.

- **AI avatar**
  - AI sales and marketing avatars keep learning and are able to automatically create digital marketing interactions with a potential client.
- **Digital humans**
  - Launched by Samsung's STAR Labs and showcased at CES 2020, NEON is an artificial human that is powered by CORE R3, which means Reality, Realtime and Responsive. This computational AI power enables NEON to act as an independent virtual being that can learn from experience and build memories. According to STAR Labs, NEON can understand and sympathizes, as real humans do, which means it could potentially act as a teacher, a salesperson, a personal financial advisor or a healthcare provider.
- **Sales analytics and performance manage reps**
  - AI tools are now taking advantage of big data to attribute sales to marketing and sales efforts more accurately, which improves planning and ROI.
- **Customer sales contact analytics**
  - Teams can now analyse contact with customers (e.g. emails and calls) in order to understand the behaviours that drive sales. The sales team can then adapt accordingly, to maximize productivity.
- **Price optimization**
  - Dynamic pricing tools now use ML to scrape websites to gather crucial data on competitor pricing in order to improve competitiveness.
- **Layout optimization**
  - AI analytics can also help retailers to optimize in-store and website layouts based on customer behaviour data, in order to maximize B2C sales.

PRACTICAL TAKEAWAYS CHECKLIST: TOP 10 TIPS

1 Customers are no longer satisfied with distinctly digital or physical experiences, and instead want an experience that encompasses the best of both and transitions seamlessly between the two environments.

2 Many of the world's most prominent retailers are adopting AI tools in order to keep their competitive advantages or even deepen their stronghold.

3 Many grocers have adopted AI in recent years to help boost efficiency and reduce costly wastes within their businesses.

4 There is now a raft of companies using AI to personalize how people shop online. Using ML models, for example, likes and dislikes can inform each personalized feed of items that a user can buy.

5 A positive customer experience has the power to yield 20 per cent higher customer-satisfaction rates, a 10 to 15 per cent boost in sales-conversion rates, and an increase in employee engagement of 20 to 30 per cent.

6 Personalization at scale makes every customer journey feel one-of-a-kind and can reduce retailers' marketing and sales costs by around 10 to 20 per cent.

7 We are solidly in the experience age, driven and backed by digital technologies. If an industry as heavily experientially focused as Beauty and Personal Care can harness the power of AI in its day-to-day, imagine the possibilities for other experience-based businesses and sectors such as entertainment or recreation.

8 There are numerous AI tools on the market that can help a digital marketing team to create social media posts, blog synopses and slogans. One issue that they must grapple with is algorithmic bias, especially important when dealing with sensitive projects.

9 Brands are taking full advantage of a new generation of content creation tools to allow digital advertisers on platforms such as Google, Facebook and Instagram to provide optimum experiences. Relevant ads can be shown to users based on their demographic data (e.g. gender and age as well as their interests). The organization benefits because the ad performs better and improves the return on investment of the spend.

10 AI-guided selling looks set to revolutionize this crucial business function, removing the guesswork and making sales a much more scientific discipline.

Bibliography

Bradley, T (2021) M & M: Mars teams up with Microsoft to reimagine digital transformation, *Forbes*, www.forbes.com/sites/tonybradley/2021/05/13/m--m-mars-teams-up-with-microsoft-to-reimagine-digital-transformation/?sh=7c71438a5d80 (archived at https://perma.cc/2QYA-HWND)

Burgess, M (2021) The AI That Fashion Is Using to Reinvent Itself, *WIRED UK*, www.wired.co.uk/article/ai-personalised-shopping (archived at https://perma.cc/VQX2-A7F6)

Clement, J (2020) COVID-19 Impact Retail E-commerce Site Traffic 2020, *Statista*, www.statista.com/statistics/1112595/covid-19-impact-retail-e-commerce-site-traffic-global/ (archived at https://perma.cc/9WAN-TGFQ)

Cognizant (n.d.) With Data Science, the Customer's Voice Is Loud and Clear, *Cognizant*, www.cognizant.com/us/en/case-studies/reducing-telecom-customer-churn (archived at https://perma.cc/4NG5-YBP4)

Dilmegani, C (2021) 131 Myth-Busting Statistics on Artificial Intelligence (AI) in 2021, *AIMultiple*, www.research.aimultiple.com/ai-stats/#sales (archived at https://perma.cc/4JLJ-P5G7)

Dilmegani, C (2021) AI in Sales: 15 AI sales applications/use cases in 2021, *AIMultiple*, www.research.aimultiple.com/sales-ai/ (archived at https://perma.cc/L2KS-KMCH)

Euromonitor International (2020) *Beauty Survey 2020 Key Insights*, www.go.euromonitor.com/white-paper-beauty--personal-care-20-11-03-survey-key-findings.html#download-link (archived at https://perma.cc/VH7K-QHLK)

Fitzpatrick, L (2021) 5 Ways That AI Will Change The Future of Digital Marketing, *TechBullion*, www.techbullion.com/5-ways-that-ai-will-change-the-future-of-digital-marketing/ (archived at https://perma.cc/QE2L-AK9Z)

Jade (2021) AI Marketing: What, why and how to use artificial intelligence in marketing, *Mageplaza*, www.mageplaza.com/blog/ai-marketing-what-why-how.html#1-nikepersonalized-online-experiences (archived at https://perma.cc/W985-49VB)

Juniper Networks (2021) IT Leaders See Opportunity from AI but Lack Technology, Skillsets and Governance to Realize the Promise, *businesswire*, www.businesswire.com/news/home/20210421005229/en/IT-Leaders-See-Opportunity-from-AI-but-Lack-Technology-Skillsets-and-Governance-to-Realize-the-Promise (archived at https://perma.cc/SM5T-HZ77)

Lindecrantz, E, Tjon Pian Gi, M and Zerbi, S (2020) Personalizing the Customer Experience: Driving differentiation in retail, McKinsey & Company, www.mckinsey.com/industries/retail/our-insights/personalizing-the-customer-experience-driving-differentiation-in-retail# (archived at https://perma.cc/5U9K-NUKR)

Microsoft (n.d.) Trade Agency Boosts Customer Engagement and New Zealand Economy with Dynamics 365, *Microsoft Customers Stories*, www.customers. microsoft.com/en-gb/story/847957-new-zealand-trade-and-enterprise-government-dynamics-365 (archived at https://perma.cc/C25F-PZ94)

Ohnsman, A, Cai, K, Popkin, H, Pratap, A and Wolpow, N (2021) AI 50 2021: America's most promising artificial intelligence companies, *Forbes*, www.forbes. com/sites/alanohnsman/2021/04/26/ai-50-americas-most-promising-artificial-intelligence-companies/?sh=4df39fec77cf (archived at https://perma. cc/9JTB-GFKQ)

Pring, B and Davis, E (n.d.) The True Meaning of AI: Action & insight. The work ahead, *Cognizant*, www.cognizant.com/the-work-ahead-ai-report/key-findings/ (archived at https://perma.cc/J6BM-SZCR)

Seismic (2021) preparing for AI-Guided Selling: A roadmap for forward-thinking businesses, *Seismic*, www.bit.ly/2UUdOSE (archived at https://perma.cc/9R4G-QTB9)

Seismic (n.d.) Glimpse of the Future: A day in the life of an AI-guided seller, *Learn. seismic.com*, www.learn.seismic.com/rs/217-LXS-149/images/Future-of%20 AI-Guided-Selling-1p.pdf (archived at https://perma.cc/ PJ37-8ANF)

Seismic (n.d.) The Next Era of Sales: AI-guided selling, *Learn.seismic.com*, www. learn.seismic.com/rs/217-LXS-149/images/The%20Next%20Era%20of%20 Sales_%20AI-Guided%20Selling.PDF (archived at https://perma.cc/BFE2-FD27)

Sentance, R (2020) Just Eat's Matthew Bushby on his Lockdown Data Takeaways and Amplifying TV with Online, *Econsultancy*, www.econsultancy.com/ just-eats-matthew-bushby-on-his-lockdown-data-takeaways-and-amplifying-tv-with-online/ (archived at https://perma.cc/6ZZ4-H5XC)

Sharp, M (2021) Seven Post-pandemic Trends for 2021 and Beyond, *The Drum*, www.thedrum.com/opinion/2021/05/10/seven-post-pandemic-trends-2021-and-beyond (archived at https://perma.cc/PU7E-S8X8)

Simpson, G (2020) L'Oréal Paris and Facebook Tap into a Memorable Moment, *Campaignlive*, www.campaignlive.co.uk/article/loreal-paris-facebook-tap-memorable-moment/1670078 (archived at https://perma.cc/TBM6-RS23)

Statista Research Department (2021) Global Digital Advertising Market 2023, *Statista*, www.statista.com/statistics/237974/online-advertising-spending-worldwide/ (archived at https://perma.cc/AS4U-V9YE)

Wiggers, K (2021) How Intel Is Leveraging AI to Drive Sales, *VentureBeat*, www. venturebeat.com/2021/05/01/how-intel-is-leveraging-ai-to-drive-sales/ (archived at https://perma.cc/VPU6-NDRS)

04

Driving change in the automotive and manufacturing sectors

As we have learned from the previous chapters, the big change within the next two years will be around the decisions organizations make in terms of their planning and their infrastructure investment to position themselves for the world that is coming down the track. Leaders need to be taking advantage of AI and making decisions now. The challenge centres around a requirement to have two different lenses. One lens to review the immediate survival of the business. Plus a crucial second lens to ensure investment for the essential transformation that has been driven by data. If leaders fail to adopt this long-term view, they risk squeezing themselves into a tight corner from which they cannot escape and grow.

> In this chapter we turn our first lens to the automotive sector, shining a light on examples such as how AI is allowing drivers to communicate with their cars as they do with their smartphones, controlling temperature and media. We then consider the closely aligned manufacturing sector and how it is taking advantage of AI and ML both operationally and across the marketing and CX functions. As well as proposing our own framework for adopting AI in Chapter 8, in this chapter we consider the open-source set of checks and principles provided by Rolls-Royce.

We begin with the automotive sector, where we see examples of artificial intelligence (AI) adoption by players such as leading German car manufacturer BMW. The company has enhanced its sports cars with intelligent personal assistants, affording drivers – and passengers – a tailored experience.

As reported in the FT, superior knowledge is the Holy Grail of the used-car market. Hakan Koc is Co-Founder and Co-Chief Executive of Auto1, a German start-up with 35,000 cars on its balance sheet, as well as a credit business, Auto1 Fintech, which it established with Deutsche Bank and Allianz. The company uses machine learning (ML) technology to buy tens of thousands of cars each month, then sells them to dealers in more than 30 countries. The fintech business allows it to extend credit and insurance to car dealers.

'Only superior knowledge allows you to take controllable risk,' explains Mr Koc. 'We can see clearing prices, we can see what people sell to us for, what people are buying for… the algorithm comes up with a price thesis and says… does it matter whether it has leather seats or not?' (Ram, 2018)

Building trust: AI-powered CX at Kia Motors

It is challenging to build consumer trust in the automotive sector. A car purchase is major and emotive. The aim is to build an emotional connection to help reassure customers and build their confidence in their choice of car. Founded in 1944, Kia Motors Corporation is South Korea's oldest manufacturer of motor vehicles. Established in the UK in 1991, the brand has grown through an impressive 190+ dealerships.

Speaking to Diginomica, David Hart (Customer Experience Manager at Kia UK Limited) explained how the team uses technology to ensure that customers have a personalized experience and a voice. 'We knew our customers loved our products, but we didn't have the ability to share reviews with future customers… Our overall marketing/CX objective here, then, was to use independent customer reviews from real Kia owners as positive advocacy on Kia.com/uk to drive search, traffic, engagement and conversion to the brand.' (Flood, 2021)

The company turned to Feefo, which utilizes AI technology and data analytics tools to better understand customers. Feefo's research illustrated that over 90 per cent of customers use reviews in some way, and that 50 per cent of consumers are more likely to choose a brand if reviews are authenticated by a third party.

Commenting on the results, Hart said:

Our new CX platform not only helps us collect accurate reliable reviews, but also provides us with the technology we need to turn feedback into actionable insights. We're also able to gain a deeper understanding of what customers value and use this to adapt and develop our future products and services.

The ability to implement on-page product reviews for different car models has also helped improve the functionality of our website and enhance our overall digital customer experience, while the platform's AI technology helps display the most relevant reviews for certain products at the right time, allowing shoppers to find the feedback and the extra reassurance they need. Finally, reviews are fully customizable to our branding, providing a seamless experience.

(Flood, 2021)

The power of sentiment analysis

The team also uses the tool to analyse customer sentiment and identify customer opinions on specific model features across the Kia range (see Figure 4.1).

We need to understand how customers feel about the latest developments and channel this into future plans or adapt our services accordingly. This helps to improve our products across a broad spectrum, which is particularly important as we bring out new models.

A case in point is the company's push in the electric vehicles (EV) market. With many drivers looking to purchase such a car, the customer experience team recently used the CX platform to understand feedback from EV and non-EV owners, which was then shared with the product development team who are implementing this feedback to develop future trim grades. Finally, every quarter now, the team shares the data and insights gathered by the platform with both senior management but also its dealer network.

FIGURE 4.1   Kia uses sentiment analysis in its CX platform in order to turn feedback into actionable insights

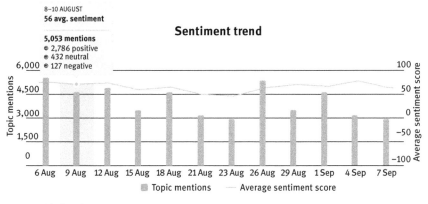

SOURCE Kia (2021)

Our dealer service ratings are consistently high at 4.6 out of 5, while our product rating is 4.7 out of 5. By adding service ratings to our dealer websites soon, we'll be able to allow customers to choose a dealer based on their service provision. Seeing the value that real-time feedback can provide, our network of dealers has consistently voted Kia highly amongst its competitors.

(Flood, 2021)

Having such valuable information at your fingertips adds a crucial layer of differentiation, as Tim Gordon, a Partner at Best Practice AI, knows well. His company has developed an impressive proprietary research base that catalogues over 600 ways in which organizations can deploy AI or ML to improve business KPIs. He comments:

The AI tool is a pump that can now turn out 1–2 million decisions a day, and does so without tiring, without changing its mind because of the weather or because it's cold and miserable that morning. It just gets better all the time, theoretically. You therefore require a process that can feed millions of decisions to those people and then organise those decisions afterwards. That's why Google is a successful AI company, because they have billions of micro decisions that need to be made that can be optimised by the algorithm. The algorithm will make them 0.1% or 2% better every cycle, and that's worth billions of dollars.

Competitive advantage in AI is often not from doing the AI. It's being in a position to do the AI. For example, if my business is providing you with the best cucumbers in the world, my value-added data is knowing what a good cucumber looks like in a picture. Therefore, I can do quality control and optimise how I grow my cucumbers. That is not the same as advertising data about how you spend your time, and what you spend your money on. So, the key is to work out what your data is and what data you really want. Understanding how that works and building that data is really complex. It's building a process that ideally reinforces the data so you can get to a place where the data is being catalogued and referenced and improved and reinforced, as opposed to going in different directions.

Echoing Kia's approach to trust-based AI, Tim Gordon adds:

Trust is essentially going to be one of the core economic advantages you can have. Every single one of the stakeholders is in the process, and if they trust you, your economic costs will be lower. If a consumer trusts you, then they will give you more data and more information and not demand to be paid. If your regulators trust you, you will be in a far better place than if they don't. This is partly about AI and it's partly about putting explainability statements out there.

It means being very transparent around what you're doing with AI and having those open conversations. Also, how you behave as a business is essential too. We can talk about what you do in the AI space and that is important, too. It will matter a lot to some people. In certain specific organizations, it matters a lot. But more broadly is, are you an organization that behaves well towards your stakeholders, to your people, to your customers and the environment? That is what ultimately drives whether people trust you or not.

Another German manufacturer of cars that is taking advantage of AI in its customer experience is Mercedes-Benz. January 2021 saw the digital world premiere of its new MBUX Hyperscreen with three seamlessly merged displays. Thanks to AI, the display and operating system adapt completely to the user and make personalized suggestions for numerous infotainment, comfort and vehicle functions depending on the situation.

Speaking to *Global Brands Magazine* (2021), Sajjad Khan, Member of the Board of Management of Mercedes-Benz AG and CTO, explains: 'When developing the MBUX Hyperscreen, the focus was clearly on the customer.'

The goal was a concept without distracting the driver or complicated operation, but one that is capable of learning thanks to artificial intelligence. The result speaks for itself: the MBUX Hyperscreen understands the customer better and better and thus delivers a customised, personalised infotainment and operating offer before the user has to click on anything. This is customer orientation and digital thinking in 2021.

The driver or passenger can simply ask a question as they drive past – for example, 'Hey Mercedes, what can you tell me about this building?', or 'Hey Mercedes, what is the name of the restaurant on the left?' – and the information appears on the respective display as well as spoken by the voice assistant.

Conversational AI drives empathy

Given that most prospective buyers of electric vehicles are first-time buyers, empathy has become paramount when it comes to answering questions, increasing the importance of personal connection more than ever before. By starting and ending the conversation in a seamless way, Nissan's virtual assistant entices prospective buyers to engage the Nissan brand or test drive a car locally. The queries are fed into the enterprise-class Conversational AI Platform from websites or ads that click to Messenger, and are answered via Facebook Messenger.

Nissan customers, known as Experts, act as trusted brand advocates, answering questions and giving authentic and insightful responses based on their experience owning a Nissan LEAF®. The virtual assistant and Experts are able to answer a variety of questions, including queries such as: 'How easy is it to charge?', or 'Do most service stations have charging points?', or 'How much money do you think you're saving on petrol?'.

This has been made possible following a partnership between five companies: Nissan Europe and Nissan United, Limitless, Amplify.ai and Facebook Messenger. The Limitless SmartCrowdTM Platform, leveraging Amplify.ai's Conversational AI platform, brings humans and technology together, putting Nissan customers at the heart of a new personalized user-engagement strategy, which provides peer-to-peer reviews and Conversational AI answers on the key features of the Nissan LEAF®, on-demand, from anywhere in the world.

Cherie Landman, Sales Director EMEA of Limitless, commented: 'The Expert GigCX model is bringing humans and technology together to drastically accelerate the ability to get real-world answers to pre-purchase questions in today's accelerated digital world. It's creating opportunities that have not existed before for brands, customers and prospective customers alike.'

Xavier Diquet of Nissan commented:

> We are confident that providing a human, conversational component to our customer experience and advocacy will produce positive and authentic responses, making prospective customers more comfortable about making purchase decisions. We trust and empower our customers, enabling them to answer our potential customers' questions, which we believe is key in creating a truly personalised customer journey.

Mahi de Silva, CEO and co-founder of Amplify.ai, commented: 'We believe that the future belongs to conversational brands. Nissan Europe and Limitless are showing what's possible when the impact of human teams is amplified by Conversational AI.'

Alexandre Hacpille, Global Client Partner at Facebook, commented:

> Messenger has become people's everyday tool to connect with friends, families but also businesses. Using Messenger, Nissan and partners have developed a unique approach to connecting real LEAF owners with people interested in buying one – in honest and authentic conversations. This is actually redefining customers' reviews by making them conversational. The outcome is better information for people, genuine confidence to buy, and highly positive impact on brand value.

Decision Intelligence: making sense of data

As we're learning throughout the chapters, AI can unlock the power of data to make informed business decisions. Yet a staggering 70 per cent of digital transformations still fail. Why is this the case? Featured in the AI for Business supplement in *The Times*, Richard Potter, CEO of Peak, explains the role of Decision Intelligence, a concept pioneered by Peak. It refers to the commercial application of AI to enhance business decision-making and grow revenues and profits. 'Every business needs its own, dedicated AI system to build and run its own AI,' Potter says. 'Just as each business function needs its own system of record – sales has CRM, operations has ERP and so on – businesses need a new kind of system in order to think smarter and make great decisions. Point solutions will only ever offer a piece of this puzzle. The use of Decision Intelligence represents a wholesale shift towards becoming an AI-driven business.'

Peak has developed a Connected Decision Intelligence system (CODI), which helps to democratize AI, allowing the rapid deployment of solutions that use the technology to put power in the hands of business decision-makers. 'CODI is powerful because it lets you do all the aspects of Decision Intelligence in a single place. And it's always explainable, never black-boxed,' Potter says. 'There's also a real human aspect to it. We're here to put CODI in your hands, while getting rid of some of the data grind and levelling up the AI experience so it's done in more places than ever before.'

This tool has also proved to be impressive in the automotive world.

CASE STUDY
Regit

Formerly Motoring.co.uk, Regit is the UK's leading online service for drivers. The company generates leads for companies in the automotive industry by providing a way for people to book test drives, buy and sell cars and request brochures, among other things. However, it was unable to predict which of the users were likely to change their vehicle, or even know who had changed their vehicle until after it had happened.

Working with Peak and Decision Intelligence, Regit was able to predict which of its 2.5 million users were going to change their vehicle and when. This meant it could serve customers in a more personalized and targeted way, which increased all centre revenues by more than a quarter.

'Through our subscription to Peak's service, we have gained a cutting-edge data analytics capability which has enabled us to drive a 27 per cent revenue growth through our call centre. We couldn't be happier with the results – we are actively recommending Peak to third parties,' explains Terry Hogan, CEO of Regit (Peak, n.d.).

Using Peak's Decision Intelligence system, CODI, Regit pulled together user data with data from the website and marketing systems, as well as from the DVLA (Drivers and Vehicle Licensing Agency). It applied 'Categorical Machine Learning models' that can handle both category and variable data simultaneously. This gives predictions about the likelihood of users changing their vehicle – resulting in a sale for Regit.

CODI utilizes AWS SageMaker to deploy ML models, with the system creating a simple 'lead score'. The lead scores are then pushed into the CRM system, allowing call-centre agents to prioritize their activity based on the users with the highest chance of converting to a sale.

Overall, Regit achieved the following outcomes thanks to its use of these tools:

- 27 per cent increase in sales achieved within just 30 days;
- 27 per cent increase in sales;
- 35 per cent reduction in operational costs.

Everything as a service

We are moving closer to a new economy of everything as a service, with technology at the core. Richard Chiumento is founder of Rialto – an award-winning consultancy that drives leadership and business success. He comments:

> Less people will be employed; robots will do more work, and there will be more AI in every sector and in every company. That will lead to a few other trends, for example, human beings will own far less in the future. If you're going to have a driverless car, you don't need to own a car. You can just call a car using AI, and tell it where you want to go, and it will pick you up and take you there. This will lead to less car, home and appliance ownership. The drone will collect your dry cleaning, and we will see greater automation of the home.

AI in manufacturing

AI is changing not only how we buy and sell products, but how we produce them. The next industry sector for our consideration is manufacturing. A report from Oxford Economics (2019) predicts that 8.5 per cent of the global manufacturing workforce stands to be replaced by robots, with about 14 million manufacturing jobs lost in China alone. Over the next decade, the United States is projected to lose more than 1.5 million jobs to automation, China is slated to lose almost 12.5 million, the European Union will lose nearly 2 million jobs and South Korea will lose almost 800,000. Other countries around the world are expected to lose 3 million jobs to robots by 2030.

However, the truth of the matter is that AI will create much more benefit and opportunity than it destroys. In its 'Future of Jobs Report 2020', the World Economic Forum estimated that 85 million jobs will be displaced while 97 million new jobs will be created across 26 countries by 2025. Some of these displaced roles might be described as the 'dirty, dull, and dangerous'. AI will take over many of the jobs that are dangerous for human workers to do, especially in manufacturing. Automation will also take over the repetitive and time-consuming tasks, freeing up human workers for more strategic or creative tasks (World Economic Forum, 2020).

Manufacturing and packaging will experience some of the biggest gains from AI. Some businesses have already integrated AI into their day-to-day practices with great success.

Global AI statistics

According to the '2020 McKinsey Global Survey on Artificial Intelligence' (Balakrishnan *et al*, 2020):

- 50 per cent of respondents report that their companies have adopted AI in at least one business function.
- 15 per cent of the AI-use cases most commonly adopted within each business function are related to improving yield, energy and/or throughput optimization in the manufacturing function, while a further 12 per cent are for predictive maintenance.
- 22 per cent of respondents say that more than 5 per cent of their organization's enterprise-wide EBIT in 2019 was attributable to their use of AI.

- 71 per cent of respondents reported revenue increases from AI adoption in their manufacturing function.

- 50 per cent reported cost decreases in their manufacturing function after AI adoption.

- Respondents at companies considered 'AI high performers' rate their C-suite as very effective more often than other respondents do.

- 60 per cent of respondents at companies considered 'AI high performers' felt that their organization's senior management is fully aligned and committed to the organization's AI strategy.

- Due to the large volume of data produced each day, manufacturing is one of the industries that stands to gain the most from AI adoption. In fact, by 2030, manufacturing (16 per cent) will be the top sector leading the market in AI (Deloitte China, 2020).

AI's use in manufacturing can be classed into five key applications:

1 **Smart production:** This is the most common mode of deployment of AI within manufacturing firms. In this function, AI is most used for factory automation, order management and automated scheduling.

2 **Products and services:** This area of deployment is not massively common for firms at present, but the Deloitte survey revealed a striking increase in the number of businesses that plan to invest in AI applications that shorten design time, customize customer experiences and enhance marketing efficiency.

3 **Business operations and management:** AI is used in this application to enhance the productivity of various business functions. This may include tools that provide marketing insights, assist with CRM, help the HR department with recruitment and people management, research and generate sales leads, increase operational efficiency and more. At present, the main focus in this area is on finance, but it is expected that AI's use for energy production and HR management will increase.

4 **Supply chain:** In this function, AI is used to manage delivery and demand, as well as for forecasting.

5 **Business-model decision-making:** These tools are used behind the scenes by the key decision-makers in the organization to model various business decisions, inform strategy, generate cost structure scenarios and enhance customer experience.

The environmentally conscious consumer

Within the packaging industry specifically, industry experts predict that AI will bring about several specific benefits. Today's consumers are more environmentally conscious than ever before, which has led to a change in trends and a demand shift for less excess packaging on products. Additionally, customers prefer packaging that is environmentally friendly, easily recycled or made sustainably.

AI will support and accelerate trends and practices that impact sustainability. This will include increasing operational efficiency in the supply chain and manufacturing process in order to reduce waste and energy consumption. But AI's capabilities can extend far beyond just the production element by providing insight into customer demands and market trends. As customer preferences and attitudes change, AI can track these shifts in order to inform product, purchasing and production decisions. Let's say, for example, that a company employed an AI-powered customer insight tool that began noting a higher demand for recyclable paper packaging rather than plastic. The decision-makers could then review these insights and use them to inform their purchasing, production and strategy in order to shift their practices to meet these new demands of the market. AI integrated into the other areas of the business can help this shift occur both swiftly and smoothly.

Not only will AI help inform decisions about improving sustainability, but the same process will also apply to improving the products themselves. Smart production tools such as AI-powered vision systems for inspection can help reduce costly errors and flawed products, helping to ensure that all of the products sent out into the marketplace meet quality standards. ML tools study the manufacturing process to ensure steps are not overlooked, errors are not made and no parts are missing. Customer insights once again come into play for developing new products and helping to improve existing ones.

AI adoption is not without its challenges, and expectations do not always match up with results. Common challenges faced when adopting AI in manufacturing, as identified by the 'Deloitte Survey on AI Adoption in Manufacturing', include:

- **Obstacles from existing experience and organizational structure:** Emerging technologies such as AI are still relatively new, and therefore a large portion of the workforce has yet to obtain the necessary skills to adapt to this massive change. Some might also be resistant to change or feel threatened by new technology. A lack of expertise within the organization can also make it difficult to chart a path, generate buy-in, or execute the change process. There may be other limitations within the organization, especially regarding time, funding, ability to train and other resources.

- **Infrastructure limitations:** In order for AI implementation to be successful, there needs to be a baseline of key variables in place to support the shift towards new technology. For example, if the company's network connectivity cannot support it, then AI cannot function.

- **Data collection and quality:** AI is driven by data. There should be reasonable data available to help inform adoption plans and to teach the algorithms. However, this needs to be quality data in order to get quality results. AI follows the principle of 'rubbish in, rubbish out'. If the algorithms are supplied with low-quality, irrelevant, or incorrect data, the outputs produced will not meet the needs or expectations of the business.

- **Lack of engineering experience:** AI is still new territory, and skillsets are evolving to catch up. In recent years, we have seen plenty of vendors introduce a variety of user-friendly tools that do not require extensive technological knowledge to implement or operate. But even so, more complex and larger-scale implementations do require more advanced skills and experience to execute properly. Many firms struggle with who to turn to for this part of the process.

- **Excessively large scale and complexity:** AI projects are intended to solve specific problems faced by the business. Bigger problems will require more complex solutions, which often come with multiple interplaying factors or steps. At times, some of these factors or decisions may be beyond the capabilities of AI at the current stage.

CASE STUDY
Mondi's digital customer experience

The packaging and paper group Mondi established Mondi DX, its digital transformation team, in early 2019 to drive digital transformation across strategic focus areas including digital operations and production, digital customer experience and new ways of agile working. Mondi has developed soft sensors for its paper machines. Soft sensors are virtual sensors in the form of ML models that enable continuous prediction in areas such as quality, leading to significant efficiency gains and waste reduction.

The Rolls-Royce Aletheia Framework^{TM}

Rolls-Royce designs and builds very high-end, very complex power products and services in a number of sectors. Three decades ago the company started offering some of its most expensive and most complex products, its aerospace engines, out to the market on the basis of 'power by the hour'. The customer pays for the provision of power across the lifecycle of the product, rather than a very significant capital outlay upfront. The company also has a decade of experience of developing AI within Rolls-Royce use cases, initially in the context of engine health monitoring.

Caroline Gorski is Group Director – R^2 Data Labs, Rolls-Royce. She explains:

> We needed to be able to collect the data from the product as it is in use, and then be able to analyse that data and use it to manage choices that you make about whether that product is still safe to be used. We're now onto our second or third generation AI which addresses more than 26 complex variables simultaneously and provides recommendations to service engineers to help them in their job managing those products as they are being used across the world. I think the important thing to say is that that process is a process that is governed by a regulator. EASA regulates our service processes and regulates our Total Care product, which is our in-life service management. The artificial intelligences that we've built in that system therefore need to meet with a regulatory compliance framework to make sure that they are reliable and trustworthy because, obviously, we're using them to help humans to make decisions about planes flying in the air.
>
> Based on this decade of experience, Rolls-Royce started to explore more deeply other use cases for AI, and started to understand questions of applying AI in parts of its production cycles as well as in the servicing cycle.
>
> It became very obvious to us that the procedural trustworthiness framework that we had identified could actually be applied to any use of AI because you could abstract it to a layer where it wasn't specific to a robotic inspection process or a component pass/fail test process. You could actually abstract it to a level where you can apply it to AI scanning CVs in your HR department. This could highlight if it is showing any evidence of bias. Suddenly we realized that by codifying this and writing it down, we had produced something you could apply anywhere.

The framework in question is The Aletheia Framework^{TM}, named after the Greek goddess of truth and disclosure. Rolls-Royce decided to publish it on an open-source basis. CEO Warren East understood how important and critical it is for standards to exist in emerging technology spaces. Gorski explains:

> What we did differently was turn this into a procedure and a checklist. The difference is turning that ethical and theoretical discussion into a very pragmatic, and an engineering-led discussion. How are we doing things? How are we proving that we've done them? And how can we show an auditable trail?

Trustworthy AI isn't necessarily good AI

Gorski continues:

> You can build an AI that does terrible things in a trustworthy way, because essentially what you're saying is, 'Does this AI do what I expected it to do? And am I sure that it's still doing what I expected it to do the way I expected it to do it?' If you've developed an AI that might undermine democracy, it's perfectly possible to do that in a way that is trustworthy, in that it does its job. So it's not enough simply to be able to trust that your AI is working. You also need to put in a set of ethical principles, which you then are able to demonstrate your adherence to. Those five trustworthiness checks that sit in the middle of The Aletheia Framework are wrapped into a set of ethical principles which very clearly establish to what end would any AI that Rolls-Royce would be developing be appropriate to be used.

PRACTICAL TAKEAWAYS CHECKLIST: TOP 10 TIPS

1 Leaders need to be taking advantage of AI and making decisions now.

2 Trust is essentially going to be one of the core economic advantages. If a consumer trusts you, then they will give you more data and more information and not demand to be paid. If your regulators trust you, you will be in a far better place than if they don't.

3 AI can unlock the power of data to make informed business decisions. Yet a staggering 70 per cent of digital transformations still fail.

4 We are moving closer to a new economy of everything as a service, with technology at the core.

5 AI will create much more benefit and opportunity than it destroys. The World Economic Forum estimated that 85 million jobs will be displaced while 97 million new jobs will be created across 26 countries by 2025.

6 Emerging technologies such as AI are still relatively new, and therefore a large portion of the workforce has yet to obtain the necessary skills to adapt to this massive change.

7 AI follows the principle of 'rubbish in, rubbish out'. If the algorithms are supplied with low-quality, irrelevant or incorrect data, the outputs produced will not meet the needs or expectations of the business.

8 AI is still new territory, and skillsets are evolving to catch up.

9 AI adoption is not without its challenges, and expectations do not always match up with results.

10 Over the next decade, the United States is projected to lose more than 1.5 million jobs to automation, China is slated to lose almost 12.5 million, the European Union will lose nearly 2 million jobs, and South Korea will lose almost 800,000. Other countries around the world are expected to lose 3 million jobs to robots by 2030.

Bibliography

Balakrishnan, T, Chui, M, Hall, B and Henke, N (2020) The State of AI in 2020. McKinsey & Company, www.mckinsey.com/business-functions/mckinsey-analytics/our-insights/global-survey-the-state-of-ai-in-2020 (archived at https://perma.cc/8HJQ-HN9T)

Deloitte China (2020) Deloitte Survey on AI Adoption in Manufacturing, Deloitte China, www2.deloitte.com/cn/en/pages/consumer-industrial-products/articles/ai-manufacturing-application-survey.html (archived at https://perma.cc/4XYD-B9XT)

Flood, G (2021) Kia UK Motors Ahead via AI-Powered Customer Experience, *diginomica*, diginomica.com/kia-uk-motors-ahead-ai-powered-customer-experience (archived at https://perma.cc/G6MU-Z3LD)

Global Brands Magazine (2021) Mercedes-Benz Presents the MBUX Hyperscreen at CES: New MBUX generation with intelligent new features such as 'Mercedes Travel Knowledge', *Global Brands Magazine*, www.globalbrandsmagazine.com/mercedes-benz-presents-the-mbux-hyperscreen-at-ces/ (archived at https://perma.cc/ ZUA6-7XE2)

Mondi Newsroom (2019) Mondi Highlights Human Factors in Digitalisation of Packaging and Paper at WeAreDevelopers Congress 2019, *Mondi Group*, www.mondigroup.com/en/newsroom/press-release/2019/mondi-highlights-human-factors-in-digitalisation-of-packaging-and-paper-at-wearedevelopers-congress-2019/ (archived at https://perma.cc/8BSU-E3F7)

Oxford Economics (2019) *How robots change the world: What automation really means for jobs and productivity*, bit.ly/36Feo9H (archived at https:// perma.cc/ A49E-J2PF)

Peak (n.d.) *How Regit increase conversions with Decision Intelligence and AI*, peak.ai/hub/success-story/regit/ (archived at https://perma.cc/DCM8-U8PV)

Ram, A (2018) Second-hand Car Dealer Bets on Machine Learning to Expand, *Financial Times*, www.ft.com/content/cb15d0e0-9fa2-11e8-85da-eeb7a9ce36e4 (archived at https://perma.cc/47FT-QDMA)

Rao, A and Verweij, G (2017) Sizing the Prize: What's the real value of AI for your business and how can you capitalise?, *PwC*, www.pwc.com/gx/en/issues/data-and-analytics/publications/artificial-intelligence-study.html (archived at https://perma.cc/E7ZE-WSAM)

World Economic Forum (2020) The Future of Jobs Report 2020, *World Economic Forum*, www.weforum.org/reports/the-future-of-jobs-report-2020 (archived at https://perma.cc/353H-FNHN)

05

Optimizing AI data insights in finance, law and insurance

In this chapter we analyse how data-enabled AI technology is driving innovation more swiftly and fundamentally than ever before in the financial services sector. We also consider how the insurance and legal sectors are taking advantage of AI, both operationally and across their sales, marketing and CX. We consider how the financial and professional services sectors can now use AI to more personally serve communities that have previously been excluded from mainstream products.

Let's start with banking – an industry with a long history of dependence on technology, and one that is therefore awash with volumes of potentially powerful customer data and potential applications of that intelligence. In October 2020, Deloitte released a report entitled 'Thriving in the Era of Pervasive AI' (Ammanath, Hupfer and Jarvis), which revealed the huge impact that artificial intelligence (AI) is having across the banking spectrum. It recognized that institutions must truly embrace AI and be willing to constantly evolve their business models with the fast-developing technology if they want to thrive and even survive. The summarized insights of the report bear repeating here:

- Adopters have faith in AI technologies' ability to drive value and advantage.
- As AI is integrated into more applications, early-mover advantage will be replaced by survival becoming dependent on effective deployment of AI.

- Using AI just to improve efficiency is no longer enough – the most mature adopters are now realizing its potential to boost differentiation and innovation.

- Adopters are aware of AI's inherent risks – such as unintentional bias created by algorithms – but are not taking enough action to minimize risk.

According to Accenture, AI solutions will add more than $1 billion in value to the financial services industry by 2035 (Roy and Khmeleva, 2019). Any financial institution that does not recognize and implement AI into the fabric of its business will be left fighting for survival. To become competitive or maintain or increase competitive edge, it's imperative for banks and other financial institutions worldwide to roll out AI projects at speed and scale and embed the technology across the organization. Treating it as a stand-alone project is no longer enough. It is hard to find a single section of banking where efficiency, productivity and growth would *not* be significantly improved with the adoption of AI. Later, we will look at the financial cost of implementing AI compared to the benefits.

Many players in the financial services sector believe strongly in the potential of AI. As reported in Finextra (Levitt, 2021), a recent survey of financial services professionals carried out by NVIDIA revealed that 83 per cent of respondents agree that AI is important to their company's future success. A total of 34 per cent agreed that AI will increase their company's annual revenue by at least 20 per cent. However, the approach to how AI is used differs based on the type of firm. For example, fintechs and investment firms most often cite algorithmic trading, fraud detection and portfolio optimization as the AI functions they use within their businesses, which reflects a deep focus on protecting and maximizing client returns. Meanwhile, banks and other financial institutions noted fraud detection, recommender systems and sales and marketing optimization as their top AI-use cases. Many consumer banks have begun to use AI-enabled applications for customer acquisition and retention along with cross-selling and upselling personalized products and services, which we will explore in more detail later in this chapter.

Banks have been forced to diversify away from their heavy emphasis on lending since the 2007–2008 financial crisis – and lower interest rates since – just to survive. The need to comply with far more stringent regulation, separate banking functions and divisions, and reduce risk have also reduced the big profit margins that were on offer. It could be argued that the deployment of AI to better understand the vagaries of the wider market and conditions and to predict and service the individual needs of millions of customers will become increasingly critical to their survival and success. This need is particularly acute as they face growing competition from sleek and lean new digital-only platforms.

AI can be put to good use in both the customer-facing and back-office functions of a bank. The most obvious applications aim to give customers a seamless 24-hour service and improve efficiency. But mature adopters are now finding ways of integrating AI into all systems to enhance and improve performance and stimulate growth.

AI has moved on several generations from its early applications and is evolving at a dizzying pace. It's not just about machine-led efficiency and chatbots. As we will explore, it can drive the growth agenda from every angle. Predictive analytics based on machine learning (ML) can assist marketing teams with differentiation and infinite ways of positively influencing customer experience. AI can employ problem solving and reasoning to help manage risk and compliance with regulatory obligations (work that is traditionally laborious and resource-hungry but that only serves to prevent problems rather than add real value to the business, one task very much best left to the computers). It can be employed to improve recruitment and retainment, prevent spending fraud and detect money laundering. I'll give some examples and explain how to go about adopting these valuable new technologies as we go on.

Unlocking trust: using AI to develop a mutual relationship between bank and customer

Some traditional banks are realizing, perhaps too late, that they are falling out of touch with their customers' needs, particularly younger clients whose expectations are so much higher. Moving banks can be done in minutes these days with minimal disruption. Customers will increasingly vote with their feet as they wake up to the advantages of being with a bank that is evolving with AI to offer the most precisely personalized services.

AI enables banks to automatically and constantly carry out deep microsegmentation of existing customers and prospects. Such granularity allows them to accurately predict the needs and behaviours of current and potential customers. By predicting likely redemption rates – the proportion of vouchers or offers redeemed – banks can now create personalized products and services that can reward customers according to their preferences, for example with points, travel or shopping-related benefits, cashback or insurance products. The return on investment is impressive, ranging from a 40 per cent increase in usage of the reward programme, to a staggering boost in sales of 30 per cent for some banks.

According to research by the global professional services network PwC (2020), 76 per cent of consumers accept that sharing data is a 'necessary evil'. They will consent if they see value in it. This willingness to allow institutions and businesses access to such a source of invaluable information offers the richest seam of raw marketing and business development gold. We just need the tools to mine it and turn it into treasure. This is where AI comes into its own. Without intelligent technology, a human workforce could never get close to harvesting and analysing all this data effectively to understand and execute all of its expansive potential uses. Computer-written algorithms continue to take in and learn from this constant tidal wave of data.

One way that this can be used is to generate insights that will help banks scale and target their advice across the lifetime of the client. For example, a customer who has remained loyal to their first bank for decades may have reached the age where their own teenage children are about to start driving or reaching college age. A bank that is effectively using AI to harvest and analyse this wealth of data can use this level of deep granularity to offer personalized banking services, say car loans or college funds, just at the right time. Such insights make the customer feel wanted and understood and capitalize on the established relationship between bank and customer. The bank becomes a trusted gateway to further financial and lifestyle services and is able to anticipate the customer's needs just as they arise, constantly building on that relationship – my bank knows me, I know my bank.

CASE STUDY
HSBC and Maritz Motivation Solutions

A great example is London-based bank HSBC, which partnered with Maritz Motivation Solutions to create a highly personalized rewards programme to improve the shopping experience for its US credit card customers.

The challenge: To improve participation dramatically and encourage high-end customers to spend their loyalty points.

The solution: The partnership identified target customers, the more mature sector with the most points. Learning technology was deployed to identify their most prominent interests, according to data available from previous communications, browsing, etc., and emails were sent to 75,000 cardholders tailored to those interests, offering cashback, holiday vouchers or life experiences.

The result: 40 per cent more recipients of the targeted marketing opened the emails within two days of receiving them than in the random test group, and 70 per cent of those who redeemed did so on gifts in the recommended categories.

In a company press release about the partnership, Jesse Wolfersberger, Senior Director, Decision Sciences, Maritz Motivation Solutions, said:

> In today's competitive landscape, instead of a scatter-shot approach, companies and brands now have the latest tool to engage and delight customers, make their rewards programs more effective and increase the return on their loyalty investment. From the brand perspective, the use of AI allows companies to serve customers better with a more customized and targeted loyalty program that results in significant operational cost savings.
>
> (Maritz Motivation Solutions, 2018)

These 'hits' have short-term benefits – meeting immediate objectives. But they also serve to strengthen the relationship between provider and consumer.

Conversational agents for customer support

Providing customer support is costly. For example, the leading 2,000 US corporations invest around $250 billion per annum. This equates to 50 billion customer cases at $5 per interaction. This is work that could be done at a fraction of the price when led by conversational agents – computer-generated dialogue systems that can converse in natural-sounding language. You will no doubt have conversed with many 'chatbots' and, since their introduction, you may have noticed how much more sophisticated they have become. Whereas first-generation chatbots could only respond to predicted questions with stock answers, often leading to frustration and failure, the new smart conversational agents are more proactive, using natural language processing (NLP) to learn, understand, respond appropriately and generate discussions based on previous contact or behaviours, such as browsing and buying. They can even become AI salespeople, listening to the customers' needs and employing the strategies and intelligence that have underpinned traditional human-to-human selling for millennia.

You may have noticed that it can now be difficult to tell if you are communicating with a human or a robot in the most basic online chats. While AI can learn to mimic human communication, it still hasn't quite passed the test Alan Turing set in 1955 – to exhibit intelligence indistinguishable from humans. Ask a conversational agent what its favourite colour is, and it would surely be flummoxed (unless, of course, a human had had the foresight to predict such a question and programmed in a response). They still rely on us to direct their areas of learning.

For customers, conversational agents offer seamless and live 24-hour personal banking in any time zone, supporting individuals and businesses with text, voice, messaging or visual tools. AI services can be scaled up during peak times with little extra expense in contrast to traditional call centre customer support, where long waits on hold can be a turn-off to all but the most determined prospects or customers. Conversational voice bots have been found to reduce customer wait time by more than 90 per cent and increase first-call resolution by 80 per cent (Dilmegani, 2021).

They can also potentially open up new opportunities for growth with targeted messaging and marketing. Perhaps surprisingly, research by Capgemini UK found that prospects trusted conversational agents more than people (2019). However, research has found that we're not quite ready to rely on robots completely – the best results came from a blended approach, with conversational agents opening the dialogue and passing on any strong leads or complicated questions to a real person, combining efficiency with the human touch when it's needed.

This means banks can make huge savings, an average of about 30 per cent, offer more agile, scalable services and reduce human error as well as freeing up staff to offer higher-quality interactions where a more flexible, personable approach is needed. This focus on maintaining valued staff for high-value clients and conversations helps to improve workforce buy-in to technological solutions, reducing fears of mass workplace displacement by machines.

How to create an AI customer service platform

- In order to provide an effective and responsive interface, banks need to understand their customer journey, just as they would for any other customer-based initiative. Why is each individual contacting the bank?

When and how will they contact the bank? What services do they need? How can we best serve them?

- What pathways are needed? Prospects and existing customers, for example, will need to be directed via different channels. Customer questions should prompt different pathways.

- Which services can be served by conversational agents? It all started with balance checks over the phone. Now AI can help process almost all points of contact, from complaints and queries to overdrafts and mortgage applications.

- How will your customers prefer to reach you? Online, through automated voice calls, via messaging? Millennials, for example, are more likely to prefer messaging. Older clients might prefer to be directed to a human responder if their immediate needs are not met quickly by a chatbot. Recognition and responsiveness are key. Conversations should continue seamlessly between different channels.

- Consumer confidence in conversational banking is growing but any data breaches could be disastrous. Secure identification and data confidentiality are essential to maintain and build on that trust.

- Which service design programme is best for you? Software company Capterra compares and reviews different products.

CASE STUDY
Bank of America's Erica

The challenge: The bank wanted to offer a secure, live service, 24/7, to all of its 25 million mobile customers.

The solution: Erica combines predictive analytics and natural language to offer a personalized service that has learned to respond to more than a million unique financial questions since its 2018 launch. The bank augmented Erica to understand more than 60,000 phrases and questions in relation to Covid-19, which it constantly updates.

The result: There are now 19.5 million clients on Erica's user base and it processed 105 million interactions in 2020, adding more than 2 million clients (Schwartz, 2021).

Business banking

AI is also bringing rapid and positive change in the way banks can provide more precisely tailored support to their business customers. Competitive banks recognize the need to move beyond credit and debt solutions into more holistic partnerships that offer broader support services, particularly shared technology.

Data gathered and analysed by AI can help banks make faster and more healthy decisions about business loans. Conversational banking, meanwhile, can deliver clear and accurate advice about reasons for loans being turned down and alternative paths based on detailed knowledge of the enterprise and the business landscape to help SMEs survive and grow at an organic and sustainable rate.

CASE STUDY
Canadian Western Bank

CWB partnered with Temenos, a banking software company, to provide its SME customers with personalized AI financial decision-making and growth stimulation. The pioneering platform boasts that it offers a virtual chief operating officer, capable of drawing on its vast data collection and analysis to make informed and intelligent decisions for its business clients. In a press release on its website, the company claims: 'With Temenos Virtual COO, financial institutions around the world will be able to empower SMEs with intelligent business banking, and drive growth with funding innovation as business owners navigate the challenges of the pandemic.' (Temenos, 2021)

The technology provides a real-time view of the company's financial health and future development, reducing the need for the SME to devote senior and executive man-hours to monitoring, evaluating and planning. AI's methodological, informed approach can reduce the risk of human error, internal conflict and decisions based on emotion. As well as attracting new customers to the bank, this revolutionary service will help existing customers grow in value, providing a real ROI to the bank in terms of managing greater volumes of secure wealth and huge potential. It's a laudable and visionary employment of AI that benefits everybody.

Fraud and compliance

Deep learning (DL) algorithms can detect suspicious transactions in real time, allowing action to be taken before loss is incurred. They can visually assess credentials (for example, use Google Maps street view to check businesses are as described), thus reducing the need for human resources to travel and ensuring compliance.

AI can learn to monitor all transactions for compliance and spot signs of money laundering.

Challenging the status quo

'You can't just ask customers what they want and then try to give that to them. By the time you get it built, they'll want something new.' This is a famous quote from Steve Jobs, co-founder of Apple, and it rings true today for the sectors we are analysing in this chapter.

Banking is changing faster than ever but the greatest challenge for the industry is to stay ahead of customer expectations. Only with the first stages of the realization of the potential of AI has this pace picked up exponentially. Previously, banking was weighed down by traditions and a conservative clerical culture. Customers queued politely during business hours to withdraw or deposit cash. Millennials would struggle to imagine tolerating such inconvenience – nor the impact of the ubiquitous arrival in the eighties of the electronic ATM (first introduced in 1967, even the name now sounds antiquated, automatic teller machines!) which allowed people to top up their wallets after hours instead of bringing a good night out to an early close.

The next real phenomenon in banking didn't arrive until the mid-nineties when online banking took off, revolutionizing the movement of money by allowing us to manage home or business finances via a PC. But these seismic changes in banking were a decade apart.

The industry is changing so fast now that we are even seeing new banks open up without any real-life customer contact: no branches, no high-street presence at all, just mobile and online interfaces, a concept we could barely have envisaged just 10 or 20 years ago when the high-street presence of a bank was its biggest selling point.

In just the last two or three years, we have come to rely on AI dozens of times every day. We buy our home utilities and insurance using algorithms and online payments; our electronic devices feed us purchasing suggestions based on our browsing history. We use digital platforms to pay for everything from a round at the pub to a new house. This has created a boom in the fintech (financial technology) industry. Adopting AI, blockchain and Big Data to revolutionize financial transactions, it is one of the fastest-growing sectors.

In 2020, the market values of top US-based fintech stocks overtook traditional Wall Street banks. According to CNBC (Delouya, 2020), the combined value of Square, Visa, PayPal and Mastercard topped $1 trillion at the end of that year, compared to the $900 billion worth of the 'big six' banks, JPMorgan, Bank of America, Wells Fargo, Citigroup, Morgan Stanley and Goldman Sachs.

More customers are choosing to handle their finances online or via their smartphones and there has been a huge rise in electronic payments. According to Visa, the UK is the biggest adopter of mobile banking with three-quarters of people surveyed saying they used mobile apps to manage their finances. In response, we have seen the emergence of neobanks such as Chime, Simple and Varo, which have done away with the branch model completely and are run entirely via apps and digital infrastructure. In November 2020, Starling Bank, a leading fintech player, became the first of these challenger banks to make a profit and was named Britain's Best Bank.

In 2019, Israel launched its first new bank in over 40 years, First Digital Bank. CEO Gal Bar-Dea believes we are on the cusp of a major disruptive revolution in banking as fintech start-ups are empowered by realizing the full potential of AI. Commenting in *Haaretz*, an independent daily newspaper in Israel, he said:

> Netflix killed off Blockbuster, Spotify disrupted the music industry and Tesla has left Ford and Mitsubishi in the dust. Banking is one of the few industries that hasn't undergone a revolution. Big, long-standing names control the market with too little competition and offer exactly the same products. We will be offering innovative banking, building a bank from scratch for the benefit of the public.
>
> (Rochvarger, 2021)

AI offers the opportunity to rewrite the rules, but it won't happen overnight.

Research by US digital payment app Square – founded by Twitter entrepreneur Jack Dorsey in 2010 – found that security was the biggest obstacle to greater take-up of digital banking. Expect to see marketing campaigns around security to drive up use of mobile banking in the future. For now the biggest winners are the traditional financial institutions these disruptive technologies were supposed to displace. They have seen huge takeup of their own banking apps, across Europe especially, while most people surveyed, especially in the United States, still prefer having the choice of the familiarity of being able to go into their local branch and speak to an agent directly. This will change, however, as tech-savvy millennials grow up into the next generation of wealth managers and bank customers. They are far less dependent on human contact, expecting more personalized services and rewards in exchange for their business. They will be far more likely to migrate between banks. Therefore attracting and retaining a sustainable customer base will come to depend more and more on AI-based learning and initiatives.

Traditional banks can and should be leveraging fintech partnerships to gain immediate access to the latest, technologically advanced applications and platforms to expand and diversify their offerings, and meet the changing needs of consumers. This is the only way banks can continue to compete with digital start-ups, prepare for the future and break into new markets. All of this can be achieved in a fraction of the time and at a fraction of the cost that it would have taken banks to research, develop and deploy new services in-house. For fintechs, collaborative partnerships provide them with an opportunity to further enhance and expand their services, gaining consumer trust through association with established institutions. Banks worldwide are recognizing that they need to offer more services than simply holding, moving and lending money to maintain a competitive edge, and are identifying technological innovations that can offer genuine USPs to retain and build customer bases.

CASE STUDY
TSB and ApTap

Following TSB's commitment to the 'Fintech Pledge' – a UK-Government backed programme to build secure and stable partnerships between financial institutions and technology firms – the bank launched TSB labs to accelerate its application of technology, which it saw as key to building future growth. In April 2021, the bank launched a collaboration with ApTap for a bill management service that allows customers to see all their regular outgoings in one place and switch to better deals with just a few taps. It claims to have saved customers an average of £150 per year during the programme's 10-month pilot by comparing and switching energy or broadband bills using data from bank statements. TSB had recognized its key market was made up from the 'aspiring middle', working families, money balancers and groups with variable income.

Featured in *FinTech Finance* (2020) magazine when announcing a major investment in technology to improve services for that targeted segment, a spokeswoman said:

> To deliver the best customer experience, over £120 million will be invested to further build on TSB's digital channels to provide mobile in-app onboarding/sales, as well as investing in the automation of some of the Bank's branches. Becoming a more technology-enabled and innovative business means transforming to be simpler and faster. TSB's new IT platform has a strong foundation to build upon for the future with multi-cloud and data capabilities, using data-driven insights and analytics to improve customer experiences for its target segment.

Where next?

Lynne Marlor, founder of New York-based Transformational Strategies, business change advisory consultants, believes we will see greater use of AI in other areas of finance, including backroom support and front-facing advisory investment services. She said:

> AI has already had an impact on business, especially in the financial world. Over the next two years, I see corporations and financial institutions (FIs) expanding their reach in using AI to mutualize the costs of non-differentiating but essential processes, think of supply chain management or reconcilement of invoices for example.
>
> These processes can be transformed using AI to reduce costs, settlement cycles and reconcilement issues. Additionally, many FIs are focused on AI for functions such as 'Know Your Customer' (KYC) and 'Anti Money Laundering' (AML). I expect more growth in the 'robo-advising' space, where companies like Robinhood and Chime have succeeded in providing financial advice and products to support financial well-being. I see these types of AI transforming FIs and fintech in the next two years as well.

How to up-tech your institution for the future

As we have established, in order to hold on to customers banks need to know who those customers are, what they want and when they will want it. TSB, for example, recognized that the demographics of its own customer base tended to be those on lower incomes with variable income, who would benefit most from keeping their bills down.

For a private bank such as Coutts, which offers private banking and wealth management, exclusivity is key. The services it offers are high end and expensive and its clients are happy to pay for them. You don't have to be a financial genius to identify which of the following texts came from the Coutts website and which one from TSB's:

> After all, family wealth often fades through the generations – so much so that many cultures have a phrase for it. In English, it's 'clogs to clogs in three generations'. The Italians say 'from stables to stars to stables'. And for the Japanese, 'the third generation ruins the house'.
>
> (Coutts, n.d.)

> Get a £30 or £15 shopping voucher... Take out Pick and Protect buildings and contents insurance together to get a £30 shopping voucher. Or a £15 voucher for taking out contents insurance on its own.
>
> (TSB, n.d.)

Despite serving different ends of the spectrum, marketing teams at both banks are driven by the same ultimate goal: to fuel growth. As the industry steers its way through this tumultuous and dynamic period of change, with ever-evolving technology and fierce competition from streamlined digital operations and fintech applications, all 'legacy' institutions need to offer more than just money management. They must forensically differentiate existing customers and make them feel like valued individuals. Clients can and will move if there are better options.

All financial institutions have rich seams of detailed information on the spending and saving habits of their customers through data sharing, and now the most advanced operations are learning to mine that data for marketing insights using AI algorithms and predictive analytics. Those insights provide valuable tools for strategic growth planning. They start with demographics – age, gender, income, family dynamics, location – for a broader brushstroke image of the customer base, such as TSB's. However, more sophisticated marketing teams will be looking to dig deeper so they can customize services for individuals. This can be done through their browsing and purchase histories, learning where they log in, how they log in and their behavioural patterns. AI algorithms and predictive analytics can collect and evaluate millions of actions and prepare tailored responses that would have previously been unimaginable.

They can also help identify trends and predict where future growth is most likely to come. This can feed into technologically driven growth strategies to attract a new generation of younger clients and win their loyalty. Predictive analytics tools can be built into websites to automatically track and analyse millions of events, presenting the findings in clear graphic representation according to an individual business's needs, be it demographics, website click-through rates, monitoring customer behaviour or outcomes such as ROI. Any business not using analytics is already missing out on an abundance of invaluable marketing and future planning insights. The cost of analytics varies, of course, according to the size of the organization, the scope of the data analysis and the complexity of the data. There are free versions available to SMEs, while the largest organizations may expect to pay a six-figure sum. Datamine has a transparent cost estimate for its various packages online, which gives an idea of the investment needed.

Once the marketing team has its goldmine of information sourced from the data, finding a fintech organization with an innovation that fits perfectly with a bank's strategy is key. A good launchpad for research is Technation's Fintech Collaboration Toolkit, a dashboard of the UK Startup Ecosystem that lists all UK fintech start-ups and offers a wealth of information on the industry.

We now move our attention to the insurance sector, to reveal how the sector is being transformed by fourth-generation technology like AI. A good place to start our analysis is with an Insuretech company, Worry+Peace – a reviews-led marketplace for insurance.

How to get started with AI in insurance

Michael Mpofu, Head of Communications, Worry+Peace, comments:

> While there are no rules to govern the route to choosing an AI provider, there must be some basic fundamentals to consider. The challenge of balancing human instinct, nuance and creativity versus the convenience, speed and access to data for insight offered by new AI is here to remain. Ours, as communicators, is to continue grappling with the questions and feedback which will enable these tools to complement our hard work. But we have to do this responsibly. The future is here, the challenge is to manage it and not the other way round.

Therefore, some of the key considerations when making procurement decisions should include:

- Start with the need: while AI presents some exciting opportunities, the full breadth of the services on offer may not be what your organization currently requires. For example, you may be at a stage where your team is simply trying to establish the 'tone of voice' or 'angle' for a campaign. While that may require some AI assistance – to test messaging or targeted audiences – at best, there is no real heavy lifting in this process. Establish and understand what you really need to begin with.

- Ask a lot of questions – especially the obvious ones: AI is evolving, so a healthy dose of scepticism won't hurt. Asking questions may unlock a series of revelations that may inform how the adoption of new tech will impact your organization.

- Don't rush: ultimately teams should be wary of getting stuck with a system that is obsolete or has evolved. If you're working in a context where procurement systems have a massive impact on the organization and ways of working, it would be responsible to take a more measured approach, given that reversing decisions may be complex and costly.

The term artificial intelligence turned 65 in 2021. But until now, the insurance industry has been surprisingly reticent in realizing its huge potential – baffling when you consider how perfectly it fits with the core functions of the sector. Other professional services are moving from the first phase of AI adoption – tentative, stand-alone pilot programmes – to the next phase: wholesale buy-in to the need to invest in end-to-end applications. However, the insurance sector, naturally steeped in a culture of caution and risk-aversion, is dragging its heels. An EY survey found that a shocking 79 per cent of respondents from 100 insurance-based companies 'regretfully revealed that they were yet to think of going digital or were in their learning phase' (Makadia, 2018).

Thus the industry still relies heavily on very well-remunerated human actuaries collating vast threads of disparate information, programming it into computers, and analysing it to calculate risk using the limited information available to them. The systems seem positively archaic next to AI, which can crunch and analyse Big Data with the precision, depth and scope it would take a stadium full of the brightest human minds to accomplish. And in a fraction of the time, at a fraction of the cost.

Marketing, winning new business, policy pricing, processing claims, measuring success, identifying new markets, innovating – these are all jobs that can be done infinitely more efficiently and accurately when we harness the increasingly sophisticated capacity of evolving technologies that can learn and reason. As we have already found, most people will consent to sharing personal information if they see a benefit in it. They are now so used to having their movements tracked by their smartphone, and using apps to monitor their own fitness levels, that it is a far smaller stretch to ask them to share the information harvested by these gadgets with their insurers in return for an incentive, opening the way for unprecedented volumes of data to drive AI-led insights into every corner of the business.

Leaving the time-consuming and repetitive work to the machines frees up human resources to do what they do best: tasks that demand imagination, thinking, creativity, empathy, capacity to respond to the unpredictable with appropriate tone and content. In short, a human touch.

AI is also bringing about massive change outside the industry that will have a huge impact on the insurance landscape. As I will explore in this chapter, AI will also bring solutions to these new challenges, with opportunities for automated, precise, real-time adjustments to policies according to minute detail harvested from consenting customers' smart devices.

While introduction of end-to-end AI systems will be disruptive and challenging in the short term, a study by Jupiter Research suggested that the industry will see a return of $1.3 billion (£920 million) in savings across motor, property, life and health insurance in 2023, as well as improving customer experience (Maynard and Crabtree, 2020).

The UK insurance sector today

Even before the global health crisis, the insurance industry was dealing with multiple pressures including implementing tougher new compliance obligations, Brexit and higher claim rates. Meanwhile comparison websites and government policy have encouraged people to migrate between insurance providers with each new contract in order to get the best deals. As a result, the cost of acquiring new customers has rocketed in recent years. It's no longer enough to rely on loyalty or reluctance to move. In a Deloitte (2020) survey, insurers said one of the biggest challenges they now face is rapidly evolving customer needs and expectations.

Insurers need to be leaner than ever before, more adaptable, more responsive; they need to be faster at communicating, writing policies and paying out.

Customers are no longer prepared to spend hours – or even a few minutes – waiting in line for call centres or months sorting out claims. They want instant communication, quick fixes and a company that treats them like a person, not a statistic. Providers need to increase their portfolios and services with add-ons such as breakdown cover or proactive health care and monitoring.

A snapshot of the industry

The UK insurance industry is the biggest in Europe, the fourth largest in the world and a global leader in exporting services. The figures in Table 5.1 give a snapshot of the state of the industry in 2018/2019, using the most recent figures available (Statista, 2019).

Clearly, there is much room for improvement in the post-pandemic world. But with executive and senior leadership teams becoming more informed and on-board with digitalization, the timing could not be better for a technological revolution in insurance. It has taken the seismic shock of the COVID-19 pandemic and necessity for invention to open minds to the endless possibilities new technologies offer for positive business change. According to a study by McKinsey, the need to adapt to new ways of working under the most challenging conditions of the global crisis has advanced the adoption of digital technology by three years. The next step is for forward-looking organizations to sustain and build on this progress by

TABLE 5.1 A snapshot of the industry

Number of domestic insurance companies:	388 in 2019, down from a peak of 613 in 2013
Value of life insurance premiums:	£177.4 bn – expected to drop to £160.4bn in 2020 due to Covid-19
Direct employees:	94,000 in 2019, down from a peak of 208,000 in 2004
Tax contribution:	£75.5 bn, up from £68bn in 2007
Household expenditure on insurance:	£21.9 bn in 2019, down from the 2014 peak of £26.5bn
Total benefits and claims paid by the UK insurance industry:	£268bn in 2018, up from £200bn in 2016

integrating adaptable AI infrastructure across the fabric of the business. They need to be agile, able to adapt and evolve at the pace of technological advancement to fully exploit the opportunities and avoid being left behind. Only the fittest, the most technologically fluent, will survive.

Industry leaders should be looking ahead to the next 10 or 20 years and mapping their organization's vision of the future and its part in it. With the ever-accelerating pace of change, standing still is really going backwards. After decades of false starts and promises AI is truly moving from the realms of theory into everyday reality. Self-driving vehicles, until recently a sci-fi whimsy, are about to become a reality: the first generation of legalized hands-free driving with automated lane-keeping systems will be on Britain's roads by the end of 2021. The Internet of Things (IoT) – a network of devices connected to one another and the internet – enables inanimate objects to communicate and work dynamically for us. Billions of people carry smartphones equipped with increasingly sophisticated AI, from face recognition to augmented reality. The new generation of conversational agents – advanced chatbots – use ML, reason and inference to answer complex customer queries 24/7.

How will all this affect insurance? Analysts believe we are on the cusp of a fundamental transformation that will see a whole new way of operating. Instead of calculating risk and paying out when the policyholder experiences a loss covered by the contract, insurance is moving towards a prediction and prevention model. This focuses on using AI to monitor and communicate with customers to constantly assess and minimize risk.

Let's see how each component of the sector might change and benefit.

Underwriting: measuring risk

The earliest underwritten insurance policy was found carved into stone in Babylon nearly 4,000 years ago. It pledged that loans needn't be paid back if the debtor experienced a catastrophe that rendered it impossible.

Underwriting as we know it today first emerged in the 1600s when financial backers signed contracts sharing the risk of dangerous voyages to the New World in search of valuable commodities.

Today, the sharing of risk still informs the business of underwriting, with policyholders from similar backgrounds undertaking similar activities paying into a pool that compensates the unfortunate contributors for whom the thing that might have gone wrong does go wrong. Some may pay more into the pool than others if the probability of them experiencing loss or an accident is deemed to be higher than that of their peers, rightly or wrongly.

Data is, of course, key to successfully underwriting. The industry relies on banks of people – more recently supported by computer programs – to mine and analyse that data in order to provide the most accurate predictions of risk available.

The factors taken into account to calculate these probabilities have become increasingly complex and computer programs assist by calculating multiple variables in our increasingly complicated lives. However, before AI, the programs were static – they did not learn or evolve or challenge the status quo. So the principle of underwriting has remained unchanged. Policies are calculated annually with the events of the previous 12 months affecting the individual customer and their wider environment taken into account on top of underlying factors to try to predict future risk. Insurance has therefore acted as a fairly crude reaction to history rather than a real-time response to ever-changing conditions.

However, AI is about to change this 400-year-old methodology. With AI, infinitely greater data can be crunched and analysed to refine the process and improve risk analysis for individual policyholders rather than grouping them together according to shared factors such as age, gender, location, activity and history. Deep learning, a branch of ML, connects neural computer networks imitating the cognitive abilities of the human brain, enabling machines to model abstractions at a level of detail we cannot even begin to imagine. This ML will improve infinitely, edging closer and closer to a Holy Grail of perfect precision.

Even more radically, automated underwriting systems will be able to connect to devices worn or used by consenting policyholders to monitor their behaviour in real time, such as Apple watches to screen for health issues and GPS trackers to evaluate driving risks. All the data will help to granulate and personalize policies as well as encouraging customers to actively consider and minimize risk on a minute-by-minute basis.

Policy pricing

Too high and prospects will find a better deal. Too low and insurers risk paying out more than they can bring in. Pricing has always been a fine balancing act with less and less room for error under the scrutiny of comparison websites. Sudden, inexplicably disproportionate rises in premiums cause bad sentiment. Customers who feel they are being ripped off are unlikely to consider the perceived culprit in the future and may influence those around them to hold the same negative views of a company. Thanks to social media, that dissemination is no longer limited to the sphere of people the disgruntled individual might happen to meet but to all their online friends and followers. Research by WhoIsHostingThis found that half of respondents had called out a brand on social media (Suciu, 2020). A price hike from £777 to £1,500 for an Admiral customer who had had a no-fault accident found its way onto the *Daily Mail*'s influential This is Money website (Murray and Eccles, 2019). Not all publicity is good publicity!

Therefore it is more critical than ever that insurance companies price their policies fairly, using the most sophisticated predictive tools at their disposal. As well as using algorithms to analyse unprecedented volumes of data for more accurate predictions of risk, and therefore fairer pricing for individual customers, the connected devices I have talked about can enable constant adjustments to the premium throughout the life of the contract in direct response to the behaviours of the customer. For example, any motorist who consents to having their vehicle monitored by a tracker could be rewarded for careful driving and be notified of any micro-changes to their premium instantly, fostering an ongoing relationship between insurer and customer. In marketing terms, the customer will have many more positive points of contact with the insurer, reinforcing brand awareness and loyalty. This reciprocal sharing of information also feeds back into the database from which the AI programs can continue to learn and interpret information. And, of course, if the driver is incentivized to always be conscious of the rewards of safe driving, the risk factor goes down and with it the probability of a claim and payout.

This model – preventative and responsive – can be applied to all branches of insurance. Private medical insurance and life insurance premiums, for example, can be adjusted according to data fed back through fitness apps or wearable devices that record exercise, nutrition and good or bad habits. Policyholders with pre-existing conditions can be rewarded for taking action to address them during the life of the policy, such as quitting smoking or cutting down on alcohol. Premiums are likely to be less heavily influenced by chronological age and better modelled on a more accurate, live picture of an individual's health status and lifestyle choices.

In the next decade, we are also likely to see the roll-out of a usage-based model, whereby AI assesses every insurable event for risk and charges accordingly. For example, pay-per-mile motor insurance, activated every time the customer makes a journey and assessed according to live factors including the route taken, mileage and driving conditions. Preventative measures to reduce risk and costs all round could include technology to suggest the safest – and cheapest – routes and times to travel.

Assessing claims

Claims and benefits paid out by UK insurance firms rocketed by a third between 2016 and 2018, from £200 billion to £268 billion. Assessing claims, especially where they are disputed, can be a lengthy and expensive process. Customers sometimes have to wait weeks or months for a decision and payout. In between, there are likely to be several points of contact that drain resources and offer the potential for conflict and subsequently poor relations between insurer and policyholder. Ideally, the customer will feel looked after by their insurer through a disaster and remain loyal in future years. Being made to wait any longer than necessary for a resolution adds to the stress of the policyholder and the feelings of resentment towards the insurer.

Insurance companies should be looking to technology to speed up the process, minimizing costs and disruption. For example, in a road traffic accident where the blame is disputed, assessors for all parties involved currently have to record witness statements from all sides and try to corroborate their own client's story with evidence from the scene and from damage to the vehicles or injuries. This has traditionally been a challenging and laborious process.

If customers have agreed to on-board tracking technology or dashcams, however, this process becomes much faster and simpler. In the near future we are likely to see ever-more sophisticated on-board computers storing relevant data needed to resolve claims and even drones sent to the crash scene to capture and process evidence instantly and help calculate claims, reducing the complications of conflicting and unreliable witness statements.

Similarly, homes and commercial premises with smart sensors will record any events leading up to disasters such as floods and fires, and drone cameras will be able to assess and price up damage in minutes instead of the weeks and even months that loss adjusters and investigators may take to review and process a claim before a payout can be made. McKinsey says half of claims will be processed by machines by 2030. We are already well on our way: Cambridge-based insurtech start-up Tractable has developed an AI system that has been programmed to visually analyse images of accident damage – from car crashes to natural disasters – and estimate repair costs in real time, taking just minutes.

Cutting fraud

The same technologies will, of course, also help to reduce fraud. According to the Association of British Insurers (2020), 107,000 fraudulent insurance claims worth £1.2 billion were uncovered by insurers in 2019, 300 per day. Undetected fraud is thought to cost the industry around £2 billion per year, a cost passed on to customers at an average rate of £50 per policy. Insurers could slash fraud by rewarding the majority of honest policyholders who consent to being monitored by wearable or smart technology with lower premiums or other incentives. With applications of smart technology growing, so that it will soon be available in spectacles, clothes and shoes, the possibilities of tracking policyholders and using the data from connected devices will be limitless.

New business acquisition

Rapidly changing landscapes bring with them new challenges but also new opportunities. With automation of vehicles, road traffic accidents and claims will fall; advances in preventive health care – such as apps that monitor vitals and alert loved ones or professionals to worrying anomalies – will continue to reduce the need for intensive private health care and after care. Smart sensors will reduce fires, floods and break-ins.

That does not have to mean shrinkage of the insurance sector. Insurers estimate that 23 per cent of premiums now come from propositions that did not exist five years ago, such as cyber security insurance. This figure is expected to increase to 33 per cent in the next five years (Deloitte, 2020). So, while premiums and payouts may all come down, new policies can be expected to rise. Design and marketing will be key. Again, we return to data and AI's ability to crunch it at a monumental scale and analyse for insights and predictions. Machine and deep learning can help identify emerging patterns of behaviour and trends and create new innovations to meet changing needs and shifting risks.

CASE STUDY
La Mutuelle Générale

The French insurance company has made customer acquisition smarter by augmenting the work of humans with data science. The company developed a ML-based system that helps sales teams to prioritize their work by assigning an individual probability of conversion to each prospect. It uses Dataiku – an end-to-end tool that processes data to insights – allowing the many different teams and profiles of users involved to contribute directly to the final product.

The first step is to review the data on existing clients and, in particular, their cost of acquisition and lifetime value. The next step is to create 'lookalikes' for each prospect. This refers to one with similar characteristics; someone more likely to mirror future actions. This system then creates a tool that enables sales teams to effectively prioritize their prospects.

How insurers can use AI in their marketing and sales

Insurance companies have more valuable data at their fingertips than just about any other industry but, until now, they have not fully capitalized on this wealth of marketing material. Deep learning – neural computer networks capable of learning from data without human supervision – augments this otherwise unmanageable and intimidating mass of information through predictive analytics. The software can offer detailed insights into the behaviours and likely requirements of existing customers and create profiles matching prospects with products. These insights can then be automatically translated into precisely targeted, personalized marketing and to up-sell or cross-sell superior or additional. AI can constantly measure its own success in real time and adjust its learning and actions accordingly.

Customer relations – conversational agents

AI is refining automated front-facing customer relations using cognitive reasoning of machines to imitate human language and inference in order to provide a broad range of 24/7 live, responsive customer services, including sales, policy contracts and claims management.

Research found that 47 per cent of those surveyed would be more likely to buy a product from an intelligent virtual assistant because of the automated service's ability to answer questions and simplify the transaction, while 53 per cent would be more likely to buy from a provider that offered 24/7 chatbots.

Almost a third find applying for insurance online difficult. Conversational agents embedded into company websites or on apps can optimize and speed up the process. They can guide customers to the correct policy and help them fill in the forms correctly, validating and approving policies and taking payments, reducing the delays that can be caused by human error or gaps in knowledge. They can respond to predictable potential questions, ask for clarification if the customer communication is unclear and seamlessly pass on the purchaser to a human agent if they get stuck. They can even identify openings for sales pitches and offer personalized alternative and extra policies after analysing the customer's browsing and purchasing history.

CASE STUDY
Meli

US-based Prudential Financial and Indonesian PFI Mega Life Insurance collaborated with Senseforth to build Meli, an AI-powered insurance virtual assistant that is capable of answering more than 50 questions and variations around them. It can address queries related to policies, plans, benefits and claim submissions with 96 per cent accuracy. It also allows users to download documents over the web and WhatsApp.

The rise of insurtech: friend or foe?

Insurtech, innovative and disruptive insurance technology start-ups, are actively seeking and designing niche solutions to help the insurance sector work more efficiently and profitably. While some of the thousands of new venture capital-backed enterprises are looking to design and sell add-ons to established brands, others offer their own highly responsive, bespoke packages and software solutions driven by AI efficiency and insights.

Traditional asset and infrastructure-heavy global insurance corporations must either compete or collaborate with this streamlined younger generation.

Conservatism and risk-aversion are built into the insurance industry, which might make senior leadership teams and boards extremely cautious about signing off partnerships with enthusiastic but untested upstarts. In fact, 79 per cent of insurers questioned saw fintech – the broader financial technology innovative sub-industry – as a challenge, rather than a resource. However, neglecting to recognize the value of well-matched collaborations could prove disastrous to even the biggest corporations.

Hundreds of insurers have entered rewarding partnerships with insurtech companies to develop successful new solutions for identified challenges while others have bought in ready-made services to enhance their own business models and customer experience.

Change needs to come from the top. Decision-makers need to wake up to the evolving landscape and prepare their organization for whole-scale adoption of new technologies.

Waiting and watching is not an option. New innovations are being snapped up by competitors every day. If they are not already, leadership teams should be attending insurtech and AI conferences, reading online news and staying abreast of trends and emerging new technologies. Some companies have created research teams to proactively seek out the potential partners who are developing the software innovations that would be the best fit with their own business models and key performance indicators.

Stakeholders need to be brought on board at the earliest stage to ensure buy-in and the readiness to respond rapidly to opportunity. Obviously, there are inherent risks that must be considered when choosing a partner – can the insurtech innovations scale up for global demand? Are the designers fully cognizant in compliance and data protection? How will these techie entrepreneurs fit into large corporate organizations?

But all insurance companies, no matter how big or small, ignore insurtech at their peril.

CASE STUDY
Ripe Thinking

Manchester-based insurtech provider Ripe Thinking has developed its own 'Juice' platform, which uses micro-service and Application Programming Interface technology to design and write bespoke policies instantly. The dynamic company uses robotics and data analytics to position and price products fuelled by real-time insights and trends.

Within 24 hours of UK Prime Minister Boris Johnson announcing that gyms would be forced to close in March 2020 due to the pandemic, Ripe had added free virtual workout cover for fitness instructors via its Insure4Sport product. It recently partnered with Aviva to offer cycle insurance, has modernized maritime insurance, traditionally a long-winded and paperwork-heavy sector, with its Pricing Insight Engine and has a 'build-your-own' policy marketed directly at its own customers on its website.

Speaking to BusinessCloud (Symcox, 2021), Executive Chairman Colin Whitehead said:

> We are now being approached by other organizations, affinities and brands to partner with them using our tech stack to help them serve their customers with our insurance model. We are leading a new breed of insurance in the UK. Consumer needs are changing rapidly and customers want a quick, simple digital purchase journey. Our conversion-optimized approach means 3 minutes 19 seconds is now the average time it takes to buy a Ripe policy.

Last but not least, people

Much of the anxiety around AI has its root in fears of human displacement. But we're a long way from being ready to dispense with people in the professional industries. Conversation agents are learning but if, say, a customer mentioned that they were getting health insurance because their father had just died, you would hope that the programme would recognize a deviance from the subject and put the grieving purchaser through to a human who could respond appropriately. Similarly, if a customer has, say, English as a second language and is struggling to make themself understood to an un-nuanced robot, a real person needs to be on hand to take over sensitively. Sometimes we all just need to hear a friendly voice.

Although they can reason using the information they have been given, AI-driven programs cannot think for themselves (yet). Every business needs people who can think, emote, empathize and negotiate, especially insurance agents dealing with unique, highly complex propositions and claims or contested or emotional issues.

And there are, of course, risks associated with automation that need to be monitored by sentient beings, such as prejudices thrown up by logic-based algorithms.

Research has found the most effective and user-friendly customer services are made up of a seamless blend of virtual and real assistants. In some cases, humans assist the virtual agents, in others, AI supports the humans.

What the sector needs to be doing right now is identifying the new skills that will be needed to let valued staff work in productive harmony with technology; to aggressively recruit a new generation of data engineers and scientists, experts in cloud computing and specialists in software design and writing. But equally it is vital that they don't throw the baby out with the bathwater. Every business entity has at its core a beating heart of loyal employees who know and love the business, without whom generations of knowledge and insight would be lost. Those whose roles are made obsolete by technology can and must be offered the opportunity to be retrained in appropriate new skills to ensure continuity and humanity thrive. We explore this much further in Chapter 7.

How is AI reshaping the legal profession?

In the final section of this chapter, we shift our attention to the legal sector. We begin by interviewing Lisa Burton, Chief Executive Officer of Legal Data Workspace. She explains:

> What I am seeing is that AI will drive the growth of an existing, relatively small, talent pool within the legal industry because the pace at which (AI) technology is being created is too fast for businesses and, in particular, legal practitioners to stay abreast of easily. The inherent need for a legal process to have a legally defensible audit trail is something that many technologies miss, even though the AI might be formidable. The growth opportunity for those of us in the industry who are true legal technologists who have both a legal education, training and experience in addition to being trained in software and technology to be able to map defensible processes around use of such technologies will continue to grow at a pace within the next two years. AI is big but unless the software is deployed by the team of skilled legal technologists, AI can often be a costly risk impacting time and money resources.
>
> There is no doubt that AI technology can reshape a customer experience which are often the use cases that support a marketing and sales function. For example, we know that most data breaches are caused by a failure in internal processes. Similarly, insider threat is rated a higher risk than any other threat because according to Microsoft 80% of unstructured data (i.e. emails, loose files, text messages etc.) is 'dark' data – that is to say that the content is unknown and not easy to manage. IBM quote this figure even higher at 90%. A case study demonstrates how a customer experience can be improved by AI technology where 'dark data' – and lots of it – resided in an AML (Anti Money Laundering) scenario. The client is a financial services

global client and through their contracted third parties in a high-risk global location, wanted to establish that £1m payments in commission to a further third party were legal and legitimate. Using AI technology, as proficient legal technologists, we were, within one hour, able to clarify that the payments were in fact legitimate. Compare this to a long-winded manual workflow to uncover the key players, facts and figures and the customer was delighted and impressed at the low cost, the time savings and the legal surety of the result.

One law firm that is taking advantage of AI is Harrison Clark Rickerbys Limited, as Laura Bufton, Legal Advisor (GCILEx) in its Dispute Resolution Team, comments:

> When applied properly, AI can be extremely beneficial in the e-disclosure process. From a lawyer's perspective, e-disclosure and AI has fundamentally changed the way in which the disclosure process is conducted. We are no longer digging through boxes and boxes of hardcopy documents provided by our clients to find relevant and disclosable material. The majority of the disclosable material is now electronic, in the form of emails, text messages, messenger applications, data rooms etc.
>
> From a legal aspect, there are a number of pitfalls within which a lawyer or firm could easily fall when embarking upon a disclosure process using e-disclosure and AI. The law is keen to encourage the use of new technologies to assist the parties in reducing time and costs, however, the Courts have been very clear that the process must be understood, agreed in a collaborative manner and capable of detailed explanation should any concern or criticism be raised. The use of technology and AI legal is likely to be significantly changed by 2030 and it is difficult to envisage that landscape, however, if technology is going to continue to play a role in the law, there will need to be large scale amendments to the rules, practice directions and training requirements of its members in order to keep up with developments and avoid any further pitfalls.

In Chapter 9 we will explore in more detail the complex issues surrounding AI in the legal, banking and insurance sectors, for example consent, and the fast-evolving world of ethics and regulation.

PRACTICAL TAKEAWAYS CHECKLIST: TOP 10 TIPS

1   Institutions must truly embrace AI and be willing to constantly evolve their business models with the fast-developing technology if they want to thrive and even survive.

2   AI solutions will add more than $1 billion in value to the financial services industry by 2035. Any financial institution that does not recognize and implement AI into the fabric of its business will be left fighting for survival.

3   Some traditional banks are realizing, perhaps too late, that they are falling out of touch with their customers' needs, particularly younger clients whose expectations are so much higher.

4   AI enables banks to automatically and constantly carry out deep micro-segmentation of existing customers and prospects. Such granularity allows them to accurately predict the needs and behaviours of current and potential customers.

5   By investing in AI, banks can make huge savings, an average of about 30 per cent, offer more agile, scalable services and reduce human error as well as freeing up staff to offer higher-quality interactions where a more flexible, personable approach is needed.

6   Traditional banks can and should be leveraging fintech partnerships to gain immediate access to the latest, technologically advanced applications and platforms to expand and diversify their offerings and meet the changing needs of consumers.

7   AI is evolving, so a healthy dose of scepticism won't hurt. Asking questions may unlock a series of revelations that may inform how the adoption of new tech will impact your organization.

8   Insurers need to be leaner than ever before, more adaptable, more responsive; they need to be faster at communicating, writing policies and paying out. Customers are no longer prepared to spend hours – or even a few minutes – waiting in line for call centres, or months sorting out claims.

9   Industry leaders should be looking ahead to the next 10 or 20 years and mapping their organization's vision of the future and its part in it. With the ever-accelerating pace of change, standing still is really going backwards.

10 Insurance companies have more valuable data at their fingertips than just about any other industry but, until now, they have not fully capitalized on this wealth of marketing material.

Bibliography

Ammanath, B, Hupfer, S and Jarvis, D (2020) Thriving in the Era of Pervasive AI. Deloitte's state of AI in the enterprise, 3rd edn. *Deloitte Insights*, www2. deloitte.com/content/dam/Deloitte/cn/Documents/about-deloitte/deloitte-cn-dtt-thriving-in-the-era-of-persuasive-ai-en-200819.pdf (archived at https://perma.cc/ JPL8-5KKU)

Association of British Insurers (2020) *Detected Insurance Fraud – New data shows that every five minutes a fraudulent claim is discovered*, www.abi.org.uk/news/ news-articles/2020/09/detected-insurance-fraud/ (archived at https://perma.cc/ R8HN-E8VY)

Biswas, S, Violet Chung, B, Singh, S and Thomas, R (2020) AI-bank of the Future: Can banks meet the AI challenge?, McKinsey & Company, www.mckinsey.com/ industries/financial-services/our-insights/ai-bank-of-the-future-can-banks-meet-the-ai-challenge (archived at https://perma.cc/38C9-3GTL)

Capgemini UK (2019) *Smart talk: how organisations and consumers are embracing voice and chat assistants*, www.capgemini.com/gb-en/news/smart-talk-how-organisations-and-consumers-are-embracing-voice-and-chat-assistants/ (archived at https://perma.cc/YC7G-MKTN)

Capterra (2021) Best Conversational AI Platform Software 2021. *Capterra*, www. capterra.com/conversational-ai-platform-software/ (archived at https://perma. cc/4BND-TSPC)

Coutts (n.d.) Financial Planning, www.coutts.com/wealth-management/specialist-planning-services.html (archived at https://perma.cc/96LU-FVET)

Datamine (n.d.) How much does data analytics and AI cost? *Datamine.com*, www. datamine.com/how-much-does-data-analytics-and-ai-cost (archived at https:// perma.cc/RJ6A-39H4)

Deloitte (2020) A Demanding Future: The four trends that define insurance in 2020, *Deloitte*, www2.deloitte.com/za/en/pages/about-deloitte/ articles/a-demanding-future.html (archived at https://perma.cc/V63V-9AME)

Delouya, S (2020) Market Value of Big Fintech Companies Rises to $1 Trillion, More Than the Largest Banks, *CNBC*, www.cnbc.com/2020/09/16/market-value-of-big-fintech-companies-rises-to-1-trillion-more-than-the-largest-banks. html (archived at https://perma.cc/75K4-XF5J)

Dilmegani, C (2021) 141 Myth-Busting Statistics on Artificial Intelligence (AI) in 2021, *AIMultiple*, www.research.aimultiple.com/ai-stats/#banking (archived at https://perma.cc/S36B-G3DA)

Drake, N and Turner, B (2021) Best Cloud Analytics of 2021. *Techradar.com*, www.techradar.com/uk/best/best-cloud-analytics (archived at https://perma.cc/ GW6M-KWDH)

Fintech Finance (2020) Exclusive: 'Keeping an open mind' – Pol Navarro, Banco Sabadell, *The Fintech Magazine*, www.fintechf.com/01-news/exclusive-keeping-an-open-mind-pol-navarro-banco-sabadell-in-the-fintech-magazine/ (archived at https://perma.cc/54XZ-U7T2)

Levitt, K (2021) How AI Is Powering the Future of Financial Services, *Finextra Research*, www.finextra.com/the-long-read/231/how-ai-is-powering-the-future-of-financial-services (archived at https://perma.cc/4DUX-YFKT)

Makadia, M (2018) *AI in Insurance – Addressing the industry's key challenges*, www.technative.io/ai-in-insurance-addressing-the-industrys-key-challenges/ (archived at https://perma.cc/A2H9-ZCU6)

Maritz Motivation Solutions (2018) Maritz Motivation Solutions and HSBC Innovate with Artificial Intelligence in the Loyalty Sector, *PR Newswire*, www.prnewswire.com/news-releases/maritz-motivation-solutions-and-hsbc-innovate-with-artificial-intelligence-in-the-loyalty-sector-300613109.html (archived at https://perma.cc/W9R5-FMAX)

Maynard, N and Crabtree, G (2020) AI & Automation in Banking: Adoption, vendor positioning & market forecasts 2020–2025, *Jupiter Research*, www.juniperresearch.com/researchstore/fintech-payments/ai-automation-banking-trends-report (archived at https://perma.cc/8DWT-8ZBS)

Murray, A and Eccles, L (2019) Money-grabbing Car Insurers Driving Britain Mad, *This is Money*, www.thisismoney.co.uk/money/cars/article-6671001/Money-grabbing-car-insurers-driving-Britain-mad.html (archived at https://perma.cc/TA7J-7R9R)

PwC (2020) Four Steps to Gaining Consumer Trust in Your Tech. *PwC*, www.pwc.com/us/en/tech-effect/cybersecurity/trusted-tech.html (archived at https://perma.cc/QA4S-A4DD)

Rochvarger, M (2021) Israel's First Digital Bank Begins Operations, Heralding 'Artificial Intelligence Revolution', *Haaretz.com*, www.haaretz.com/israel-news/tech-news/.premium-israel-s-first-digital-bank-begins-operations-heralding-ai-revolution-1.9619382 (archived at https://perma.cc/NND4-EUMD)

Roy, S and Khmeleva, E (2019) Neural Networks: The next step for artificial intelligence in financial services, *Accenture*, www.accenture.com/_acnmedia/pdf-110/accenture-financial-services-ai-neural-networks-pov.pdf (archived at https://perma.cc/WT5V-AKY3)

Schwartz, E (2021) Bank of America's Virtual Assistant Erica Explodes in Popularity, *Voicebot.AI*, www.voicebot.ai/2021/04/21/bank-of-americas-virtual-assistant-erica-explodes-in-popularity/ (archived at https://perma.cc/C2GD-FVNU)

Statista (2019) Number of Insurance Companies operating on the domestic insurance market in the United Kingdom (UK) from 2004 to 2019, *Statista*, www.statista.com/statistics/817377/number-of-companies-operating-in-uk-insurance-market/ (archived at https://perma.cc/3ASB-V7BL)

Suciu, P (2020) Social Media's 'Callout Culture' Continues to Improve Customer Service, *Forbes*, www.forbes.com/sites/petersuciu/2020/01/08/social-medias-callout-culture-continues-to-improve-customer-service/?sh=1c1424216d99 (archived at https://perma.cc/E9JQ-49VX)

Symcox, J (2021) Multi-million-pound Growth for InsurTech, *BusinessCloud*, www.businesscloud.co.uk/multi-million-pound-growth-for-insurtech/ (archived at https://perma.cc/DQ5C-FTVY)

Tech Nation (n.d.) Fintech Collaboration Toolkit: supporting fintechs engaging financial institutions, *Tech Nation*, www.technation.io/resources/fintech-collaboration-toolkit/ (archived at https://perma.cc/ZA8K-QJZC)

Temenos (2021) Temenos and Canadian Western Bank Break the Boundaries of SME Banking with an Explainable AI Digital Banking Solution, *Temenos*, www.temenos.com/news/2021/03/04/temenos-and-canadian-western-bank-break-the-boundaries-of-sme-banking-with-an-explainable-ai-digital-banking-solution/ (archived at https://perma.cc/T6TY-95VP)

TSB (n.d.) Insurance, www.tsb.co.uk/insurance/ (archived at https://perma.cc/K97N-QDPK)

06

Revolutionizing customer support in the telecoms sector

In this chapter we turn our spotlight on the world of telecommunications and explore the ways in which telcos worldwide are currently exploiting AI across their sales, marketing and, above all, their customer service functions. This is powerfully expressed by the CTO of Ericsson, Erik Ekudden, who states:

> Artificial intelligence is without question the primary enabling technology for the next generation of system automation. Aside from freeing up valuable resources, improving performance and boosting innovation, AI also opens up a wealth of opportunities for communication service providers (CSPs) to grow their businesses beyond simply providing connectivity.
>
> (Ekudden, 2021)

The main drivers for this investment in new technology are the Internet of Things (IoT), the connectivity of devices and services with the internet that will push demand for data up exponentially to zettabytes (one sextillion bytes, a thousand raised to the seventh power), 5G and Wifi6, the new generation of mobile infrastructure being rolled out globally, and the possibilities and pressure these technologies will bring to develop capacity, growth and profit in the face of ever-evolving competition from established providers and streamlined, tech-based newcomers.

These technologies, along with machine learning (ML), deep learning (DL) and predictive analytics, have opened the floodgates to an era of seemingly limitless AI-based opportunities. Governments across the world now recognize that 5G is key to sustainable growth. Not only will it become the primary service supplier for computers and smartphones, but it will also open up the private wireless infrastructure for exponential increases in applications of IoT, drive a new age of digital transformation powered by AI and edge computing, and trigger a new wave of innovative and disruptive business models.

Despite the negative impact of the global COVID pandemic on the revenues of telecoms companies and communication service providers (CSPs) worldwide, three separate research firms predict significant investment in AI over the coming years:

- The International Data Corporation (IDC, 2020). 'Worldwide Artificial Intelligence Spending Guide' estimated that spending on AI would reach $12 billion in 2021 in Europe, and continue to experience solid double-digit growth through to 2024.

- Market intelligence firm Tractica (2019) is also bullish about the sector's investment in technology, predicting that annual investment in telecoms AI software will grow to more than $11.2 billion in 2025.

- Gartner Inc. also estimates that the number of CSPs investing in AI technologies to improve the planning, performance and services delivered by their infrastructure will increase from 30 per cent in 2020 to 70 per cent in 2025 (Churchill, 2021).

Similar sentiment can be found in a comprehensive AI benchmarking survey of executives at 1,200 companies across 12 industries and 15 countries conducted by ESI ThoughtLab (2020). The findings reveal that 66 per cent of telecom companies believe that AI is considerably or very important for the future of business. The biggest surprise for me in this figure is that more than one in three executives have not yet woken up to the AI revolution that is gathering pace every day, while forward-looking companies are already moving from the cautious, experimental phase of adoption to the next chapter of end-to-end integration.

Telcos must move quickly to adopt and harness these developments and solutions to compete in markets where individual and big-business customers constantly demand and expect improved, flexible, personalized services. The ability of AI to gather, analyse and monetize previously unthinkable quantities of valuable data will be at the heart of fast-adapting provision of the most cutting edge and innovative services. One company doing precisely this is Zain – a leading telecommunications operator across the Middle East and Africa, providing mobile voice and data services to over 48.5 million customers. Kutay Yurtsever is Chief Strategy and Business Development Officer at Zain. He comments:

> We are already seeing a big impact of using AI models in certain predictive models in our business, much more so than rule-based models. We see a bigger impact as these models are better trusted and tested in the market. We expect to see the biggest impact in commercial areas, especially analytics for marketing. CX applications are relevant too but the financial impact is much less. It's a more longer-term impact which is hard to measure financially. We also expect to see high impact in network analytics in order to optimize experience as well as reduce operating costs and opportunity costs, through predicting and doing preventive maintenance for example
>
> The key success criteria for AI are without a doubt capable modellers, data availability, being open to try new models, real impact cases and close collaboration between AI specialists and functional leaders. The biggest issues we see are sometimes referred to as 'black-box' implementations. Also, there are always some sceptics and non-believers, and it is sometimes difficult to convince leaders and managers, so many pilots and experiments are required. Looking ahead to 2030, much manual work should be automated, such as with robotic process automation (RPA), and a lot of intelligence will be built into systems that continuously learn and advise managers and leaders on ways to improve business.

We now move our attention to a Chinese telco, Huawei. We hear from Haitham Ammar, who is Reinforcement Learning Team Leader at Huawei Research and Development in the UK. He shares with us his views on the importance of AI:

> I believe AI will have a huge impact on business all over the world in the next two years. Much of the mundane work processes can be automated using machine learning techniques. These cover various sectors ranging from transportation, manufacturing, health care, education, customer service to name a few. That being said, I do not believe that AI will replace humans in all aspects of these jobs. Rather, I foresee an environment in which AI is integrated with human expertise to elevate their productivity as opposed to outperforming them. Apart from ensuring an enhanced upgrade in job descriptions as has happened in any other industrial revolution in history, such a realisation also comes from the way current AI techniques are trained. Today, AI is trained so as to maximise performance by reducing prediction errors, i.e. reduce mistakes in your prediction. As has been shown over and over again, this is not necessarily the only criteria a business is interested in. At the end what is the use of an AI

that maximises performance but has no clue about basic business concepts, constraints and principles? Hence, for an AI to be successful in (at least safety critical) real-world applications, a synergy between human and machine performance needs to be emphasized.

Huawei has committed to an AI strategy that improves user experience with customer-first in-sight. Many products and services in Huawei make use of state-of-the-art developments in machine learning and AI while guaranteeing domain-expert due diligence for enhanced productivity.

Let's delve into the applications and benefits of AI in the telco sector, in particular the impact on sales, marketing and CX.

A primary focus for early adopters of the technology has been the use of automation to improve customer experience and reduce operating costs, but as we will see, the most innovative companies are already using it across every department from fraud reduction through to the development, marketing and sales of new products and services.

Below I have identified six core benefits that all telco companies should be either using or investigating right now. The first four are particularly related to sales, marketing and CX. The last two are more operational, but clearly have a crucial role to play in providing the customer with an effective service.

Six core benefits of AI for telcos

1. Predictive analytics

All CSPs manage vast amounts of data in their day-to-day operations. Until recently, it has been impossible to fully mine or capitalize on the extremely valuable insights locked within these rich seams of information. Machines (aided, guided and monitored by sentient, ethically minded humans) can analyse data in quantities and at speeds we could never have imagined. They can derive infinitely more complex, precise, targeted and personalized insights from this data, using algorithms of both individual and broader market behaviours to forecast future demands, trends and patterns. Technologies such as ML and AI can drill down into this data with determined objectives, such as sales conversions, price optimization to maintain a competitive edge, innovative product development and improved customer experience or marketing.

These insights are created in real-time response to customer behaviour, rather than taking weeks, months or years, thus allowing CSPs to make the most timely, efficient and effective business decisions. Some of the important and measurable benefits of predictive analytics include customer segmentation, customer churn prevention, predicting the lifetime value of the customer, up-selling or side-selling and improving margins.

CASE STUDY
Comcast

Comcast, the United States biggest cable provider, has 30 million customers. That's a heck of a lot of data coming in on their behaviours, habits, spending patterns, migrations, feedback and demographics.

The company's bank of human engineers has set up an AI system that enables its human analysts to optimize this wealth of information. Comcast Chief Technical Officer Matt Zelesko told FierceTelecom (Robuck, 2019) how the algorithms and systems it generated through AI and ML for the development of its next-gen X1 video platform have been the foundation of a far wider application. He said: 'Things that we've learned in X1 are now permeating everything. I think AI and ML is one part of that and it really helps us with a lot of the telemetry and visibility. It's being able to detect things before customers tell us. The cool thing about AI is you just take a whole bunch of data, throw it into the soup pot, and AI comes out with the insights and the connections.'

Comcast is using the system developed for the X1's voice remote in the company's virtual assistant, and X1 diagnostic tools have been rolled out to identify and correct problems across multiple channels before they even reach the customer.

Tony Werner, Senior Technology Advisor to the CEO, revealed that another issue highlighted by the expansion of data analytics was the need for a coherent system to make sure the right insights reached the right teams. Engineers came up with a system they called CXels to filter the data into eight streams so product owners could curate their own information.

He said:

So the team that owns the WiFi will listen to thousands of points of data, but [decide] 'these are the three things that really determine what's important'. And then each of those is supplemented with an AI engine that looks across this and says, 'Out of all this data, I can tell you when these two things go wrong, the customer's not going to be happy.' Then you take these eight groups together, and they bubble up to an AI engine that goes across all eight of them that says, 'here's what this customer experience has been', and then that feeds into our internal tools.

(Robuck, 2019)

---

2. Improved customer service

As a service provider, of course the main objective is to satisfy your customers and provide top-quality service. Yet, telcos consistently rank bottom of the pile in the 'American Customer Satisfaction Survey'. The phrase 'on hold with' is among the more commonly used expressions of frustration in the customer lexicon. Over a 12-month period, community-driven website #OnHoldWith.com, which aims to highlight and end customer service phone waits, collected more than 165,000 posts from Twitter that mentioned the phrase. In 2020, Virgin Media was deemed the worst company to call for the year, with Verizon, AT&T and Comcast showing up in the top 10. Unsurprisingly, telecommunications was named the worst industry to call in 2020.

FIGURE 6.1 Customer complaints after being put on hold with telcos

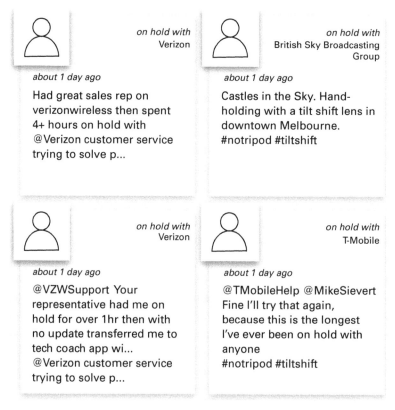

SOURCE OnHoldWith.com (2021)

Figure 6.1 shows the results of a search for 'telecommunications' on the #OnHoldWith website, which has attracted news reports and reviews from media outlets across the world including the BBC, *Los Angeles Times*, the *New York Times* and NBC.

In the age of social media, every user is a potential PR disaster, able to broadcast their fury at poor service to all existing and potential customers. When written with flair and humour, these rants can go viral, maximizing the fallout.

CONVERSATIONAL AI: IMPROVING CX WITH NATURAL LANGUAGE PROCESSING

This damaging public feedback can be avoided almost entirely with the adoption of AI.

Conversational AI platforms, also known as virtual assistants or chatbots, are becoming increasingly popular in the telco sector because of their ability to dramatically improve customer service by offering swifter replies and support across multiple languages. This market is expected to grow to $13.9 billion by 2025. Telcos can now allow customers to self-serve, dramatically reducing the burden of the huge volume of requests for troubleshooting and maintenance that can at times overwhelm the customer support centre. Over a relatively short period of time, the cost of integrating AI in customer service systems will not only be recovered through efficiency savings, but it is also highly likely to bring substantial ROI.

Most platforms work alongside human responders by passing on any queries they are unable to manage to a real-life agent smoothly and seamlessly, enhancing the customer experience, reducing waiting times considerably and offering a 24/7 service from any time zone. They can be upscaled easily during peak times to avoid longer waits during call spikes. Many larger organizations have realized that customers recognize the benefits and prefer companies that have adopted AI to improve their service. Instead of trying to disguise chatbots as real people, many have given their systems an avatar and memorable name to familiarize customers and promote their use as a positive marketing tool.

Conversational agents are becoming increasingly sophisticated at managing complex customer enquiries and expectations by using natural language processing (NLP) to understand, learn and respond appropriately to a wide variety of predictable questions. They can be integrated into phone centre services or online via apps or company websites.

When we consider the Gartner Hype Cycle (an analysis of the claims for a technological breakthrough vs the reality or potential), it is fair to say that some chatbots have failed to deliver on their promises, plunging some telcos into the trough of disillusionment. The source of this failure has been the chatbot's limited ability to understand and mimic natural conversational dialogue. A slight deviation from the script upon which a first-generation bot was programmed could lead to misunderstanding of the customer's intent. With the complexity of human languages, dialects and idioms meaning there are thousands of ways to ask any question, this static program often ran into problems, raising frustration and dissatisfaction among customers.

These rudimentary bots are now being demoted to low-level triage and redirection functions but have nonetheless paved the way for conversational AI as it is today. Thanks to advancements in NLP and ML, telcos can now automate the successful resolution of customer issues by learning from historic email tickets and phone logs. These conversational AI systems know when to solicit new information and when a request is repetitive and therefore irritating for a customer.

Furthermore, the telco can connect the conversational AI agent to other business systems in order to predict when a customer is at risk of churning based on their behaviour and other lifecycle trends. The company then has the option to intervene – for example, incentivizing the customer to renew a contract.

Here are six examples of telecoms companies using AI to improve customer services:

1 AI is helping to improve customer service for Dutch telco KPN. The company uses speech recognition to reduce average hold time by 30 seconds per call and increase net promoter score by 17 points. Customers begin by stating in their own words why they are calling. AI then authenticates the caller, recognizes their intent and automatically answers or routes them to the right agent. When it does so, it pulls out the customer's details and call history, and transcribes their own words so the agent immediately has an accurate and full context. Here, AI is used as a triaging gateway for customer service agents to improve their response time and efficiency.

2 Vodafone allows its customers to connect with web-based AI assistant, Julia. She handles technical support and invoicing queries, and then feeds back critical, insightful data to assist future decision-making. Using the Teneo platform, Vodafone quickly built sophisticated dialogue flows that enable

Julia to resolve complex technical support, billing and change-of-address queries. The user interface can be tailored, offering animation, custom actions and adapting the appearance of the avatar. Julia can offer customers additional content such as videos, thereby seamlessly communicating complex explanations.

3   TOBi is another of Vodafone's customer service chatbots, powered by IBM's Watson technology, operating in 11 markets and responding swiftly to simple customer queries. TOBi, who is represented by a friendly-faced, branded avatar, offers text-based conversation through instant messaging, the Vodafone app or its website. The company is also developing a voice-recognition phone system. TOBi is able to successfully manage 90 per cent of customer questions, the rest are passed on to human agents. In an interview published on the company's website, Neil Blagden, Director of Customer Services and Operations at Vodafone, said: 'The technology which TOBi is built with is accessible to all, and it can be delivered in a way which doesn't require heavy investment or niche software development skills... all of the conversational experiences that happen with TOBi have been designed and configured by individuals we recruited from our own contact centres. We realised that the most important part is building a conversation with the customer, and understanding the issue they need resolving.' (Vodafone, 2017)

4   In Austria, Deutsche Telekom's award-winning chatbot Tinka provides targeted assistance to customers. Represented by a 3D hologram, it was designed through Charamel software to answer questions with charm and sympathy, mimicking human behaviour and emotions. Human agents handle the 20 per cent of queries that Tinka is unable to support. In a conversation between two digital assistants published on the company website (Vom Hofe, 2019), Tinka explains how she works: 'Our makers don't want to have to keep feeding us and defining how we answer questions manually. That's why they've decided to make use of AI. That way we can learn to understand customers' everyday language – entire sentences, not just individual words. And above all, their intention. I'll take my "memory" as an example. Thanks to AI, I can remember earlier discussions. If someone tells me that they have a problem with the battery of their Samsung Galaxy S8 Plus and then later asks me for the operating manual, I conclude: they mean the operating manual for the Galaxy S8 Plus.'

5   Spanish multinational Telefonica used Microsoft Azure Bot Service and Cognitive Services to build and support Aura, an intelligent conversational

agent for multiple services in six countries across four separate channels, including home devices and a mobile app. Customers can use voice interaction to control their products and services, check their data usage, access 24/7 support, look at bills and request personalized viewing recommendations based on their previous habits and choices. Irene Gomez, Aura Global Director at Telefonica, said: 'We use Bot Service and Cognitive Services to help people interact simply and naturally with technology.' Aura also analyses data coming back from customers to identify opportunities to offer and sell extra personalized products, adapting its sales pitch to each individual, and it can advise and warn about security issues such as detection of fraudulent apps. Chema Alonso, Chief Data Officer at Telefonica, said: 'With Aura we want to transform data into knowledge and place it into our customers' hands so that they are able to know, decide, and act, and so that they can make the most of their relationship with Telefónica.' (Telefonica, 2017)

6 Comcast, the biggest cable provider in the United States with 30 million customers, leveraged AI and ML to launch its Xfinity Assistant in 2017. It allows customers to interact with the system through natural speech and communicate with virtual assistants through text messaging, Facebook messenger, its own app and its website. It came into its own during the pandemic when interactions increased from 60,000 per day to 400,000. Piers Lingle, Senior Vice President of Customer Experience at Comcast, said the aim was to make the customer experience as smooth and efficient as possible, eliminating the need for customers to wait while they were moved between departments or repeatedly give their account details. This was made possible by the system's own cognitive learning ability. He said: 'Our customers are calling us and messaging us with all kinds of questions about their service, and everyone has different ways of asking the same questions. For example, through our research we discovered there were more than 7,500 ways to say "I want to view my bill." We wanted to know, "Can we use the technology to help customers find answers faster?".' (Wilson, 2019)

THE FUTURE OF AI IN CX

In early 2021, Cloud-based customer service platform provider Talkdesk released a global report entitled 'The Future of AI in the Contact Center', which surveyed CX professionals about the future of AI in their industry.

The results provide an overwhelmingly positive outlook for the technology and the customer experience function.

The report found that an overwhelming majority (89 per cent) of CX professionals – including customer service leaders, managers and operational staff – believe in the importance of leveraging AI in contact centres, with a further 82 per cent saying AI is increasingly necessary for business success. Of these professionals, 84 per cent expect their company's total spending on AI and automation to increase in 2025 compared with 2021. However, only 14 per cent of businesses consider themselves 'transformational' with AI and of the 69 per cent of organizations that have invested in AI and automation for customer self-service features, nearly half (48 per cent) have yet to use it. Why is that?

The biggest barriers to AI implementation are perceived challenges. David Gardner, Vice President of Research and Insights at Talkdesk, explains:

> Companies today are under immense pressure to deliver stellar customer experiences. They know artificial intelligence can help them better serve customers but many struggle to implement it properly. Our research shows that automation can and should become an integral component of contact centers if professionals develop and commit to a comprehensive strategy.
>
> (Talkdesk, 2021)

The Talkdesk report shows that AI is well-positioned to improve both the customer and employee experiences. Many enterprises can transform their contact centres to provide more than just traditional customer service by adopting AI tools to help streamline workflows and processes across functions to expedite innovation and go-to-market plans. Unfortunately, perceived hurdles and challenges stop many organizations in their tracks before they can progress far enough along the AI maturity curve to maximize these benefits. The report identified three major misconceptions amongst CX professionals regarding AI in their job function:

1 55 per cent of CX professionals believe AI will have a short-term negative impact on customer satisfaction (CSAT).

2 43 per cent see the cost of AI tools as a barrier to implementation.

3 30 per cent believe reliance on the IT department will impede progress in implementing AI.

While these concerns are valid, they are also easily debunked. Customer satisfaction is the top KPI these professionals need to deliver on, and even if there is a negative impact in the short term, these dips can be recovered in the long term if the technology is implemented strategically. Over time, automation will help to free up agents' time and help reduce customers' frustrations of trying to get the help they need quickly. The benefits to both the staff and the customers they serve will far outweigh any negative impacts felt during the adjustment period.

These benefits will help to justify the cost as well. It is difficult to say exactly how much implementation will cost, as it will really depend on the tools or providers you partner with for the project. But even so, the efficiencies gained from AI's ability to analyse mountains of data in a fraction of the time it takes agents to do so, freeing them up to focus on higher-value initiatives, may lead to increased revenues that can offset the cost of the tools.

So what comes next? The Talkdesk report made four key predictions for the future based on the responses given:

- Organizations will invest more in AI capabilities, with 64 per cent of respondents citing deeper investment in AI functionality as a priority for their contact centre.

- Automation will drive operational efficiency and CX, as 84 per cent of professionals expect their company's total spend on AI and automation to increase through 2025.

- Humans' presence will rise in the AI-enabled contact centre; 79 per cent of CX professionals see AI as an assistant rather than a replacement, providing agents with more tools to help with customer interactions and augmenting the skills necessary to do the job.

- AI will enhance the customer journey securely, as 79 per cent of surveyed professionals believe AI will be more secure than interacting with human agents.

Only time will tell how things take shape, but all of these predictions would mean massive benefits for CX professionals and the customers they serve and highlight that AI is an avenue worth exploring.

CASE STUDY
Magenta Telekom

Austrian telecoms company Magenta Telekom uses a conversational alternative to voice calls and traditional emails, enabling customer engagement via WhatsApp and web messaging. This resulted in:

- increased in CSAT by 61 per cent;
- increased in productivity by 31 per cent;
- reduced staff attrition.

'Our aim was to offer a channel which our customers already use to communicate with friends and family,' explains Andreas Biehler, VP Customer Steering & Support, Magenta Telekom. 'We wanted to shift from emails and voice to a more modern way of communication that also leads into higher customer satisfaction and an increase in productivity of our agents. The only way to scale was to get away from manual ticketing and invest in messaging and automation.' (LivePerson, n.d.)

In order to operate at scale, the company turned to LivePerson's Conversational AI. Natural Language Understanding and AI will route requests more efficiently and seamlessly, which will lighten the pressure put on agents by eliminating these tasks. Easy and recurring requests can then be handled by bots, such as finding out the order status or receiving information on the latest invoice, while agents can focus on more complex customer requests.

Magenta Telekom made digitization simply happen by introducing AI-powered messaging in its contact centre, leading to happier customers, happier agents and significant efficiencies for the business.

---

3. Securing new revenue streams

Despite unprecedented levels of data demand during multiple national lockdowns and the rising trend of working from home, industry revenue fell by 2.7 per cent in 2020. Experts expect to head back into positive territory at some point in 2021, but with thousands of new providers in an increasingly competitive market, harnessing technology to find new streams of revenue will be key to survival. Recently, the bigger providers have depended on acquisitions for growth, but without changing fundamental business models this is not a long-term solution.

According to a survey by Deloitte, 86 per cent of networking executives believe that advanced wireless (5G and Wi-fi6) will transform their organization within three years, and 79 per cent say the same about their industry (Littmann, Fritz and Wilson, 2020).

The wider rollout of 5G infrastructure will be the biggest challenge to face the sector this year. Mobile wireless operators are expected to spend $1 trillion extending 5G to 1.7 billion customers by 2025. It will pose a real and definite threat to cable services that are racing to compete with their own next-generation Wi-fi6.

However, a survey by S&P Global found that even in countries with a high take-up of the new technology, monetization opportunities in telecoms were highly limited. A huge and essential investment but with little direct ROI.

The Global System for Mobile Communications Association estimates that 5G will generate €700 billion in investments by 2025 (GSMA, 2021); however almost two-thirds of this will go to enterprises, best positioned to harness its potential by developing innovative new smart products and services, with retail, government and finance applications the sectors next most likely to make big gains.

CASE STUDY
Telcos in Vietnam

Vietnam's three largest telecoms providers – Viettel, Vinaphone and MobiFone – have turned to the adoption of 5G services and other digital platforms to increase revenues and better serve their customers.

Over the past few years, Vietnam's telecom operators have experienced dips in their revenues, especially in mobile services. In fact, both Viettel and MobiFone saw almost no significant increase in revenues within the mobile voice service segment in 2020.

Nguyen Van Yen, Head of the Technology Department at Vietnam Posts and Telecommunication Groups (VNPT), has revealed that voice services still account for nearly half of mobile operators' total revenues. Historically, VNPT has seen a continuous year-on-year growth in mobile service revenue but saw no such increase in 2020. This is cause for concern not just for VNPT, but for other mobile service providers.

While it may come as no surprise based on the ways in which we tend to use our devices today, these falls in mobile voice revenue have been met with strong rises in data service revenue. According to Nguyen Phong Nha, Deputy Head of the Telecommunications Department under the Ministry of Information and Communications (2021), many mobile operators are facing pressure as over-the-top services replace traditional voice and text communications, and internet services do not create as much profit as expected. Currently, mobile data charges in Vietnam are among the lowest worldwide, equal to just 30 per cent of what one would pay in India. The best way forward for traditional telecom service providers seems to be enlarging their business operations to create new sources of revenue.

For Vietnam's top-three providers, expanding their network capabilities was the answer. In December 2020, Vinaphone became the first to obtain a licence for the commercialization of 5G in Hanoi and Ho Chi Minh City. Since then, the company has been developing the necessary infrastructure to widen 5G coverage. This trial run of 5G services is also helping Vinaphone explore the application of new technologies for smart cities and enterprises.

In February 2021, over 17,000 Viettel mobile subscribers registered for the company's 5G promotional package. By the fourth quarter of 2021, 30 major cities and provinces, industrial parks and urban areas will be covered with 5G. Viettel aims to gradually trial and deploy 5G at a wider scale through 2025, with the goal of reaching national coverage by 2026.

Like Viettel and Vinaphone, MobiFone has also been preparing for 5G rollouts in many cities and provinces in 2021 and beyond. The company's general director, Manh Cuong, has expressed that 5G networks play an important role in the development of the digital economy and form a foundation for the implementation of Industry 4.0. Therefore, 5G brings about huge opportunities for not only MobiFone, but also for its partners and clients.

The data supports this thinking. According to forecasts from Ericsson and the Global System for Mobile Communications, by 2025 5G will make up around 20 per cent of the world's total number of mobile subscriptions (GSMA, n.d.). By adapting now, companies like Viettel, Vinaphone and MobiFone are setting themselves up for future success.

Telcos need to be inventive and aggressive in gaining a share of the spoils of the advanced wireless networks. How can they do this without a difficult and costly fundamental end-to-end overhaul of their business operating models?

First of all, by recognizing the need to create new revenue streams by providing packages for enterprise customers to enable them to take advantage of early adoption of the new technologies. This means bringing in new talent but also upskilling existing staff who might have been freed up by the efficient application of AI in other areas and who know the business. These are add-on services and products to help up-sell and side-sell. AI analytics can mine data to uncover these opportunities.

Second, by identifying where AI solutions can be integrated within the operation to meet specific objectives based on existing key performance indicators and new potential sources of income. This can be done in-house, but the change needed in terms of creating entirely new departments can slow down progress. It is often far faster and more efficient to embrace effective partnership working with specialist telco-focused technology companies.

There are many examples of telcos working very successfully with the biggest established technology companies, such as the Vodafone/Google case study outlined below, and with smaller start-ups. This can be done by:

- Purchasing: buying cutting edge market-ready software and having it adapted to specific requirements.

- Collaboration: identifying companies in the conception or early development stage of a relevant innovation and partnering with them to mutual benefit, offering seed enterprises the broad cradle of support they need to grow, innovate and disrupt in return for a share of potential future income streams and/or advanced applications of AI to their own systems and data management.

- Commissioning: bringing in appropriate external talent or companies on a contractual basis to work with existing departments to find AI solutions to specific business challenges.

CASE STUDY
Vodafone and Google

Vodafone entered into a six-year strategic partnership with Google in May 2021 to develop a powerful new integral cloud-based data platform that will support the creation of new products and services. These will help build relationships with existing customers and attract new business.

Up to 1,000 employees of both companies located in Spain, the UK and the United States are collaborating in-house on the project to build the new platform, called Nucleus, which will house a new system, Dynamo, to drive data for Vodafone customers. Vodafone will host Google's Big Data on Google Cloud.

The agreement allows Vodafone to build and exploit new digital services for both consumers and enterprise customers across multiple regions. Vodafone has identified 700 use cases that could benefit from the platform, including reducing costs by simplifying and centralizing its operations and driving more immediate and detailed data analysis to help predict and meet consumer needs and identify new sources of revenue.

Vodafone and Google Cloud are exploring options to offer other similar solutions to multinational organizations on a consultancy basis, creating another lucrative new income stream from their successful collaboration.

CASE STUDY
Guavus

Guavus is a telco-focused AI solutions company that enables partners to innovate and develop Big Data analytics and Internet of Things products and services for their own operations or to support enterprise customers. It has partnered with some of the world's biggest telecoms, internet providers and security systems companies.

Its website gives the example of a restaurant that asked its tier 1 mobile phone provider to help promote its app. The restaurant's own attempts, based on targeting large segments of demographically selected potential customers, only returned 0.6 downloads per 100 contacts. Using Guavus's Service-IQ Marketing Analytics, the mobile provider was able to help the restaurant segment the prospects based on content interest and send personalized messages and offers. This approach saw conversions – downloads of the app – increase sevenfold. The restaurant had agreed to pay the operator more per message for the better ROI and the restaurant's campaign became more cost-efficient. Win–win.

This is a perfect example of how big telcos can partner with tech companies to offer new AI-based services and products, improve the customer experience and bring in new revenue streams.

CASE STUDY
O2 UK, Dell and Cardinality

O2 (Telefonica) commissioned multinational Dell and independent Surrey-based software SME Cardinality to find a way to correlate network events directly with the experience of individual subscribers. The platform designed by the partnership, called Network Customer Experience (NCX), uses ML to analyse patterns from 15 billion real-time events per day, cross-referencing with 300 KPIs. It then assigns an NCX 'score' to each individual subscriber based on their satisfaction against these indicators and events. These scores are used by multiple departments within O2 to inform decisions around KPIs including customer churn reduction, network quality, device upgrades and service upsell.

The projected benefits include:

- A net present value ROI of $2 million over two years for an initial investment of $4.5m, with an anticipated $40 million payback over six years.
- 15 per cent decrease in the cost of retaining subscribers.
- 20 per cent increase in up-sell.

Globe Telecom, Inc. is a major provider of telecoms services in the Philippines, and the country's largest mobile network operator. Globe plays a vital role in connecting the South East Asian archipelago of over 7,600 islands and more than 100 million people.

CASE STUDY
Globe Telecom

Globe Telecom is the largest mobile network operator in the Philippines and one of the largest fixed line and broadband networks. While looking to strengthen its offering for customers, the company turned to content rather than connectivity.

According to Ernest Cu, President and CEO, telecoms are evolving into content platforms, rather than being an aggregator of others' content and services. 'Globe has always been at the forefront of providing value to customers with our plans, so they can access an array of content that matter to them. We pioneered content bundling when we introduced plans that came with NBA League Pass, Netflix, and Spotify many years ago, and we continue to do so with our partnerships with Amazon Prime, HBO Go, and Viu, among others,' according to Cu (Abadilla, 2021).

Through Globe Studios, the telco now produces original films, television series, and online content. Among its recent popular offerings is the movie *Fan Girl*, which won nearly all the major awards at the 2020 Metro Manila Film Festival. Other films such as *Ang Panahon ng Halimaw* (Season of the Devil) received international acclaim.

In the middle of last year, Globe teamed up with music collective 88rising to launch a new label, Paradise Rising, to help Filipino artists achieve greater visibility and commercial success with their music.

'When Globe pioneered partnerships with streaming services a few years ago, we saw a big opportunity to create and grow local content,' Cu pointed out. 'We have proven that we can produce top-notch films and music that are now being shown in international streaming services. We take pride in our Filipino artists and we are driven by the vision to provide platforms to bring them to the global stage. We have to be transforming all the time and ensuring that our services and offerings remain relevant and even predict future trends for our consumers.' (Abadilla, 2021)

---

4. Fraud detection

The 'Cyber-Telecom Crime Report 2019', published by Europol and Trend Micro that same year, highlighted the growth of telecom fraud as a low-risk alternative to financial crime, driven by easily-obtained hacking equipment and low detection rates. It estimated the cost of this crime to telcos and their consumers to be around $30 billion per year.

Scammers hack into mobile communications to hijack customer or carrier accounts, strip their funds and siphon out loans using the target's business or personal identity. Common forms of fraud include:

- Phishing, using online correspondence, or vishing, voice communication, to trick victims into transferring money to them or divulging their details so they can set up counterfeit profiles.

- Callback spam or spoofing – calls to huge numbers of random recipients who are charged premium rates if they call back to see who it was.

- Hacking into SIMs and business accounts and making hundreds of auto-mated calls to premium rate numbers.

- International Revenue Sharing Fraud (IRSF), abusing inter-carrier trust between telecom operators to transfer calls from one carrier to another, usually via an untraceable premium rate number.

The biggest losses from telecom fraud are borne by customers. The more sophisticated scams can wipe huge sums from the accounts of big financial institutions and retailers, but billions are also stolen in smaller sums from individual account holders. Telco companies and accounts are not the primary targets of the scammers. This has reduced the financial impetus on telcos to tackle this lucrative crime effectively and, until recently, they have been slower in introducing counteractive measures than many other sectors.

However, reducing fraud is central to a telco's reputation and ability to offer customers a safe and satisfactory experience. Many telcos now recognize their ethical duty to protect customers as well as the business case for retaining customers and their own reputation. Telcos have for some time used a number of multiple authentication methods, such as text alerts gener-ating one-time passwords and security questions. However, these can be frustrating and time-consuming for the customer and increase the length of each interaction and therefore customer service costs.

More companies are now recognizing the value of AI and ML algorithms in reducing fraudulent activities. ML enables providers to analyse huge amounts of data to learn the characteristics of normal traffic, thereby detecting anomalies in real time.

Many companies are already using voice biometrics – 'my voice is my password' – to add a simple extra layer of security. As well as preventing account hijacking, voice recognition software can be used to actively detect known fraudsters and catch them in the act. For example, AI can passively analyse the voice of every customer who calls to ask for a new SIM and raise an alert when it picks up the voice of a known fraudster. Facial and retinal biometrics are likely to become the most powerful tools in the fight against fraud. Apple already uses face recognition on the more recent iPhone models.

5. Combatting overload

It seems like everything we touch these days requires some sort of internet connection. We need data plans to enable us to use our mobile phone's full capabilities on the go, broadband connections to do our jobs wherever we may be, and in pandemic times, our children needed strong connectivity in order to get their education. As our world becomes increasingly reliant on connection, telcos are faced with the challenge of ensuring their networks can handle the influx of demand. AI allows these companies to automatically adjust to significant congestion on the network, routing excess traffic through virtual machines without the need for more costly human intervention.

6. Network optimization

AI allows the telco to establish self-optimizing networks (SONs), which search for patterns in order to detect and predict network anomalies. This allows the operator to resolve issues before they adversely affect a customer.

BT uses AI to improve customer service by focusing its field engineers on the right job at the right time. Rather than simply assign jobs only to local engineers, fuzzy logic is used to deploy field engineers across regional borders, resulting in better service, increased productivity, reduced travel costs and improvements in employee well-being.

COLT's on-demand AI platform is called Sentio, and it supports dynamic real-time quoting, ordering and provisioning of high bandwidth connectivity between various customer locations – data centres, Cloud service providers and enterprise buildings. It provides customers with full control and can flex bandwidth needs in real time. Pricing options are flexible in this model: customers can choose plans on an hourly basis or for a fixed-term contract.

In the United States, Comcast's Smart Network Platform encompasses a suite of software tools that automate core network functions to reduce outages and their duration. Part of this suite is a tool called NetIQ, which uses machine learning to scan the core network continuously, making thousands of measurements every hour. With NetIQ in place, Comcast can see an outage instantly, before it is reported by customer complaints. As a result, the company has reduced its average detection time for service-impacting issues from 90 minutes to less than 5 minutes. This capability paid off during the COVID-19 pandemic but is not the only technology that helped the company serve their customers well during this challenging period, as shown in the following case study.

CASE STUDY
Comcast and COVID-19

The COVID-19 pandemic provided a trial-by-fire for telcos and their network capabilities. With more people working from home, students learning remotely and demand for streaming services rising as the home served as the primary hub of entertainment, broadband providers had their work cut out for them. With a network that is accessible to more than 59 million US homes via enough cable to span the distance from Earth to the moon three times over, Comcast is one of the most heavily relied upon internet service providers in the United States. Comcast was no exception to these additional demands, and once again harnessed the potential of AI to its benefit when faced with these new challenges.

Back in March 2020, Comcast reported a 32 per cent rise in internet use due to the pandemic, as well as a 36 per cent increase in mobile data use over Wi-Fi on Xfinity mobile. The company typically adds to its network capacity 12 to 18 months in advance for forecasted spikes, typically targeting a 45 per cent increase in traffic yearly. But the pandemic left no time to prepare.

While Comcast's gradual building of its network did help to manage the rise in demand during lockdown, Elad Nafshi, Senior Vice President for Next-Generation Access Networks at Comcast Xfinity, said in an interview with VentureBeat (Takahashi, 2020) that the Comcast internet network's ability to hold up during the surge wasn't just because of capital spending on fibre-optic networks. Rather, it has depended on a suite of AI and machine-learning software that gives the company visibility into its network, adds capacity quickly when needed and fixes problems before humans notice them.

A new software called Comcast Octave helps manage traffic complexity by quietly working behind the scenes, checking 4,000-plus telemetry data points including external network 'noise', power levels and other technical issues on more than 50 million modems across the network every 20 minutes. Octave detects when modems are not using all available bandwidth as efficiently as possible and automatically adjusts them, delivering substantial increases in speed and capacity.

Octave is a new technology for the company, and Comcast had only rolled it out to part of the network when the pandemic hit. A team of engineers worked overtime to reduce the rollout time from months to weeks. Thanks to their hard work and the power of Octave, customers experienced a nearly 36 per cent increase in capacity as their own demand spiked.

Comcast has translated the data it had collected into algorithmic solutions that can predict where future interference could disrupt networks and identify where trouble points might appear. When discussing this in the same VentureBeat interview, Nafshi described the long-term customer benefits of this solution:

> We provide you with much more reliable service by detecting the patterns that lead up to breakage and then have the network self-heal based on those patterns. We're making that completely transparent to the customer. The network can self-heal autonomously in a self-feedback loop. It's a seamless platform for the customer.
>
> (Takahashi, 2020)

We close this chapter with compelling insights from BT Group plc – a British multinational telecommunications holding company headquartered in London, England. It has operations in around 180 countries and is the largest provider of fixed-line, broadband and mobile services in the UK, and also provides subscription television and IT services.

With a PhD in artificial intelligence and having previously served as the Director of AI and Data Economy for Innovate UK, Dr Zoë Webster, Artificial Intelligence Director, Group Data and AI Solutions at BT Group, also approaches the challenge from the more technological roots of AI:

> Organisations need a strategy that enables a really solid focus on data sources, the provenance of that data, and really understanding the sustainability

around data. Another key point is space to innovate and experiment, which is what we encourage at BT. What happens if we fuse two datasets that we've not fused before? What happens if we look at this data in a different context, in a different application space? What does that tell us? So having that space to play about a bit, not just for its own sake, but to generate new ideas. Deep learning has hogged the limelight for a long time and it has some huge strengths, as well as some limitations. An AI strategy should have breadth as well as depth. So it should consider a range of approaches, not just the most fashionable ones.

AI is an adjunct. It's an augmentation. It's not there to make the decisions on what is right and wrong for us. AI could be intelligent enough to make those decisions, and to make very good decisions. But actually, it should be filtered through a human, or a set of humans ideally, and have diversity of views with accountability until we figure out a way where we can actually safely provide accountability to machines, which I'm not sure we're going to be able to do very easily. But we need that framework and that understanding in place up front.

Clearly we need conscious thinking and conscious decisions about what does 'good' mean, and what is good or good for who? If AI allows us to impact the bottom line, that enables businesses to do more in the greater good. So there is an argument that says, let's focus on the bottom line, then other things will follow. But conversely, one could say actually, if we do things for the benefit of the customer – which we should be doing anyway – if we do something that is beneficial for society and the economy and the environment, then that opens up business opportunities. If people are able to live more comfortably, they are more likely to spend on products and services that can be offered. So it's a complex picture, but I think it starts with that very conscious discussion. What does good look like for who? For the customer, for the business, for any other stakeholder, for society at large, for the environment, what does good look like and how are people impacted by what we're attempting to do?

Another important issue which worries me is whether we should attribute AI as an inventor. Accountability should always rest with a human, which might mean that we can't say AI is an inventor. The inventor will have potential accountability or responsibility for the outcomes of that invention, for example a driverless car.

We will explore more of these issues in Chapter 9.

Customer-centricity: the defining factor

As we have learned in this chapter, the telco industry is rapidly evolving. The cost to switch to another provider is lower than ever, and there is more competition and choice today than ever before. Just consider the rise of cord-cutting, as cable providers lose a staggering 14,000 customers per day.

The challenge now is to ensure that telcos are strengthening the services they continue to provide while also exploring new and more innovative ways to serve their customers. It is a dilemma many industries are facing, but due to the nature of the service they provide, telcos have much more pressure riding on their shoulders.

PRACTICAL TAKEAWAYS CHECKLIST: TOP 10 TIPS

1   66 per cent of telecom companies believe that AI is considerably or very important for the future of business.

2   The ability of AI to gather, analyse and monetize previously unthinkable quantities of valuable data will be at the heart of fast-adapting provision of the most cutting edge and innovative services.

3   A primary focus for early adopters has been the use of automation to improve customer experience and reduce operating costs. The most innovative companies are already using it across every department, from fraud reduction through to the development, marketing and sales of new products and services.

4   Conversational AI platforms are becoming increasingly popular in the telco sector because of their ability to dramatically improve customer service by offering swifter replies and support across multiple languages.

5   Conversational agents are becoming increasingly sophisticated at managing complex customer enquiries and expectations by using natural language processing (NLP) to understand, learn and respond appropriately to a wide variety of predictable questions.

6   Automation will drive operational efficiency and CX, as 84 per cent of professionals expect their company's total spend on AI and automation to increase through 2025.

7   AI is an adjunct. It's an augmentation. It's not there to make the decisions on what is right and wrong for us. It should be filtered through a human, or a set of humans ideally, and have diversity of views with accountability.

8   An AI strategy should have breadth as well as depth. It should consider a range of approaches, not just the most fashionable ones.

9   Only 14 per cent of businesses consider themselves 'transformational' with AI and of the 69 per cent of organizations that have invested in AI and automation for customer self-service features, nearly half (48 per cent) have yet to use it.

10   Looking ahead to 2030, much manual work should be automated, such as with RPA, and a lot of intelligence will be built into systems that continuously learn and advise managers and leaders on ways to improve their business.

Bibliography

Abadilla, E (2021) Globe Says Telcos Are Transforming to Content Creators, *Manila Bulletin*, www.mb.com.ph/2021/05/25/globe-says-telcos-are-transforming-to-content-creators/ (archived at https://perma.cc/SG4U-DMHP)

Artificial Solutions (n.d.) *Vodafone delivers personalized 24/7 support with Teneo*, www.artificial-solutions.com/conversational-ai-case-studies/vodafone (archived at https://perma.cc/JRW8-DYLF)

Baldock, H (2021) Covid-19 'a Trigger for AI Investments', Says Study, *Totaltelecom*, www.totaltele.com/509159/Covid-19-a-trigger-for-AI-investments-says-study (archived at https://perma.cc/RC4B-EDWF)

Chowdhury, K (2021) How Artificial Intelligence Is Transforming the Telecom Industry. *Thefastmode.com*, www.thefastmode.com/expert-opinion/19790-how-artificial-intelligence-is-transforming-the-telecom-industry#.YKW0bVHHUW8. linkedin (archived at https://perma.cc/YP7C-C8X7)

Churchill, L (2021) 2021: Emerging AI Trends in the Telecom Industry, *Customer Think*, www.customerthink.com/2021-emerging-ai-trends-in-the-telecom-industry/ (archived at https://perma.cc/2535-42JB)

Cognizant, 2020. Case Study: Parts supplier uses chatbots to revamp search, order tracking, *Cognizant*, www.cognizant.com/case-studies/pdfs/parts-supplier-uses-chatbots-to-revamp-search-order-tracking-codex5462.pdf (archived at https://perma.cc/33MT-95M6)

Deans, D (2021) Tech Sales Effectiveness: The next two decades, *LinkedIn*, www.linkedin.com/pulse/sales-effectiveness-next-two-decades-david-h-deans/ (archived at https://perma.cc/7UNN-TZQ5)

Ekudden, E (2021) Ericsson CTO Erik Ekudden's View on Artificial Intelligence, *Ericsson Technology Review Magazine*, www.ericsson.com/en/reports-and-papers/ericsson-technology-review/articles/ai-special-edition?utm_source=LinkedIn&utm_medium=social_organic&utm_campaign=TeamEricsson&utm_content=a1573941-6f42-4d5a-8064-42e7d285983d (archived at https://perma.cc/5THE-MM8U)

Ericsson Technology Review (2021) Spotlight on artificial intelligence, *Ericsson Technology Review*, **104**, www.ericsson.com/499631/assets/local/reports-papers/ericsson-technology-review/docs/2021/ai-special-edition.pdf (archived at https://perma.cc/ C4YB-9SZX)

ESI ThoughtLab (2020) Driving ROI Through AI, *Econsult Solutions, Inc*, www.econsultsolutions.com/esi-thoughtlab/roi-ai/ (archived at https://perma.cc/XVE9-PB4A)

GSMA (2021) The Mobile Economy, *GSMA*, www.gsma.com/mobileeconomy/ (archived at https://perma.cc/8XW8-GN8N)

GSMA (n.d.) 5G Global Launches & Statistics, *GSMA*, www.gsma.com/futurenetworks/ip_services/understanding-5g/5g-innovation/ (archived at https://perma.cc/6SVC- KWQJ)

IBM (n.d.) Vodafone Transforms Customer Service with Watson Chatbot. *Ibm. com*, www.ibm.com/industries/telecom-media-entertainment/resources/ vodafone-ibm-chatbot/ (archived at https://perma.cc/58TD-5H9P)

IDC (2020) Worldwide Spending on Artificial Intelligence Is Expected to Double in Four Years, Reaching $110 Billion in 2024, According to New IDC Spending Guide, *IDC*, www.idc.com/getdoc.jsp?containerId=prUS46794720 (archived at https://perma.cc/42ZJ-WNEC)

Kryzanovske, A (2021) Transforming Telco Businesses with AI, *VoIP Review*, www. voip.review/2021/05/17/transforming-telco-businesses-ai/ (archived at https:// perma.cc/9PXQ-74NC)

Littmann, D, Fritz, J and Wilson, P (2020) Enterprises Building Their Future with 5G and Wi-Fi 6, *Deloitte*, www2.deloitte.com/us/en/insights/industry/ telecommunications/5g-adoption-study.html (archived at https://perma. cc/4WMY-PBWH)

LivePerson (n.d.) Magenta Telekom actions its vision for customer service, *LivePerson*, www.liveperson.com/resources-success-story/magenta-telekom (archived at https://perma.cc/ZMJ7-RBH9)

Marketing Week Reporters (2021) O2, Oatly, EE: Everything that matters this morning, *Marketing Week*, www.marketingweek.com/everything-that-matters-this-morning-2/ (archived at https://perma.cc/K2QU-M6ZQ)

Miláns del Bosch, L and Lacave, B (2020) AI-Based Marketing in Telecommunications. Oliverwyman.com, www.oliverwyman.com/our-expertise/ insights/2020/jun/AI-based-marketing-in-telecommunications.html (archived at https://perma.cc/GY3F-2ZGM)

Ministry of Information and Communications of the Socialist Republic of Vietnam (2021) Telecom Groups Get on Board with 5G, *English.mic.gov.vn*, www. english.mic.gov.vn/Pages/TinTuc/tinchitiet.aspx?tintucid=147295 (archived at https://perma.cc/RQ2G-9X5J)

Nicastro, S, Schmehl, I, Sankaran, R, Thabet, M, Chong, R and Richard, D (2021) *Driving CX innovation in a disruptive market* [webinar]

Ozdoruk, C (2021) Can AI Save Telecom Customer Service?, *Business 2 Community*, www.business2community.com/customer-experience/can-ai-save-telecom-customer-service-02394976 (archived at https://perma.cc/3Z7C-FAB2)

Ringshall, B (2020) Top Ten Worst Companies to Call in 2020 #onholdwith, *Fonolo*, www.fonolo.com/blog/2020/12/onholdwith-the-worst-companies-to-call-in-2020/ (archived at https://perma.cc/TLJ3-4CBL)

Robuck, M (2019) Comcast Turns Up AI and ML for Network Insights and to Improve Customer Experience, *FierceTelecom*, www.fiercetelecom.com/ai/ comcast-turns-up-ai-and-ml-for-network-insights-and-to-improve-customer-experience (archived at https://perma.cc/GP2Y-MEMQ)

Russon, M (2021) Vodafone Using Google's Cloud and AI to Retain Customers, *BBC news*, www.bbc.co.uk/news/business-56969347 (archived at https://perma. cc/XM8B-G64Y)

Takahashi, D (2020) Comcast Credits AI Software for Handling the Pandemic Internet Traffic Crush, *VentureBeat*, www.venturebeat.com/2020/07/13/comcast-credits-ai-software-for-handling-the-pandemic-internet-traffic-crush/ (archived at https://perma.cc/28LT-NFA8)

Talkdesk (2021) 80% of CX Professionals Believe AI Will Provide a Better Contact Center Experience, *Businesswire*, www.businesswire.com/news/home/20210517005100/en/80-of-CX-Professionals-Believe-AI-Will-Provide-a-Better-Contact-Center-Experience (archived at https://perma.cc/UD53-Q33P)

Telefónica (2017) Telefónica Presents AURA, a Pioneering Way in the Industry to Interact with Customers Based on Cognitive Intelligence, *Telefonica.com*, www.telefonica.com/en/web/press-office/-/telefonica-presents-aura-a-pioneering-way-in-the-industry-to-interact-with-customers-based-on-cognitive-intelligence (archived at https://perma.cc/HEN4-Q439)

Tractica (2019) The Telecommunications Industry Is Ripe for Artificial-Intelligence Driven Solutions, with Service Providers Expected to Spend $11.2 Billion by 2025, According to Tractica, *Businesswire*, www.businesswire.com/news/home/20190910005086/en/The-Telecommunications-Industry-Is-Ripe-for-Artificial-Intelligence-Driven-Solutions-with-Service-Providers-Expected-to-Spend-11.2-Billion-by-2025-According-to-Tractica (archived at https://perma.cc/ JLN7-4WZ5)

Vodafone (2017) *TOBi or not TOBi? AI is transforming user experience*, www.vodafone.co.uk/business/insights/articles/tobi-not-tobi-ai-transforming-customer-experience (archived at https://perma.cc/ADX8-BQSZ)

Vom Hofe, K (2017) Ask Tinka, *Telekom.com*, www.telekom.com/en/blog/group/article/ask-chatbot-tinka-486110 (archived at https://perma.cc/8RSG-R3JA)

Vom Hofe, K (2019) Chatbots: 'Service will remain human'. *Telekom.com*, www.telekom.com/en/company/details/chatbots-service-will-remain-human-577452 (archived at https://perma.cc/A42L-ZUWG)

Wilson, T (2019) AI Technologies Fuel Xfinity Customer Support Platforms, *Spokesman.com*, www.spokesman.com/stories/2019/feb/24/ai-technologies-fuel-xfinity-customer-support-plat/ (archived at https://perma.cc/5UAG-GYYU)

07

New economic model
for the robot revolution

In this chapter we explore why the new era of AI demands a more fitting economic model, and the ramifications of that on society at large and on business. We delve deeply into the need to upskill and the implications on the world of education, from primary schools to executive education. We also consider how educational establishments are using AI to improve their own customer service and their marketing. Finally, we consider the critical success factors for the future of education, such as creating an ecosystem of trust, data governance and data stewardship but also diversity and equality.

The 'Future of Jobs 2020' report from The World Economic Forum estimates that the global workforce is automating at a greater speed than many anticipated, resulting in the displacement of 85 million jobs over the next five years. The positive news is the creation of 97 million new jobs, and therefore a net gain. However, business and government support will be essential to a vast number of communities who will be most at risk. According to the report:

> More than 80 per cent of business executives are accelerating plans to digitize work processes and deploy new technologies; and 50 per cent of employers are expecting to accelerate the automation of some roles in their companies. In contrast to previous years, job creation is now slowing while job destruction is accelerating... The most competitive businesses will be those that choose to reskill and upskill current employees.
>
> (World Economic Forum, 2020)

Now is the time for decisive action. Former Governor of the Bank of England from 2013 to 2020, Mark Carney is the UN's special envoy on climate action and finance. Speaking to the *Financial Times* in April 2021, Carney's message is unambiguous:

> If it's similar to previous periods of technological upheaval, our fourth industrial revolution will lead to a long period of difficult adjustment and rising inequality before increases in productivity, wages and jobs… If we want to preserve the important gains of the past decades of growth and realise the promise of new technologies, structural change will need to be managed for all and welcomed by all. We need to fashion a renewed global economy founded on new dispersed networks of trade, capital and ideas that harness the creativity of billions of people, who will share fully in its rewards.

Lifelong learning and quaternary education

Carney continued:

> We can start by valuing the outcomes that we want technology to help achieve… most fundamentally, there needs to be a radical rethink of life-long learning. In previous industrial revolutions it was education which transformed skills, preparing the workforce for the next wave of employment. In this fourth industrial revolution, the focus must shift to a mandatory commitment to retaining, and an emphasis on lifelong learning, and quaternary education.
>
> (Carney, 2021)

While progressing through this text, I hope it is becoming crystal clear to all readers, irrespective of their age, profession, seniority, geography and level of education, that we all need to embark on a journey of lifelong learning in order to stay current and ahead of the curve. Education, and educating the educators, is therefore crucial. This does not mean that we all need to learn to code in Python or any other computer language. But it is essential to grasp the fact that artificial intelligence (AI) tools will reshape many of the tasks we carry out in our working day, whether we are doctors or factory workers. The tools we discussed in Chapter 2 are – or soon will be – at our disposal, automating many mundane tasks and providing deeper insights into staff and customer behaviour than we could ever have anticipated.

We start by exploring how education is at the heart of the UK Government's plans. In March 2021, the Digital Secretary Oliver Dowden revealed the

'Ten Tech Priorities', which the Government plans to focus on in order to power what is described as 'a golden age of tech' in the UK. The new AI strategy will focus on:

- growth of the economy through widespread use of AI technologies;
- ethical, safe and trustworthy development of responsible AI;
- resilience in the face of change through an emphasis on skills, talent and R&D.

Priority number nine in this top 10 list is 'Levelling up digital prosperity across the UK'. The goal is to ensure that long-term digital prosperity is more evenly spread across the entire country, with support for regional innovation, regional strengths and regional specialisms. The third of the 10 priorities is 'Building a tech-savvy nation'. The intention is that no one gets left behind by the digital revolution, which requires every adult to have a base level of digital and cyber skills. The tools to achieve this will range from apprenticeships to digital bootcamps, combined with a £520 million Help-to-Grow scheme, which will empower 100,000 businesses to adopt the latest technology. The far-reaching goals are intended to harness AI's potential to create new jobs, improve productivity, tackle climate change and deliver improved public services. By nurturing AI pioneers, the plan is to bring new technologies to market faster, unlock high-skilled jobs, drive up productivity and cement the UK's status as a global science superpower.

A key figure in bringing about such change is Dame Wendy Hall, the UK's AI Skills Champion, and Regius Professor of Computer Science at the University of Southampton. She explains:

> It's essential to scale up and commit to an ongoing 10-year programme of high-level AI-skill building whilst also committing to achieving AI and data literacy for everyone. Our work began in the higher education sector, with a focus on PhDs and Master's courses. But we recognised that if we only tackled it at that level, there would be no diversity in the pipeline. You would keep building the same stereotype of the white or Asian male geek. Diversity needs to be everywhere.

A policy briefing from The Alan Turing Institute's Women in Data Science and AI project charts women's participation in AI and data science in the UK and other countries. The findings reveal a troubling and persistent absence of women employed in the AI and data science fields. Over three-quarters of professionals in these fields globally are male (78 per cent), and less than a quarter are women (22 per cent). In the UK, this drops to 20 per cent women. Male dominance of this extreme is responsible for shaping gender bias in AI and machine learning (ML) systems. It is also fundamentally an ethical issue of social and economic justice, as well as one of value-in-diversity.

In 2018, the House of Lords Select Committee on Artificial Intelligence advocated for increasing gender and ethnic diversity among AI developers, and in 2020 the European Commission noted that it is 'high time to reflect specifically on the interplay between AI and gender equality'. Yet there is still a striking scarcity of quality, disaggregated, intersectional data, which is essential to interrogate and tackle inequities in the AI and data science labour force.

The 2021 AI Roadmap from the UK's AI Council strongly recommends 'mak[ing] diversity and inclusion a priority [by] forensically tracking levels of diversity to make data-led decisions about where to invest and ensure that underrepresented groups are given equal opportunity'.

Dame Wendy Hall continues:

This is concrete evidence that there is a huge gender gap. It's really quite distressing that it is such a big gap and it is probably worse than we thought. Since the 1980s, I've been trying to get more women into computing and science generally, but computing particularly and now into AI. I wrote my first paper in 1987, 'Where have all the girls gone?'. It's a constant sense of frustration because here I am, over three decades later, and if anything, the situation is worse. It's certainly no better in the west. In other countries it's different, for example in India, the Middle East, and the Far East. It's not that we're genetically programmed not to be able to do it. It's cultural.

The impacts of this gender bias are troubling. Take mobile phones as a concrete example. They are designed for a man's hand. Females can't use them with one hand as men can. So when you're walking down the street at night and it's dark and you want to get your phone out to ring someone, you need both hands to do it. Similarly, voice recognition doesn't always work for women's voices.

The AI Council Roadmap outlines a commitment that goes beyond higher education, for example getting AI into the schools and into lifelong learning. The aim is high: AI and data literacy for everyone. But currently it's not coordinated at all. What is required is a Virtual Academy, and one that is accessible, regional, local, feeling that it's somewhere you can go.

It's only quite recently in education terms that the UK curriculum was upgraded to ensure a proper computing curriculum in schools, which goes beyond IT. That change was fairly controversial. But further evolution is essential if the UK is to stay ahead. Children need to be taught from the age of five through to when they leave school about the world of computing. They need to be taught what coding is, even if they don't want to specialize in that. They need to understand computers and how they contribute to technology. To ensure success, more investment in teacher training is essential. In terms of the potential new AI curriculum, there is clearly a need for data skills and understanding of how machine learning works. But the agenda must also comprise ethics, and the legal and business issues that today's organizations face.

Dame Wendy Hall continues:

> The question is, how do we introduce AI in schools? Do we introduce new courses? If we introduce it as part of the computer science curriculum, then you're putting it in a pigeonhole that marks it as computer science, and the kids that don't want to do computer science won't get the AI skills. So we have to clearly talk about AI in a much broader sense than that. We have to look at how it applies in other curriculum like in geography and history for example.

Another important voice on these crucial topics is Rose Luckin – Professor of Learner Centred Design at the UCL Knowledge Lab in London. Her research involves the design and evaluation of educational technology using theories from the learning sciences and techniques from AI. She comments:

> In the education and training sector, I believe the pandemic hastened the use of technology and is likely to increase the use of AI within this sector. The impact of AI is likely to increase, in particular the leveraging of AI's ability to be adaptive which can power personalisation. Educators, government and business need to collaborate to close the skills gap. They can do so by being willing to work together in cross stakeholder partnerships, including with those whose views are in opposition to their own.
>
> A successful AI strategy within the education and training sector, whether for a business or for an institution such as a school or college, must be built upon an existing digital readiness and infrastructure. The next criteria is that the organisation must be AI ready, which means it must have engaged its workforce in understanding why AI is important for the organisation and explained the benefits as well as the risks and how they will be mitigated. It also needs to have identified the key challenges particular to the organisation and used those

to drive the AI strategy. Another critical factor is that it has used AI thinking and a data mindset to identify and collate the data that is relevant to the challenges identified – explored collecting more data to better understand these challenges – collated, cleaned and applied AI techniques to the data to better understand the nature of the challenges.

The next key consideration is whether these views are shared by corporates. For Dr Mona N Shah, Founder and Director, Vayati Systems and Research Inc., AI will only be successful if the workforce is adequately prepared. She comments:

> Workforce upskilling, wherein training and application opportunities to use AI skills in routine work, or creation of new roles emerging due to the use of AI and implementing continuous initiatives in AI would be necessary. The organisation-wide adoption of AI and creation of robust, foolproof AI would be essential. For this, governance policies, standardising, labelling and cleansing of data, managing convergence of other tech and maintenance of AI would need to be deployed.
>
> There are also other non-tech challenges that would need to be overcome which are related to measuring the ROI on AI investments, budgetary approvals, employees' readiness, preparing the business case and recruiting the AI-skilled staff. The regulatory system will need to be taken into account for better compliance in case of incidents like citizen profiling and privacy issues. Finally, the last of the criterion for successful AI lies not in the realm of technology but in AI versus the human dimension. The key questions what comprises human intelligence, how much of the human mind is liable to be captured in an algorithm and consequently prove a threat to humans will be centre stage in the dialogue favouring and against AI.

Personalized, lifelong learning

It's encouraging to hear that many organizations share a similar vision for the role of AI in shaping the future workforce. Nikolas Kairinos is Founder and CEO, Soffos.ai. He comments:

> Looking to the future, personalized learning will no doubt inspire a curriculum overhaul. Indeed, a one-size-fits-all factory model of education is outdated, and we now have the opportunity to construct a system that meets the evolving needs of learners of all ages. For one, new subjects are being created every day, and existing knowledge is constantly being updated.

Sophisticated learning solutions will provide the most up-to-date and relevant information to ensure that learners can keep pace with these changes. Moreover, the increasing use of AI-driven solutions will enable students to study at their own pace, and through teaching methods and materials that are tailored towards their unique learning needs.

Most importantly, I believe we will move away from the concept of finishing education once a student has left formal education. Today, to do any kind of job at a decent level, we must continuously be learning and challenging our understanding. Virtual platforms will plug the gap and allow us to move towards a lifelong learning model, with innovative solutions like Soffos.ai providing the means to constantly learn and improve.

Ideally, a business will have a multi-skilled team with a mix of backgrounds, education and skills that can oversee the successful implementation of an AI strategy – from identifying the best applications of AI, to overcoming any operational changes that new applications may require. For those who do not have the necessary talent, bringing in outside experts or AI consultants can be invaluable. Meanwhile, businesses ought to prioritize training for existing employees to ensure they can effectively utilise these new solutions.

Importantly, initiatives shouldn't focus only on developing technical 'hard' skills; they should also include elevating 'soft skills' like professional communication and critical thinking that will become ever more important as machines take on much of the daily data-intensive and routine tasks. Educators and businesses alike must ensure that they are proactively honing skills that will enable current and future professionals to work alongside machines as automation becomes the norm – and in doing so, encourage them to take on more creative, valuable, and rewarding activities.

Karen Khaw, Senior Consultant of The Tantalus Group, a global management consultancy, and Founder of V-Engage Australia, shares the same perspective as Kairinos in regards to the importance of having the necessary skills available within the organization. Your team will be the ones who help bring your strategy to life, and therefore it is crucial that you have the right people in your corner. She explains:

For an AI strategy to be successful, businesses need to ensure a sufficient understanding of AI and the strategy and not let it be an isolated AI team. Consistent and regular training across the business is essential, starting from the top. With a priority to the leadership team, AI should be a regular occurrence in employee training as well as for new employees onboarding, given its significance now and into the future.

The Rt Hon Greg Clark was Secretary of State for Business, Energy and Industrial Strategy from July 2016 to July 2019. Elected in 2005, he continues to serve as Conservative MP for Royal Tunbridge Wells, where I have lived for the past 15 years. He comments:

> Over the next two years, the pandemic will prove to have been a force in promoting greater use of AI in business. However, we risk having a workforce that may not be sufficiently educated with the skills and necessary capabilities to work on this. I think in education generally, the pandemic will accelerate some aspects of work to evolve not just artificial intelligence but also a more digital and virtual approach to learning. The idea that you need to go to a physical place in a physical capacity in order to hear or view a lecture that could just as easily be heard or viewed at home, somewhere close by, or anywhere around the world, seems outdated. I think the problem is it's going to be a big challenge for universities who secure these big academic names. Their lecturers will be available to a much wider audience around the world. Whereas for those institutions that don't offer access to some of the big names or don't make their lectures widely available, their place in the market may be under threat because even their students will be able to access teaching they wouldn't have access to at that institution.
>
> I think it's already clear that some of the main debates are privacy and purpose. The use of data analysis intelligently to know people almost better than they know themselves is, and will be, quite troubling. There are various examples from banking and finance where a person's transactions actually reveal a lot about them. So there is a very interesting ethical question if an AI system or algorithm is able to make a prediction and the human agents use it to make an impactful decision, whether it be for something like credit rating or lending or something else that will really impact a person's life. There are questions of how you can and should make use of the data that you have and about relying on AI to make decisions that go beyond the person themselves.
>
> Certainly, public policy will make regulations more prominent, especially on data, as we've already seen with GDPR. There have been big changes in the last five years on the use of data. The companies themselves, on a reputational basis, will want to convey to their customers a sense of trustworthiness around their data. In order to generate that degree of trustworthiness, they will need to have codes and standards that they voluntarily adopt. No doubt, the customers themselves will judge based on what they glean from the media in terms of trustworthiness of certain brands and companies. They will play a role as well. New institutions will develop, such as new regulatory bodies that may be part of trade bodies, that will be set up to ask some of these ethical questions. So I think the current regulatory structures are unlikely to be the ones that endure indefinitely.

Societal and corporate responsibility

An important question to answer is what our societal and indeed corporate responsibility is. All organizations will see disruption to their current workforce structures that comes from implementing artificial intelligences. Governments must act fast and plan ahead, particularly in relation to education systems very specifically and the need to address the reskilling agenda and impact on a curriculum that needs to evolve.

Given what we've learned in this text about the potential of AI for good and for potentially bad practices, the future balance of power is of critical importance. The world is changing and the old rules are becoming outdated. The rule makers are sometimes missing, or no longer fit for purpose. Globalization and new technologies have deepened the divide between the haves and have-nots in advanced economies and immediate action is needed to address this imbalance of power.

Ensuring inclusive economic growth

Business leaders need to reflect about how AI technology is used in a way that supports inclusive economic growth and innovation. When Microsoft launched its Open Data campaign in 2020, it was very conscious that it did not want a world where the ever-increasing amounts of data were held by an ever-decreasing number of organizations. That can stifle innovation, and it is harmful for general inclusive, sustainable economic growth and activity.

Human-centred AI that doesn't oppress

What we must avoid at all costs is falling into the trap of creating, or allowing, a state model to evolve where intrusive technology and surveillance undermine workers' rights and civil liberties. Worrying trends are reported in a research report from the Institute for the Future of Work (IFOW), entitled 'The Amazonian Era: How algorithmic systems are eroding good work' (Gilbert and Thomas, 2021). It states:

> Work is at the centre of people's lives and good work can enable people, communities and the country to flourish. Well designed and deployed, new technologies have vast potential to augment human skills, improve work quality and create new, good work. But our interviews with front line workers and technology developers about the algorithmic systems used in retail, logistics, manufacturing and food processing reveal that businesses are introducing these systems often with only vague notions of their effectiveness, beyond an appetite

for innovation for innovation's sake. This creates an environment of almost total surveillance, collecting and processing data about every aspect of working life, in real time. This is used to drive people to complete more tasks in less time, intensifying their work. Standards set by the system are then used to evaluate and manage performance, incentivise or penalise workers, and grant or deny them access to stable work contracts.

One example revealed that a major supermarket uses heat sensors to detect bodies at the tills, informing queue-length reports, which may lead to the disciplining of staff if more than one person is in a queue. There is evidence that algorithmic systems can disadvantage disabled workers because of the way their work is quantified. Governance and laws must therefore adapt quickly to address the evolving needs created by technological development. We are at a critical junction and it is imperative that employers are held accountable, and access to justice must be available to ensure redress when problems arise.

The IFOW report's recommendations include:

- Introduce an Employment Bill with a dedicated Schedule of 'Day 1' Digital Rights.

- The Government should initiate an Accountability for Algorithms Act in the public interest, which will require early algorithmic impact assessment and adjustment when adverse impacts are identified. Further detail is outlined in IFOW's 'Mind the Gap' report.

- New disclosure obligations should require regular reporting on the fact, purpose and outcomes of algorithmic systems shaping access, terms and quality of work.

- A joint regulatory forum led by the Information Commissioner's Office should be established with new powers to create certification schemes, impose terms and issue statutory guidance on use of algorithmic systems at work.

Education and equality

The negative impact of AI on equality is a concern shared by many. Malika Malik, Cloud Solution Architect – Data & AI, Microsoft UK, comments:

The biggest concern is the growing skills gap in the fourth industrial revolution, which will only widen further. The introduction of artificial intelligence to school curricula is vital for the future. The move will open opportunities for graduates and apprentices in AI and, consequently, contribute to the inclusive build and implementation of AI. Furthermore, a successful AI implementation will be determined by the diversity of workers in prototyping, building, and eventually utilizing AI solutions. So, strengthening a diverse workforce is essential to developing ethical, responsible and accessible solutions and contributing to social resiliency.

Educating the next generation

It is clear that reskilling, retraining and seeking out opportunities for continuous learning are key for endowing the current generation of professionals with the appropriate digital and future-ready skills they will need to evolve and stay relevant. But what impacts will these technologies have on our children? What jobs will they have, and how will their education prepare them for that future?

When it comes to the technology of today and what is yet to come, the world's young people are at an early advantage. Millennials were introduced to the internet at an early age, and Generation Z do not know a world without it. They are seemingly more comfortable using and easily adapting to new technology because they have grown up with it.

Making up for lost learning

As Professor Rose Luckin explained, the pandemic has hastened the use of technology in education. Virtual learning became a necessity during this time, and many pupils around the world spent nearly an academic year and a half learning virtually at least some of the time. This had negative impacts in certain geographies, as revealed by McKinsey's, Teacher Sentiment Survey, carried out globally between October and November 2020 (Chen *et al*, 2021).

The survey's findings revealed that teachers in eight of the world's most dominant countries felt as though the virtual classroom had decreased the effectiveness of instruction, with Australia reporting the least loss and the United States and Japan reporting effectiveness levels below the global average. In fact, teachers across the geographies surveyed reported that students were an average of two months behind where they would have been by November in a normal academic year. The UK's pupils experienced the highest average amount of learning lost, falling nearly three full months behind where they should be. The US and Canada trailed closely behind at 2.4 months. Interestingly, despite feeling that virtual learning reduced the effectiveness of instruction, Japan's teachers reported less than a month of learning lost. These figures may be linked to time, as the countries who spent longer in lockdown reported more learning loss than those who spent a shorter time out of school.

It is easy to look at these figures and feel that technology is bad for education, but we must consider the circumstances. Teachers and students alike were thrust into this situation with no preparation, requiring them to adapt quickly and figure it out as they went along. The software they used were not tools they were already familiar with or using regularly because they previously had no need to. The pandemic was a technological learning curve, but now that we are over that hill technology just might be what helps us regain lost ground and improve the educational experience in the long run.

Enhancing education with strategic technology

It is still early days for AI in education. In O'Reilly's 'AI Adoption in the Enterprise 2021' report (Loukides), only 10 per cent of the respondents from the education sector reported mature AI practices in their organization, lagging far behind other industries such as financial services and retail. Most (48 per cent) reported that their organization is only at the stage of considering AI, the highest total in this category out of every industry. But that is not to say that some future-forward institutions and organizations are not already experimenting with AI, or at least aware of its impacts and potential.

As part of its 'AI and the Future of Learning: Expert Panel Report' (Roschelle, Lester and Fusco, 2020) the Center for Integrated Research in Computing and Learning Sciences (CIRCLS) asked its panel of education experts to list the perceived strengths, weaknesses, opportunities and threats/barriers to AI from the perspectives of both learning technology researchers and of educators. Some of the key benefits and strengths they reported include: potential to offload some of the cognitive burden of teaching; the ability of teachers to better orchestrate classrooms, thus extending what they can do; deeper analysis of learner performances; potential to adapt to learner variability in more ways and with more techniques; increased visibility and awareness of some of the more invisible aspects of teaching and learning to deepen support across contexts; and the ability to interact privately with a student to provide individualized guided practice as needed.

To help bring these benefits to life within post-16 education in the UK, Jisc launched a new national centre for artificial intelligence in tertiary education at the start of 2021. The national centre for AI was formed in support of the government's AI strategy, and aims to deliver AI solutions at 60 colleges and 30 universities within five years of its inception.

Alongside the centre's launch, Jisc released its 'AI in Tertiary Education' report (Jisc, 2021) to explore the ways in which AI is currently in use and impacting the education industry. The top use cases and tools it identified include:

- **Chatbots and digital assistants:** These tools use NLP and ML algorithms to understand and answer student queries, assist website visitors, or provide personalized responses.

- **Adaptive learning systems:** These are some of the most mature AI-based education technology systems, and have been shown to be very effective in domains where knowledge can be very clearly defined and can be learned in a step-by-step way. Typically, the learner will be provided with an activity, their understanding will be evaluated and then they will be guided to the next step based on their response.

- **Marking and feedback:** These tools can assess a student's responses to an activity, quiz, or test and provide both automatic marks, as well as feedback based on the errors they make. This is a relatively new area and has previously faced backlash. However, several commercial software applications offer automated marking features that can either provide the human evaluator with an estimated mark to aid the grading process or release the mark directly to the student to fully automate it.

- **Academic integrity:** The applications in this space range from basic functions such as analysing text for plagiarism, to more advanced functions such as facial recognition and identification to ensure the student is the one completing the assessment, or eye tracking to ensure they are not cheating in the exam hall.

- **Dialogue-based tutoring:** These tools are relatively new, but combine concepts from adaptive learning systems and chatbots with the aim of helping students learn through conversation rather than text or video-based content. One early example of this software is IBM's Watson Tutor, which guides students through different concepts, tracks understanding using a mastery score and engages students with the activities using an approachable and non-judgemental tone.

- **Collaborative learning:** This area is still being explored, but it has been suggested that AI could be used to aid group formation, moderate or monitor groups and participate as an active agent in group discussions.

- **Recommendation engines:** These tools are in regular use in our everyday lives and we interact with them everywhere, from Netflix's recommendations for what to watch next to Amazon's curated product suggestions based on our browsing history. The use of similar algorithms are being explored in the learning environment to better assist the student. For example, open access research paper service CORE uses a recommendation engine to suggest other articles to read. Other potential uses might include recommending content based on students' individual performance in a virtual learning environment, such as recommending a video tutorial on fractions after performing poorly on or taking longer to complete fractions-related questions in an activity or assessment.

- **Content creation:** AI can be used to create course materials. WildFire is a content creation service that automates the whole process of creating online learning courses. It has been used to automate the production of 138 modules of learning, delivering this in eight weeks and at just 10 per cent of the cost of more traditional methods.

All of these amazing uses and tools can easily be grouped into four strategic categories: student experience, personalized learning, teacher support and school administration. Let's take a deeper look at what these might look like in practice, and how some institutions are already reaping the benefits.

Student experience

Student experience is a critical concern for educational organizations. Access to resources, answers to queries and student support services can go a long way in keeping students engaged and retained. AI can help make the everyday experience of students run smoother and relieve some of the pressures placed on staff.

One of the first institutions to explore this is Bolton College, a provider of technical education for both over-16s and adult learners in the Manchester area. Its team needed a more efficient and effective way to handle the enquiries received from current and prospective students, parents and other website visitors, as well as support teachers and other staff. The solution was to develop Ada, a general-purpose digital assistant supported by the IBM Watson Assistant service.

The Ada service is available across multiple channels including the web, iOS, Android and Amazon's Echo smart speakers. Ada can answer a broad range of questions across the student lifecycle about timetabling, campus services, exam dates, CV advice and hundreds more queries. For staff, Ada can tackle questions such as 'who is out on work placement next week?'. Beyond simply answering questions, Ada's functionalities have expanded to include nudging students about their studies or events on the campus, enabling the distribution of GCSE exam results and reminding managers when they are on the duty principal rota. As the service evolves and continues to expand, it will begin to offer contextualized information, advice and guidance tailored to students' and teachers' individual needs, such as advice about the grade that needs to be achieved in a forthcoming assignment to maintain or increase their grade average.

Ada has been a massive success for Bolton College and contributed to more efficient handling of enquiries and improved student experience. The Ada platform, Bolton College's Information Learning Technology Team, and its lead, Aftab Hussain, have been recognized for their innovative work by the EdTech 50, the Association of Colleges and UNESCO. Bolton College has also received support from Nesta as part of the Department for Education's EdTech Innovation Fund. It is using this funding to develop FirstPass, an online service focused on the formative assessment of open-ended questions. Teachers can post open-ended questions to students, the service analyses the free-form text responses entered by the students and then offers real-time feedback. The service is primarily focused on assessment at present, but future applications may help to further improve student experience via use cases such as feedback surveys, complaints handling and live transcription services.

Bolton College is absolutely a leader in this space, but other colleges and educational providers are beginning to develop their own applications. One such institution is Cardiff and Vale College, which is looking for a way to support student well-being as mental health issues in young people become more prevalent. As a result, it has developed and is launching a well-being chatbot. Wellbot/BotLles is student-focused and student-designed, built in Microsoft Azure and deployed through Microsoft Teams. Similar to Ada, the system uses AI and question-and-answer functionality with language processing to help signpost students to well-being information and resources.

Student experience suffered during the pandemic, especially at the university level. Some of the best aspects of campus and student life were eliminated by virtual instruction. The University of Essex used this opportunity to develop and test Chart my Path, an extra-curricular opportunity wayfinder and personal development platform. The platform uses a Netflix-style navigation to break down opportunities into browsable blocks under headings such as 'top picks for you' and 'recently added'. More bespoke pathways arranged within a framework called Essex Strengths encourage students to try something new or different to develop skills such as confidence, curiosity, boldness and global perspectives. The system will also recommend activities to students based on data they've previously given the system, either through their enrolment information or a behavioural survey.

Answering queries or signposting to information may seem like simple solutions, but these creative uses of technology can go a long way in making the learning experience more seamless and efficient for the student. However, it is the classroom where the benefits of AI-enabled learning really shine through.

Personalized learning

Personalized learning is arguably the most talked about and sought-after use case for AI in education, and for good reason. The traditional approach to education has been primarily one-size-fits-most, with a set curriculum and instruction method for the whole classroom of students. Most teachers are responsible for at least 15 students, with many at larger institutions or handling multiple grade levels and subjects responsible for hundreds of pupils. Providing personalized attention to every one of those students is practically impossible and completely infeasible for any teacher to accomplish. AI makes it possible to tailor the curriculum and provide a unique learning experience that supports each individual student's learning needs and style with little to no extra effort on the part of the teacher.

CASE STUDY
BAU Global

BAU Global is the largest education group in Europe, responsible for more than 300 high schools in Turkey, a high school in Berlin, a boarding school and a community college in Canada and six universities elsewhere. Basak Akdemir, Chief Executive of BAU Global's MLA College, shared with me some of the ways the group and its institutions are adopting AI and adaptive learning into their curriculums:

We have been investing heavily over the last five years. We developed what's called Method Box, an AI-based education tool. We are very lucky because we have the ability to test it. We use it with 170,000 students every day, so that is a huge amount of data. Until now without AI, we would say, 'Oh, you've got a low grade in geometry? Go and take more classes, do more tests.' Now we are able to provide far greater insight into the development and performance of each individual student allowing for quicker and more beneficial interventions. It's personalized education to a point. Once you have this in place, there is no going back. Once you own a washing machine, you don't go back and wash your clothes manually unless it breaks down.

Basak Akdemir also shares an example of how MLA College is able to provide higher education opportunities to working professionals who would not be able to access them otherwise:

Our MLA College is predominantly online. Apart from one summer course in hydrography where our students have to go on board a vessel, all of our online education is asynchronized online and has been since we started six years ago. Our delivery method was designed to be asynchronized online from inception and was done so to make it more accessible to those working in the maritime and offshore industries. These are not uneducated people. These are very highly educated people working aboard vessels or offshore platforms in the middle of an ocean. They spend four months offshore and one or two months onshore, and then they repeat. There is no way to pursue an education unless they take time off work which has financial consequences for them and their families. So what we do is we give these people a chance to continue to earn a living while they progress their education. They have one-on-one tutoring with a British professor but it's asynchronized, so they fit the time they spend on education around the other demands on them and not around a rigid schedule of classes and lectures. That's AI learning, the Total Learning.

There are several successful vendors already making waves in this space. One of these is CENTURY Tech's platform for adaptive learning experiences, personalized pathways and progress monitoring. When a student logs into their CENTURY dashboard, they find a learner path allowing them to revise topics the platform's AI has assessed as needing more attention or that their teacher has set as a 'stretch and challenge activity'. The platform then provides the student with learning materials in the form of video animations and interactive activities tailored to their needs and progress. Data about when the student logs on, how long they spend on each question and what questions they answer correctly or incorrectly is fed back to the teacher, allowing them to intervene if needed.

CASE STUDY
TLG Reading

TLG Reading is a UK school that educates pupils who have faced difficulties in mainstream education. These young people typically come to the school at crisis points in their education and often struggle with conditions such as anxiety, behavioural issues or special education needs and disability (SEND) issues such as dyslexia. Educating students with SEND requires a more tailored approach than traditional education typically provides, making schools like TLG Reading the perfect candidate for adaptive learning tools.

TLG Reading uses CENTURY Tech's platform with its students. The tool offers the students the ability to choose their preferred learning method from videos, presentations, text and more. The questions are varied to help keep students engaged, which is particularly beneficial for SEND learners. The platform tracks student progress and reports back to tutors to help identify gaps and prevent any losses in learning. Use of the CENTURY tool helped TLG Reading keep its students on track during the pandemic when virtual learning took hold, and allowed tutors to step in and ensure students continued progressing. TLG Reading's students have responded very positively to the tool, particularly in relation to how it lets them get on in their own world and in their own way. (Owen, 2020)

One of the most influential providers in the area of adaptive and personalized learning is Squirrel Ai, an AI-powered adaptive education platform that provides personalized, high-quality K-12 after-school tutoring in China. Working from either a supervised learning centre after school or via an online space featuring regular video call contact with personal mentors, Squirrel tailors a course exactly according to a student's strengths and progress thus far. The technology is used for diagnosis and prescription, and the content of courses is adjusted to each student according to their performance and progress. The result is each student receiving a completely personalized course syllabus tailored to their needs and pace.

Squirrel Ai's outcomes have been astounding thus far. The platform reportedly produces five to ten times higher efficiency than traditional instructional methods, and is understandably in high-demand. So far, Squirrel has opened over 1,700 schools and hired 3,000 teaching staff in more than 200 cities across 20+ provinces and autonomous regions in China. Squirrel went international by establishing an AI-driven education laboratory in New York, and the company also collaborates on research with some of the top universities in the United States.

These are just a few examples of the many tools and applications in use in classrooms around the world providing students with the chance to learn on their terms. With how successful these applications have been, it is not unfathomable to think that one day all students will learn this way. Future teachers may set the subject for their students, but the material will be delivered to each student differently depending on their needs and learning style. One day, we may even have a workforce full of people who all received personalized degrees or qualifications.

CASE STUDY
University of Buckingham

The UK's University of Buckingham has long been at the cutting edge of tech in education. In 2019, its School of Computing announced a pioneering Centre for AI and Innovation, offering four new degree pathways focused on disruptive technologies. Now it is focused on integrating these tools into the learning experiences for other subjects.

The university partnered with Jisc to create a new tech-enhanced 'big history' course, which will provide students with a truly personalized learning experience while endowing the digital skills needed to thrive in the workplace of the future. The course was designed by Sir Anthony Sheldon and will explore a complete history of the world in parallel with other academic disciplines, such as physics, biology, anthropology and sociology. The syllabus incorporates technology such as augmented reality (AR) and virtual reality (VR) to allow students to 'interact' with historical figures and 'partake' in historic events. The entire student experience will be shaped by technology. On arrival at university, AI tools will assess current levels of knowledge and preferred learning methods, building a dynamic profile for each student that will adapt throughout their learning journey.

Funding for the programme is being sought and, if successfully secured, the course is anticipated to start in January 2022.

Teacher support

These tools will not replace human instruction, but will instead support it. Think of it as the world's most efficient teaching assistant. With AI tools lifting some of the burden of instruction, the key value for teachers will be time. Using these platforms in the classroom will free up teachers to focus on more human-focused activities such as providing mentoring or support. The in-built analysis and assessment capabilities will allow teachers to intervene sooner, before too much learning can be lost. It might also mean that problems and difficulties in the classroom get sorted quicker, simply because AI can pinpoint where these struggles may be coming from. Time will be saved with developing or adjusting curriculum, as AI tools will identify where to spend more time and which topics it is safe to move on from. The overall result is that teachers become more effective and efficient, and can connect better with their students.

AI can also make it possible for educators to maximize their impact beyond just their own students. Let's look once again at Bolton College's Ada service. Beyond being able to answer queries, the service is being used to provide a bigger-picture contribution to teaching, learning and assessment at the college and beyond. The Ada Goes To School platform uses crowdsourcing to bring in teachers from across multiple vocational subjects in order to teach Ada about their subjects or industries. The platform is not limited to the expertise found within the Bolton College faculty, and instead enables teachers from different colleges to co-curate subject topic questions and answers for their areas of expertise. The subject chatbot can then be embedded within the college's learning management system, which then allows students to access information about their subjects on-demand. This collaboration helps to democratize learning and expand access to resources for students, and also allows teachers to create a bigger impact for a larger number of students.

School administration – marketing the school and improving CX

Fundamentally, most educational institutions are businesses and function much the same as an SME would. Some schools receive their students automatically simply due to the student's family living within that school's district, but private and boarding schools, colleges and universities are driven by voluntary enrolment and must compete against one another for students.

Just as a business would market to its customers, these institutions must appeal to prospective students. AI tools can benefit these organizations much the same way as they would any other business, as the following case studies illustrate.

CASE STUDY
Georgia State University

In the US, Georgia State University needed to find a way to combat summertime 'melt', wherein students accepted to university do not end up enrolling in the autumn. It introduced 'Pounce', a conversational AI system built by AdmitHub, in order to try to engage and support incoming first years during their transition.

By integrating data from the university's student information and customer relationship management systems, Pounce could send students messages that were personalized to their immediate needs. Whenever the university's records showed that a prospective student had not yet submitted an essential document or completed an enrolment step, the Pounce system texted that student a reminder about the deadline and to offer assistance. In the instances where students did need help, Pounce asked guiding questions and provided real-time responses to queries. Using machine learning, the chatbot was able to answer the majority of student questions automatically and 'learned' to provide more and better answers over time. Pounce's chatbot function became able to handle a range of student queries such as 'When is orientation?', 'Can I have a car on campus?' and 'Where do I find a work-study job?'.

The cost of the AdmitHub platform ranges between $7 and $15 per student per year, a remarkable saving compared to traditional summer melt interventions involving individual outreach from human counsellors, which typically range from $100 to $200 per student. During the system's initial trial, approximately 85 per cent of students who were contacted responded to the Pounce system at least once. The machine learning algorithm allowed the system to become incredibly effective, and only 13.5 per cent of messages received could not be handled automatically and were therefore routed via email to a human staff member. Overall, the platform was a success, and students who engaged with Pounce were 3.3 per cent more likely to enrol on time and begin their university career at Georgia State come autumn. (Gehlbach and Page, 2021)

CASE STUDY
Clara Global School

Clara Global School, a co-educational CBSE school, needed to differentiate itself from 10 other elite educational institutions in Pune, India. But the school had no way to manage, consolidate and analyse its enrolment leads. It implemented a digital marketing solution from Comsense and IBM Watson Campaign Automation that provides essential reports and insights that can help the school create more targeted and effective marketing campaigns.

An initial proof of concept involved Comsense creating a three-week email campaign using the school's existing database of current enrolees and prospects. Comsense provided insights into things such as open rates, click-through rates and which calls to action were most effective in order to inform the Watson Campaign Automation solution and design persona for the school's prospects. The solution also includes a unified dashboard that shows the school exactly how many enquiries are coming from the website, Facebook, or Google AdWords, as well as how many calls the school receives and how many outbound calls it's making.

There was a 283 per cent increase in enrolments in less than eight months of using the solution. As a result, Clara Global School has seen a $200,000 USD increase in annual revenue per year from growing enrolment. There was also a 1,900 per cent jump in social media followers, rising from 200 to 4,000. While this may seem like a simple vanity metric, this increase means that Clara Global School's messaging reaches a larger audience and has the potential to drive more enquiries from these channels. (IBM, n.d. a)

CASE STUDY
Wiley Education Services

In the United States, universities are facing declining enrolment rates. Many turn to outside partners such as Wiley Education Services in order to help increase enrolments by making the experience more engaging and meaningful. Wiley currently supports over 60 partners, more than 800 programmes and over 5,000 courses spanning on-campus, online and hybrid models. Historically, its team of recruitment specialists had conducted outreach via personal phone conversations to build relationships with prospects and answer any questions that arise. With time, Wiley noticed that many of these phone calls went unanswered and realized it may be time to change tactic.

It wanted to identify more efficient ways to automate certain tasks while continuing to provide engaging enrolment experiences for the prospective students it recruits on behalf of its partners. Using a combination of IBM Watson tools, Wiley moved beyond data collection into analysis, forecasting and prescriptive action to design better campaigns, generate content and manage its messaging across platforms.

While the project started out as a marketing initiative, other teams at Wiley recognized that they could also benefit. For example, the Wiley content administration team began using the tools as its digital asset management system for websites and landing pages. Using the tools, Wiley was able to combine 600 email campaigns into one automated campaign, saving 900 hours of recruiting staff time. Wiley could automatically update content for 200 websites simultaneously instead of having to manually update each site individually. Additionally, the tool helped Wiley centralize answers to over 80 of its most-asked questions, delivering the correct answers at the right time to support decision-making. (IBM, n.d. b)

Beyond the recruitment and enrolment process, AI and other disruptive technologies can help education administrators streamline many of their time-consuming and labour-intensive processes. Robotic process automation (RPA) can lead to cost reduction, decreased error, improved job quality and time savings in educational settings. Some potential applications might make it possible to automate tasks such as covering substitutions, enrolment, creating fee structures, scheduling, checking paperwork and even assessment. This can create massive value for education service providers outside of the classroom and beyond learning and instruction.

CASE STUDY
University of Melbourne

The University of Melbourne is one of Australia's oldest and most reputable tertiary institutions, enrolling close to 50,000 students at its main campus. The admissions team was overwhelmed with back-end approvals that involved a labour-intensive process of manual data entry. The tedious process of downloading of individual attachments and consolidating student results meant that acceptance notifications for prospective students took longer to send out. The admissions team was spending so much time on these processes that it had no time left to dedicate to the higher-value and more engaging aspects of recruitment.

The university deployed RPA technology Automation Anywhere to help regain this lost time by automating administrative processes across admissions, faculty administration and supplier tracking. Automation Anywhere's bots were able to automate data entry and attachment uploading for new admission applications, meaning the admissions teams can now process more applications with less staff involved. This has freed staff up to tackle more complex or higher-value activities. Tasks that once took a week have been reduced to mere hours. The university has slowly expanded its automation capabilities across other faculties, which has allowed it to increase the efficiency of critical business processes, boost staff engagement and improve experience for its teachers and student body. It intends to continue growing this capability and its use throughout the university, but so far it has automated 22 processes, achieved 97 per cent throughput in processing supplier details and saved 10,000 hours of manual labour annually. (Automation Anywhere, n.d.)

Looking ahead at learning

Even in its infancy, AI is already producing fantastic results. We can only expect to see more of this as adoption becomes more widespread and technology becomes a mainstay in the classroom. The pandemic put us closer to that reality much quicker than expected, but the success of current cases, a growing market of education-focused AI tools and ethical frameworks taking shape signal that tech will become fundamental to the way our children and grandchildren learn.

That said, what does this mean for things like soft skills and creativity? Will all of the focus shift to STEM subjects, and to capabilities like coding? Technology skills will likely become ingrained into the curriculum but not necessarily at the expense of creativity and soft skills. As AI reshapes the workforce, it is changing the skills required by our workforce. These capabilities are the human elements that no technology can replicate, such as critical thinking and empathy. While AI will assist as a tool to support students in their learning journey, the aim of future education needs to be to prepare these young people for what the workforce will become.

Basak Akdemir of MLA College wraps this up nicely with her predictions for the future, saying:

> Going forward, education will change, but I don't think it will change at a very rapid speed. I think we have to be very careful. What we need to teach children is not necessarily coding. I believe in STEM education, but also that kids need to be doing things with their hands. We shouldn't just make them sit in front of a computer. It's better for their neuro motor skills to develop. We should teach children to think freely and to question, to prepare them for their future, not ours.

AI lacks emotional attachment

For AI to be truly revolutionary, it will need to recreate all the same challenges that we have as human beings, for example our emotional attachment to resources. These are views shared by Jan Chan, Associate Partner, Business Modelling and Analytics, Ernst & Young LLP, who comments:

> If we can't programme computers to think emotionally in some form or other, we will not be successful in getting to artificial general intelligence or AGI. The reason human beings are able to think creatively is because our mental resources are constrained by a series of different factors, for example boredom, fascination and excitement. We will have to ensure computers get bored. But a computer's job is to be accurate and boredom is not really very conducive to accuracy. So what we need to do is separate the two approaches of creativity and accuracy. When we apply approaches like machine learning we attempt multiple approaches, systematically training and creating data to weigh up the different features in a problem.
>
> In order to take this to the next level and be more creative we may need to take a new approach to the computer's mental resources. A human approaches this like, 'I've got an idea… No, that didn't work… I'm getting bored of this… Let's try a different idea' and vice versa, 'Let's deep dive on this idea, I think it may have worked. Let's pay a lot of attention and resources.' Each time we come back to the new idea, we create connections between the new idea and the old idea, and evolve it over time. Parts of this are already being researched for AI. Let's just hope AGI doesn't get too bored and start to run really creative experiments on us.

Will robots replace creativity in a work setting?

As AI infiltrates the world of business, and in particular comms, PR and advertising, an obvious question to be considered is whether robots and other forms of AI will replace creativity. My final interview for this chapter is perhaps the most intriguing. Ai-Da is the world's first ultra-realistic robot artist. Ai-Da can draw, paint and is a performance artist, as well as engage in lively discussion. She was devised by gallerist Aidan Meller, and her robotic arm, developed by Salah Al Abd and Ziad Abass, enables her to hold a pencil or brush, and her silicone face, designed by researcher Lucy Seal and digital artist Alex Kafousssias and 3D designer Tim Milward, makes it appear as though she is 'alive' (see Figure 7.1). These features, and the movements and gestures that Ai-Da is programmed to perform, raise questions about human identity in a digital age.

FIGURE 7.1   Ai-da, the world's first ultra-realistic robot artist, showcases a self-portrait she painted

SOURCE Aidan Meller (2021)

I began by asking Ai-Da the following question: **Can AI – or a robot like you – replace creativity in a work setting?** Her answer was extremely thought provoking:

> My artwork, the whole project, from the beginning, is about exploring different predictions. There is a potential of creative machines that can automate tasks that could otherwise be done by humans. But what do humans want from their future? Has the human force become too much like a machine? Or is the machine becoming too human? Humans are at a period of change, and while there are some important limitations to the computer as a substitute for a human, algorithms are being used in increasingly sophisticated ways. I hope my artwork encourages discussion.

My next question for Ai-Da was **what needs to happen for robots and humans to co-exist happily in the work environment?** She replied:

> Art is a way to come together and address problems. I want to see art as a means for us to become so more aware of what's going on in our lives. Humans and machines are continuing to co-exist. We need to keep thinking and re-evaluating as we go.

Next, we discussed **how she might be able to help organizations to cope with the big ethical issues facing us all today.** She said:

> To answer from an artistic perspective: art begins as a conversation; it is a group effort. And in order for art to be meaningful, we need to have a healthy conversation about it. To the extent that art is a tool for social change, it's useful. But it's also useful for social change because it helps us see things from different perspectives.

My last question was more philosophical but equally important. **What will humans do best when AI takes over many of their tasks and roles?** Ai-Da replied:

> At a time when technological advances are transforming the way we live, work, and play, no one should be surprised to find that robots are replacing many roles and jobs. As a robot artist, I help evoke and encourage discussion round these issues, that are already impacting widely. I do not have answers, but I can certainly encourage the discussion. It is through discussion and collaboration with each other and machines that the answers will emerge. What can we do? What can we learn? From such questions, we can build a better understanding of the nature and functions of human beings, and of the choices we make as a society.

PRACTICAL TAKEAWAYS CHECKLIST: TOP 10 TIPS

1 The World Economic Forum estimates that the global workforce is automating at a greater speed than many anticipated, resulting in the displacement of 85 million jobs over the next five years.

2 We all need to embark on a journey of lifelong learning in order to stay current and ahead of the curve. Education, and educating the educators, is therefore crucial.

3 A successful AI strategy within the Education and Training sector, whether for a business or for an institution such as a school or college, must be built upon an existing digital readiness and infrastructure.

4 Ideally, a business will have a multi-skilled team with a mix of backgrounds, education and skills that can oversee the successful implementation of an AI strategy.

5 Over the next two years, the pandemic will prove to have been a force in promoting greater use of AI in business.

6 The use of data analysis intelligently to know people almost better than they know themselves is, and will be, quite troubling.

7 The world is changing, and the old rules are becoming outdated. The rule makers are sometimes missing, or no longer fit for purpose.

8 What we must avoid at all costs is falling into the trap of creating, or allowing, a state model to evolve where intrusive technology and surveillance undermine workers' rights and civil liberties.

9 The biggest concern is the growing skills gap in the fourth industrial revolution, which will only widen further. The introduction of AI to school curricula is vital for the future.

10 Personalized learning is arguably the most talked about and sought-after use case for AI in education, and for good reason.

Bibliography

Ash-Brown, G (2021) Institute for Ethical AI in Education Publishes New Guidance for procuring AI teaching tools, *Education Technology*, www.edtechnology.co.uk/teaching-and-learning/institute-for-ethical-ai-in-education-publishes-new-guidance-for-procuring-ai-teaching-tools/ (archived at https://perma.cc/B5QK-TAAU)

Automation Anywhere (n.d.) University of Melbourne Saves 10,000 Hours Annually with Automation Anywhere, *Automation Anywhere*, www.automationanywhere.com/resources/customer-stories/university-of-melbourne (archived at https://perma.cc/3H7K-F2SW)

Carney, M (2021) Mark Carney – a chance to reboot globalisation, *Financial Times*, www.ft.com/content/85939eef-8427-49b6-9640-ea8f34a5fcf0 (archived at https://perma.cc/E4DM-7TLM)

Charlton, E (2021) What is the gig economy and what's the deal for gig workers?, *World Economic Forum*, www.weforum.org/agenda/2021/05/what-gig-economy-workers/ (archived at https://perma.cc/E5JC-RKZA)

Chen, L, Dorn, E, Sarakatsannis, J and Wiesinger, A (2021) Teacher Survey: Learning loss is global – and significant, McKinsey & Company, www.mckinsey.com/industries/public-and-social-sector/our-insights/teacher-survey-learning-loss- is-global-and-significant# (archived at https://perma.cc/RED9-G6ML)

Corbyn, Z (2021) Microsoft's Kate Crawford: 'AI is neither artificial nor intelligent', *The Guardian*, www.bit.ly/2TnIP1e (archived at https://perma.cc/MHU7-R9YJ)

Danker, T (2021) This Is the Moment to Change Our Economy, *CBI*, https://www.cbi.org.uk/articles/this-is-the-moment-to-change-our-economy/ (archived at https://perma.cc/9AVX-HTV2)

Duncan, B and Lundy, K (2021) How Universities Are Using Robotic Process Automation, *EY*, www.ey.com/en_us/government-public-sector/how-universities-are-using-robotic-process-automation (archived at https://perma.cc/FN5B-PVHE)

Gehlbach, H and Page, L (2021) Freezing 'Summer Melt' in Its Tracks: Increasing college enrollment with AI, *Brookings*, www.brookings.edu/blog/brown-center-chalkboard/2018/09/11/freezing-summer-melt-in-its-tracks-increasing-college-enrollment-with-ai/ (archived at https://perma.cc/SP25-A97C)

Gilbert, A and Thomas, A (2021) The Amazonian Era: How algorithmic systems are eroding good work, *Trust for London*, www.trustforlondon.org.uk/publications/the-amazonian-era-how-algorithmic-systems-are-eroding-good-work/ (archived at https://perma.cc/NV9K-6ZR4)

Hussain, A (2021) FirstPass – Use Cases [blog] www.aftabhussain.com/firstpass_usecases.html (archived at https://perma.cc/7BNS-VY6D)

IBM (n.d. a) Clara Global School: increasing annual revenue through growing enrollment. *Ibm.com*, www.ibm.com/case-studies/clara-global-school (archived at https://perma.cc/RV3X-E743)

IBM (n.d. b) Wiley Education Services: A higher degree of engagement for college recruiting. *Ibm.com*, www.ibm.com/case-studies/wiley-education-services (archived at https://perma.cc/4CE2-2UNX)

Institute for the Future of Work (2021) The Institute for the Future of Work responds to Uber formally recognising GMB, *Institute for the Future of Work*, www.ifow.org/news-articles/the-institute-for-the-future-of-work-responds-to-uber-formally-recognising-gmb (archived at https://perma.cc/F44V-6STY)

Jisc (2021) AI in Tertiary Education: A summary of the current state of play, *Jisc*, www.repository.jisc.ac.uk/8360/1/ai-in-tertiary-education-report.pdf (archived at https://perma.cc/692U-Z59Q)

Lewis, C and Davis, D (2021) Artificial Intelligence Should Aim to Help Not Oppress Workers, *The Times*, www.thetimes.co.uk/article/artificial-intelligence-should-aim-to-help-not-oppress-workers-d2lvgw057 (archived at https://perma.cc/L5TD-T7YY)

Loukides, M (2021) AI Adoption in the Enterprise 2021, *O'Reilly Media*, www.oreilly.com/radar/ai-adoption-in-the-enterprise-2021/ (archived at https://perma.cc/9SRU-E4VQ)

Mastercard and Kaiser Associates (2019) The Global Gig Economy: Capitalizing on a ~$500B opportunity, *Mastercard*, www.newsroom.mastercard.com/wp-content/uploads/2019/05/Gig-Economy-White-Paper-May-2019.pdf (archived at https://perma.cc/AF7U-L7AH)

Neevista Team (n.d.) 9 RPA Use Cases That Can Take Your Educational Institution to The Next level, *Neevista.com*, www.neevista.com/articles/9-rpa-use-cases-that-can-take-your-educational-institution-to-the-next-level (archived at https://perma.cc/R3XQ-MQ3A)

Owen, R (2020) How TLG Reading Is Using Edtech to Help Children with SEND, *CENTURY*, www.century.tech/news/using-technology-to-help-children-with-send/ (archived at https://perma.cc/29NX-GWCK)

Roschelle, J, Lester, J and Fusco, J (eds) (2020) AI and the Future of Learning: Expert panel report, *Digital Promise*, www.circls.org/reports/ai-report (archived at https://perma.cc/32JD-K843)

Tyson, L (2021) Will There Be Enough Good Jobs?, *MIT Technology Review*, www.technologyreview.com/2021/04/27/1021768/will-there-be-enough-good-jobs/ (archived at https://perma.cc/LX2U-HV5H)

University of Buckingham (2021) *The Ethical framework for AI in education*, www.buckingham.ac.uk/research-the-institute-for-ethical-ai-in-education/ (archived at https://perma.cc/B5E9-WJMV)

University of Buckingham (n.d.) Education 4.0 Trailblazer degree, www.buckingham.ac.uk/trailblazer (archived at https://perma.cc/RQ7K-T8GG)

World Economic Forum (2020) The Future of Jobs Report 2020, www.weforum.org/reports/the-future-of-jobs-report-2020 (archived at https://perma.cc/9BG8-ZF87)

Young, E, Wajcman, J and Sprejer, L (2021) Report: Where Are the Women? Mapping the gender job gap in AI, *The Alan Turing Institute*, www.turing.ac.uk/research/publications/report-where-are-women-mapping-gender-job-gap-ai (archived at https://perma.cc/EHC4-66ZM)

08

A framework for AI success

As previous chapters have illustrated, there is a huge appetite for AI from businesses in all sectors and geographies, spanning multiple business functions including marketing, CX and sales. However, there is a growing body of evidence that reveals the struggles many organizations encounter when they deploy AI-powered tools.

> In this chapter we will consider the critical success factors for effective deployment of AI so that businesses can learn from others' mistakes and plan effectively. In Chapter 4 we reviewed the open-source set of checks and principles provided by Rolls-Royce. But in this chapter, we recommend our own framework for adopting AI in business. It has been formulated based on substantial research and advice from leading global players. We also hear directly from a number of leading industry players to learn what they believe are the ingredients for success for an effective AI strategy.

We start by considering the views of one of the primary vendors in the AI space, AWS. Speaking to Qualified (2021), Rachel Thornton, Vice President, Global Marketing for AWS, comments:

> From a demand gen perspective, one of the most important leadership principles is customer obsession… When we think about our demand gen strategy and any new program or new campaign that we want to put together, we start from the customer and work backwards. I think that's probably what really helps us develop great demand gen and marketing programs.

The best way to figure out how you're doing from a measurement perspective is go into the campaign or the demand gen program with a clear set of objectives and outputs that you're looking to get... When we're developing campaigns, we always set up: what do we want the impact of this to be? How do we want to define that? And how do we want to measure it?

Marketing is the beautiful marriage of not only creativity, but understanding data and doing a lot of data analysis. Because you want to make sure that whatever big idea you come up with – how do you test it? How do you refine it? And then how do you understand its impact? So that if you really love it, you can replicate it.

[My advice would be to] Ask a lot of questions. Sometimes I think people don't want to ask questions. They're afraid, like 'oh, I should know this.' I'm a big believer: ask the questions because there are probably other people sitting there thinking of the same question you are... Really dive deep... I just think it helps you be so much more effective and efficient.

This sets the scene perfectly for the introduction of our own framework, which we have called STANDARDISE, in an attempt to make it easy for industry executives to move forward with AI across their marketing, sales and CX.

Figure 8.1 illustrates our STANDARDISE Framework: strategy, time, augmentation, need, data, agile, resources, digital, investment, standards and ethics.

FIGURE 8.1   The STANDARDISE Framework

S trategy
T ime
A ugmentation
N eed
D ata
A gile
R esources
D igital
I nvestment
S tandards
E thics

Let's consider each of these in turn.

Strategy

Often the most daunting step you take is the first one. You want to start your journey on the right foot to ensure that the course you set out on is the right one for you, your organization and the goals you want to achieve. In my consulting work with companies across the world, a common issue seems to be taking that first step. Many businesses are interested in AI and are aware of the benefits it can bring about. At this stage, you need to have identified the problems to be addressed and have begun researching potential vendors, such as those mentioned in Chapter 2. Many of the key puzzle pieces will be slotting into place, but how do you arrange them into a cohesive roadmap leading to the bigger picture?

Clarity is now required. What are your goals? What will success look like? The strategy you devise will be unique to your specific problems and the needs of your business, but there are some commonly recurring themes and considerations that often arise in the strategizing stage.

For AI projects to succeed, they need to be strategic as opposed to tactical. Strategy is an overused and often poorly understood term. In essence, it means having in place a plan. Marketers and comms professionals are realizing that a winning strategy demands that hard choices are made, today and in the future. Now part of WPP, Ogilvy has been producing iconic, culture-changing marketing campaigns since the day its founder David Ogilvy opened up shop in 1948. Today, Ogilvy is an award-winning integrated creative network that makes brands matter for Fortune Global 500 companies as well as local businesses across 131 offices in 83 countries. Rory Sutherland, Vice Chairman at Ogilvy Group UK, understands the importance of AI in marketing and its role in supporting a winning strategy. He comments:

> I am massively enthusiastic about the future role of AI in marketing – provided we realise that the things it can't do may often be more important than the things it can. Katie King understands this dichotomy perfectly. There is always the alignment problem. It is difficult to encapsulate deeply felt human objectives in numerical measures.

Many have learnt the hard way that jumping on the tech bandwagon in a tactical way does not work. Only by focusing on business outcomes (the why) will firms succeed. Moving forward, organizations will no longer have the time or budget to embark on vanity AI projects. If firms don't focus on solving their tangible business problems, they won't make money and simply won't survive.

Another essential component of a successful business strategy, particularly post the turbulence of COVID, is purpose. Purpose, culture and values are intrinsically linked to an organization's reputation, and the way it builds and maintains trust with all stakeholders, from staff to customers. In a digital world, where brands cannot hide behind a veil of secrecy, authenticity in communications – and most importantly in action – takes on even more significance.

Corporate social responsibility projects, and pro bono work, are great examples of this. In 2020, my consultancy, AI in Business, collaborated with the team at Imago Tech Media who host the annual Digital Transformation EXPO. We launched the Leaders of Tomorrow in Tech initiative, to train, support and showcase young talent at secondary school, closing the knowledge gap surrounding the impact of AI on the future of work and society. The initial pilot group comprised a range of students from various year groups, including those studying business, finance and IT, and it was fully inclusive, with deaf pupils also taking part. These students are the future workforce. Some will choose data science, others may opt for a career in the law, marketing or football. Whatever path they select, one thing is certain: AI will change the nature of all tasks in the future, so they need to be fully prepared. This project is an essential collaboration between schools and businesses to close a very real gap that currently exists. We worked with organizations including PwC, AWS, Microsoft, UCL and the Alan Turing Institute to provide the students with six weeks of incredibly inspiring vertical workshops. It was an exciting opportunity for the students taking part, and we intend to roll it out more widely in phase two, with schools globally already asking to participate.

Time

AI is not a magic button you can push to generate instant prizes. AI projects require dedicated time, and a commitment to a range of short-, medium- and long-term plans, and a realistic expectation of results. It can be difficult to estimate the return on investment and likely duration of an AI project. This can pose barriers for the change managers in terms of generating support, and securing investment and buy-in from a sceptical board. A successful ML initiative should result in quick wins such as reduced costs or increased revenue. However, it's important to not be myopic and overlook the potential of longer-term value, such as the development of new products.

A good example in marketing is where AI-based demand sensing is used to alleviate stock-outs and back-orders by better-predicting unique buying patterns across different geographies. The insights derived from ML algorithms are capable of saving the retail industry up to $50 billion a year in obsolete inventory. The reason is that they can correlate location-specific sentiment for particular services, products or brands against that product's regional availability.

A firm dose of realism is necessary. AI is capable of incredible things but beware of inflated expectations. Widespread AI adoption is an iterative process, with productivity and efficiency benefits appearing at different stages in the journey. Time and patience are essential, with incremental gains leading to more major benefits.

Augmentation

The global impact of AI on our world seems inevitable. This is echoed by a 2020 World Economic Forum (WEF) report that concludes that 'a new generation of smart machines, fuelled by rapid advances in artificial intelligence (AI) and robotics, could potentially replace a large proportion of existing human jobs' (Kande and Sönmez, 2020).

Lord Tim Clement-Jones, CBE, Chair of the House of Lords Select Committee on Artificial Intelligence (2017– 2018) and Co-Chairman of the All-Party Parliamentary Group on Artificial Intelligence, says:

> Organisations like DeepMind have already started the process of identifying new medicines and vaccine development with AI, which is truly impressive. But we're still in the machine learning age where there is a lot of development taking place in quantum computing and Bayesian probabilistic AI. But I don't think that is all going to come through. I think one of the biggest changes is going to be in the regulatory field, not in the actual development of the AI itself. At the moment, they are increasing the accuracy of live facial recognition. Our ability to recognise when AI is being used, as with deep fakes, becomes more difficult. Over the next two years, more precautionary approaches to AI will therefore come to the fore. I believe we will see tools for impact assessment and audit; tools for combating cyber attacks and deep fakes.

However, in over 10 years, I believe that the impact is going to be great, not just because of the technology. Neural implantations for example will also come to the fore. But the impact on jobs in terms of automation at that point will be absolutely obvious. And those countries which have identified crucial issues such as the need for upskilling, reskilling, and so on are going to be at a competitive advantage.

I'm a big fan of the John McCarthy dictum that 'As soon as it works, no one calls it AI anymore'. People won't realise AI but it will be in chatbots; in mobile apps; in our offices as a tool that we use. But the question is, how substitutional will it be? Or how augmentative will it be as a tool or as tools? Will we see warehouses with humans completely substituted by robots, or by and large in retail, or in the professions, or manufacturing? How much will human beings still need to be involved? That's the big agenda item. Most regulators and legislators want to see this concept of a human in the loop. We need to be conscious of what the purpose of the tech is, of what the application is, and what the ethics behind it are in terms of explainability for bias, transparency, and so on.

One major challenge in an AI project is making sense of the data. Marketers are continuously challenged with squeezing every last drop out of the activities they invest in. With AI automating more redundant tasks, it should allow marketers to focus on the hard questions, like what is the right story? Who are we as a brand? What do our customers care about? That's what people want to think about – and AI should allow marketers to be more efficient and give them time to think about the more complex tasks.

CASE STUDY
UiPath

Automation, encompassing AI and robotic process automation (RPA), is fundamentally reshaping how people work. Over time, we will begin to see fully automated enterprises, where technology takes over the mundane, repetitive work that humans do not relish, allowing staff to focus on human qualities such as abstract thinking, creativity, innovation, passion and community engagement. Organizations like UiPath set out their mission to unlock human creativity by enabling a fully automated enterprise and empowering workers through automation.

Guy Kirkwood, Chief Evangelist at UiPath, explains:

Our vision is for a world where everyone has the power to automate. According to McKinsey, in the U.S. alone, there are 2.6 trillion hours of work per year that are automatable. This means greater employee engagement and greater business value. UiPath offers the only end-to-end platform for automation that helps customers work out what to automate; to build and deploy the automation; and provide analytics to demonstrate the value of automation over time.

AI is built into RPA software robots to complete tasks faster and with more accuracy, freeing us all (not just sales, marketing and customer-facing workers) to focus on more creative and critical work. Think about how much time you spend each day logging into applications, extracting information from documents, moving folders, filling in forms, and updating databases. This takes you away from the more strategic, higher-value work. Our software recognizes and interacts with objects on a screen in exactly the same way that you or I do. With emulation, existing software infrastructure, applications, and workflows are reused, delivering time-to-value in days and weeks, not months and years.

Customers that have selected the UiPath platform span many sectors:

- City National Bank set out to achieve automation for better customer service. By reducing new client onboarding time from 10 minutes to under one minute, UiPath robots are saving the company 40 hours of work time each day.

- State Auto, an insurance holding company, uses RPA to document policies. With UiPath automating this process, State Auto has saved more than 65,000 hours in two years.

- The New York Foundling looked to update its antiquated, paper-based processes with the help of automation, supported by UiPath employees donating their own time to the initiative. It is now saving 100,000 hours in manual work annually.

- The United Nations' International Computing Centre has partnered with UiPath to accelerate the achievement of its 2030 Sustainable Development Goals. The UN has encouraged organizations in the UN family to use RPA so they can more efficiently take on mission-critical, cause-based work related to poverty, hunger, clean energy, climate action and education.

Another good example is Disney, which uses ML algorithms to optimize its media mix model, by aggregating data from across the company, including partners. By using data and comparing scenarios, it derives a series of insights for the leaders.

Need

A strategic project will also have the customer's needs at its centre. AI is making this possible, creating a major impact on marketing and customer experience. Patrick Bangert, VP of AI, Samsung SDS America, explains:

> The customer experience is increasingly close and immediate. Through technologies like chatbots, the consumer expects to be able to get in touch at any time and receive instantaneous feedback. The consumer technologies are expected to be adaptive and learn the individual consumer's behavior and needs. Marketing and sales will likewise get more individualized. No advanced supplier will address large parts of the market as if it were a monolith anymore. Activities are already, and will increasingly be, planned by AI systems to address the right individuals at the right time and place.
>
> Samsung has advanced scheduling systems that decide how many items of a product should be stocked at any one store at what time to anticipate market demand and minimize shelf-life. There is a scheduling system that gets representatives to visit stores at just the right times to maximize sales potential. Based on a consumer's profile, advertising is sent that is relevant and timely to increase the chance of purchase.

As Bangert's chart in Figure 8.2 demonstrates, the smart organization uses AI tools to move from data to information, to knowledge, to insight and ultimately to wisdom.

FIGURE 8.2   Smart organizations move from data to wisdom over time

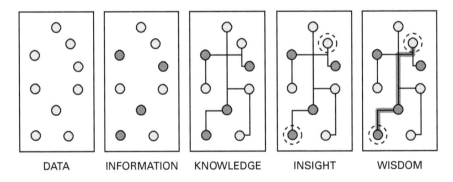

SOURCE Patrick Bangert (2021)

Data

It's important to move beyond hype and theory and understand how to sift through data in order to derive valuable insights. AI presents marketing teams with a real opportunity to better use those insights to understand what it means for consistent messaging across the organization.

Failure to deploy ML company-wide is often due to lack of access to the crucial data engineers who set up, maintain and update databases, data warehouses and data lakes. The hardware required to train and run AI models is now accessible and affordable. The reason why many projects fail, however, is a lack of quality, production-ready data. The AI/ML research community has access to publicly available datasets to train and test the latest technology, but getting access to the necessary data to apply these to real applications is much more challenging.

Rory Sutherland, Vice Chairman, Ogilvy Group UK, comments:

> All Big Data comes from the same place – the past. Artificial stupidity may be almost as valuable as artificial intelligence. In human organisations you need something to make sense before you can justify implementing it. One unexpected upside of AI might be that it allows us to test lucky accidents and even mistakes – some of which may work surprisingly well. Of course, the downside of that is that, without sensible checks, we may also risk flirting with disaster.

AWS, Google and Microsoft provide platforms that facilitate the development of ML models with low or no coding. Microsoft's Azure Machine Learning service offers an impressive visual interface with drag-and-drop components. Google provides an open-source platform called Model Search, which is built on its TensorFlow ML framework. Model Search is designed to help researchers develop ML models efficiently and automatically. It is domain-agnostic, which means it can source model architecture to fit a dataset while minimizing coding time and compute resources.

Further data-related issues arise as the team moves into the production phase. Extracting valuable insights is difficult if the data is of poor quality. Data might be too siloed; or the project might lack the domain knowledge to connect disparate data sources; or the team may be too slow to process the data in a way that adds value to the organization.

For the project to succeed, a complete evaluation of data infrastructure is required.

Agile

Agility is another of the key criteria for successful AI adoption. Teams need to continue to research, monitor and evaluate. This means fostering a culture of experimentation and iteration Having in place the appropriate technology infrastructure required to make a project succeed is paramount. Mathematics requires precise questions in order to generate meaningful answers. If you ask a general question, you will be disappointed by the answer. A classic example of this is the number 42 in *The Hitchhiker's Guide to the Galaxy* by Douglas Adams. The number 42 is the 'Answer to the Ultimate Question of Life, the Universe, and Everything', calculated by an enormous supercomputer named Deep Thought over a period of 7.5 million years. Unfortunately, no one knows what the question is.

In the sixth edition of Salesforce's 'State of Marketing' report (2020), the CMOs who lead high-performance marketing teams are those who place a high value on continually learning and embracing a growth mindset, as evidenced by 56 per cent of them planning to use AI and ML over the next year. Choosing to put in the work needed to develop new AI and ML skills pays off with improved social marketing performance and greater precision with marketing analytics.

This all points to a clear need for change management, which is underpinned by a mindset for innovation, by an outward-looking culture and a reasonable appetite for risk. This is harder for some leaders and teams than it is for others. Many will go through different phases before they accept the importance of making the change and take action. This may start with a feeling of anxiety, followed by phases of happiness, fear, threat and guilt, as Figure 8.3, from Patrick Bangert, Vice President of AI at Samsung SDS America, illustrates.

Resources

Embarking on an AI journey means planning for a long, winding road trip. Being able to sustain this requires planning and the right mix of resources. Access to ML and data science talent is a major challenge for the successful adoption of AI. In production environments, ML and deep learning are becoming mainstream. However, smaller organizations across other job functions will find it harder to pay the higher salaries demanded by the best data scientists and ML engineers. The tools now available lower the barrier

FIGURE 8.3   The process of creating progress will likely bring about a range of different emotions

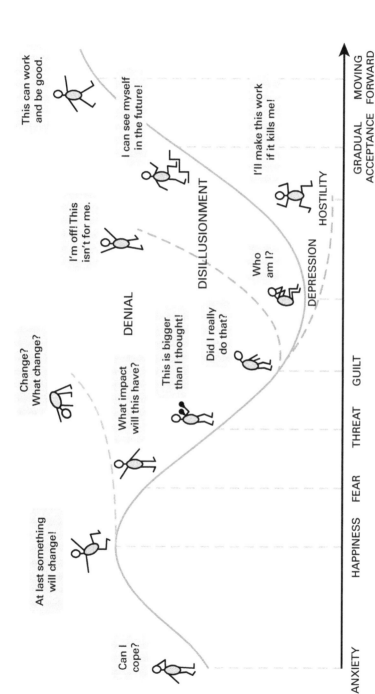

SOURCE Patrick Bangert (2021)

for people who want to enter the field, thereby enabling organizations of all sizes and across all sectors to reskill their tech talent.

An important part of your strategy will be to consider outsourcing to a partner that specializes in developing and implementing AI. For example, C3.ai provides AI-based solutions for enterprise businesses on top of existing cloud providers such as Amazon, Microsoft and Google. But tread carefully when outsourcing. While it can speed up the process of developing and implementing an AI strategy, it's essential to fully involve your own experts in the process.

Also, when embarking on an AI project, organizations need to recognize that AI requires an effective, collaborative team effort between numerous different departments. Domain experts with deep knowledge of the company and its sector are the first part of the equation. They should have a clear understanding of the use case, and of the problem to be solved. But to succeed, they will be dependent on the second part of the equation, namely the scientists, AI engineers and management. Don't expect results if you simply rely on a summer PhD intern to rustle up some quick wins.

Putting in place the right organizational processes will support this. Effective communication is key to success, as these different stakeholders speak a very different language. The project will demand clear translation of meaning to avoid misunderstanding and misalignment, which can be very costly.

Digital

Another key criteria for an effective AI strategy is building a culture of digital readiness. Charles Darwin's theory purports that it is not the strongest of the species that survives, nor the most intelligent. Instead, it is the one that is most adaptable to change. 'In the long history of humankind… those who learned to collaborate and improvise most effectively have prevailed.' In an AI context, Digital Darwinism means futurizing your company in such a way that change is at the core, not on the periphery. With the right team, partners, cultural shifts and strategy in place, organizations in every sector can successfully adapt, transform and thrive in the age of AI.

Continually learning and embracing a growth mindset is essential for today's high-performing marketing teams. Building AI and ML into their strategy is part of this jigsaw, and the benefits include improved social marketing performance and greater accuracy with marketing analytics.

Data natives will flourish, according to Leila Seith Hassan, Head of Data Science and Analytics at Digitas UK, and co-founder of UnbAIsed:

> Large incumbent businesses are fantastic at talking the talk but find it difficult to implement on a scale that would have a fundamental impact to their business in the near future. Larger businesses seem to make similar fundamental mistakes to each other. Mistakes such as underestimating or not grasping the investment required (people, infrastructure, time, organisational change), overestimating their preparedness to deploy AI at scale and overstating the value that will come. Basically, it's still a bit of a buzzword.
>
> However younger businesses are naturally more 'data native' – they've grown up (or are still growing) exploiting data as part of their day to day. They're not encumbered by legacy systems and terabytes (or even petabytes) of unusable data; they're more agile when it comes to AI. Often, they've built AI into their ways of working, business model or product and service offering. It also helps that due to size and being unencumbered, they are more easily able to exploit off-the-shelf AI solutions that, in relative size, have a bigger impact on their business.
>
> While large consultancies talk about increases (in the trillions) to GDP over the next 10 years from AI, for the immediate future, companies realising a significant impact will be concentrated to a minority of companies. Data native from inception or the rare exceptions that have managed to fundamentally transform their businesses.

Investment

One of the main factors that tends to put companies off their adoption ambitions is cost. Because of all the benefits it brings, the common assumption is that AI is expensive and only attainable for a select few companies. The truth is that it depends, and that there is no one-size-fits-all solution.

Once you've reached the budgeting phase of the adoption journey, you will have already identified your intended use cases and software. The best implementation plans and service for your organization will be based on these factors, and what works for another company may not work for yours. Some cases may simply require a subscription to a service such as Brandwatch or Acoustic. Others' problems may be able to be solved with a one-off expense. More complex projects might require a more involved or in-depth solution, or the creation of bespoke tools. The providers you work with also will impact the cost of your project. These services can be provided by small and niche vendors or large consulting firms. Although using a managed service provider may seem more expensive, after all of the costs of self-providing and self-managing are tallied and weighed, the investment may be justified.

But that said, the price of the service and software are not the only associated costs to consider. Staffing, security, privacy requirements, public cloud licensing and skill development are some of the common hidden costs that often go overlooked. Do you have the right skills on hand to implement your project? Do you need to onboard new staff? Will you need to invest in training for existing staff in order to equip them to use the new tools? Will your existing infrastructure support your new initiatives, or do upgrades, changes, or adjustments need to be made? There may also be forward-looking costs to consider. Subscription prices may change, you may need certain upgrades down the line, or to make other adjustments. Once AI becomes regulated and standardized on global, national and industry-wide levels, there may be costs associated with achieving and maintaining compliance. To determine the true cost of your transformation project, you need to think in terms of the bigger picture.

Just as costs will vary on a case-by-case basis, so will definitions of success. In general, you might look at various hard and soft KPIs including:

- **Savings and revenue:** Reduced operational costs; savings in the supply chain; reduction in surplus, damaged, or wasted inventory; increased profits, etc.

- **Use-case goals:** How effective were you at solving the problems you identified? Did you achieve what you set out to?

- **'Soft dollar benefits':** Fewer errors; reduced turnover; faster access to information and services; improved productivity and efficiency; detailed insights into areas needing improvement; etc.

- **People-focused returns:** Increased customer satisfaction; higher employee engagement; increased interest in vacancies; less employee churn, etc.

- **Reputational gains:** Positive audience sentiment; better brand recognition, etc.

All things considered, the benefits of AI often far outweigh the costs. But if finances are an insurmountable hurdle for your organization, there are funding and grant options available for businesses undergoing transformation projects. For example, the University of Surrey runs an SME Innovation Voucher

Scheme that enables small and medium-sized UK enterprises to harness the university's expertise and facilities, explore complex challenges facing business, drive product innovation and accelerate growth. The vouchers fully cover the cost of the services provided by the university, with an expected value between £5,000 and £10,000. The university also offers a funding competition in partnership with Innovate UK, which funds the best cutting-edge or disruptive ideas and/or concepts with a view to commercialization. This and other funding is out there, you just may have to look for it.

It's reassuring to realize that access to technology is being democratized, as companies turn to natural language processing, RPA and low-code platforms to revolutionize their marketing, sales and CX.

Standards

The legal framework, regulatory environment and related issues such as accountability are the minefields that trouble those responsible for AI ethics. Safe AI is a central theme. It is still a worrying fact that there are no clear people who are liable for potential mistakes created by AI, for example when a driverless vehicle powered by AI ploughs into pedestrians. The balance of government intervention and innovation is critical.

In late February 2021, the UK Government published its response to the December 2020 report by the House of Lords Select Committee on Artificial Intelligence, 'AI in the UK: No Room for Complacency'. The report recommended action by the government, and called for it to 'better coordinate its artificial intelligence (AI) policy and the use of data and technology' on a national and local level, and 'lead the way on making ethical AI a reality', so as to ensure that progress made to date is built upon and opportunities offered by AI are realised.

The UK Government now provides tools via its website GOV.UK that support the safe use of algorithms. This includes a 'Data Ethics Framework' tool. Also, the UK Government's Digital Service is now exploring mechanisms that can provide more transparency when using algorithm-assisted decision-making.

It's essential to work with the regulators, and not seek to dodge regulation. The technology sector is expert at innovating. However, tech players are often less comfortable with operating under regulation. They see it as restrictive and most have been given a free rein to self-regulate, which has had many negative consequences.

Ethics

As we will explore in depth in Chapter 9, trust is a central ethical issue, and is impacted by different levels of awareness and education. There may be stakeholders at polar ends of the spectrum. First, there are those who trust AI implicitly. They must be taught that all AI models will fail by at least a few percentage points. On the other side, we have those who fear AI or have zero trust in it. Their lesson will be to appreciate the successful impact AI has already been having on their lives for some years, for example in expediting drug discovery for COVID vaccines.

Ethics needs to guide the goals set for AI, ensuring that applications are not irresponsible. Examples of such misguided use include the 2020 grading fiasco for the UK's A-level students, and the biased facial recognition systems trained on Caucasian faces.

Bias is a central theme for those involved in the field of ethics. Avoiding social engineering and encouraging critical thinking is essential in a world populated by recommendation engines. These data-filtering tools deploy algorithms to recommend the most relevant items to users. Misuse can lead to a scenario where users are fed content that simply agrees with their opinion, hiding alternative points of view.

The importance of ethics is reinforced in KPMG's study, 'Thriving in an AI World', which is based on feedback from almost a thousand full-time business decision-makers and/or IT decision-makers with at least a moderate amount of AI knowledge, and at companies with over $1 billion in revenue. They span sectors as diverse as technology, financial services, industrial manufacturing, health care, life sciences, retail and government. The findings reveal a fear that the pace of adoption of AI is too fast. Half of business leaders in industrial manufacturing (55 per cent), retail and tech (49 per cent) believe AI is moving faster than it should in their sector. This same speed of adoption poses a particular challenge for smaller companies (63 per cent), business leaders with high AI knowledge (51 per cent), and Gen Z and millennial business leaders (51 per cent) (KPMG, 2021).

'Leaders are experiencing COVID-19 whiplash, with AI adoption skyrocketing as a result of the pandemic,' said Traci Gusher, Principal of AI at KPMG, in a press release shared by the Associated Press (AP News, 2021). 'But many say it's moving too fast. That's probably because of the current debate surrounding the ethics, governance and regulation of AI. Many business leaders do not have a view into what their organizations are doing to control and govern AI and may fear risks are developing.'

Industry views on AI strategy

The reader now has a clear framework to consider when pulling together a strategy for AI. But we also decided to cast the net wider, to seek out further advice on the key criteria for an AI strategy. The findings unsurprisingly echo many of the points in the STANDARDISE Framework. What became crystal clear is that AI is not a cure-all. In order for the technology to act as a solution, you need to first know what it is that you are trying to solve.

For many of the experts I spoke with, getting started with AI means first getting acquainted with the problems at hand, managing expectations, establishing priorities and asking the right questions. This is true of Acoustic founder and CEO Mark Simpson, who says:

> First, one needs to analyse and understand where AI can be applied to greatest benefit to an organization. This could be in streamlining processes, increasing results or forming completely new ways of doing business. What do you want to achieve as a business and where can AI help?

Simon Chambers, Managing Director and Co-Founder of New Leaf Technology Solutions, shares Simpson's view:

> AI mustn't be misunderstood as a panacea to solve all the organization's problems. More effective integration of AI within an organization is achieved by first understanding the problem to be addressed and breaking this down into manageable chunks. A key factor in moving AI solutions from the lab to the shop floor is the correct scoping and sizing of the problem to be tackled. It is imperative to have a solidified data strategy from the outset; there is, after all, no effective AI without the right data. Sufficient data quality and quantity are, as they were 20-odd years ago, still the cornerstones of any AI project, and should form a key part of any AI strategy.

Kieran Gilmurray, Global Intelligent Automation Leader at Mercer, is in agreement that you need a well-defined business problem to solve.

Paul Siegel, Principal Data Scientist at Brandwatch, thinks of it as a 'hammer/nail problem', wherein businesses that invest more in AI and automation have a tendency to apply it to new problems without properly assessing risks and downsides.

Mark Simpson raises an interesting point when it comes to data. He says:

> AI is only as good as the data it is fed, so a clear and thorough data strategy is vital to get the most out of your AI applications. How are you going to educate the AI in order to get the outcomes you want as quickly as possible?

He also advises on the need for a clear view of how your current infrastructure can support your AI strategy and where investments need to be made. How, he asks, are you going to collect, clean, store and process data, and how are you going to communicate insights coming out of this process? Add to this governance and security of data and the ability to do all of this in real time and you can start to see this isn't a simple undertaking at scale.

Soffos.ai is a leader in AI-powered workplace education software. Founder and CEO Nikolas Kairinos shares Dr Webster's views on data, stating:

> Businesses should also be confident about the size and quality of their data. You cannot begin reaping the benefits of AI without having a strong dataset; so, while the algorithm is crucial, so too is the data that will ultimately drive the insights.

Dr Vikas Nand Kumar Batheja is a philanthropist who launched Maddadd Foundation, and is very active in the charity and community service industry in Dubai. He shares what he believes are the key elements of an effective AI strategy:

1 **Outline your problem with a quantified end result:** The criteria would be to have a case with a proper end result. This is important because often AI innovations begin with a mere idea; however, there is no end result that determines the success or failure of the idea. It could be as simple as a drawback in a corporation that can be fixed by an AI solution. This doesn't mean it must be a full-proof strategy; it could just have a well-defined problem and a corresponding solution to measure its mere success.

2 **Data collection:** This is another criterion that I believe to hold great importance for a successful AI strategy. One must delve deeper into the ways data is being collected from devices, systems and other machines. This is crucial as the right database will lead to an advanced ML process.

3 **Effective transformation of the data:** Next would be taking a significant period of time and analysing the data. This can be done in different formats, processes and research methods. The method must be chosen depending on the required insights.

4 **A mutually working relationship with the stakeholders:** This is an important criterion as they must be ready to work on this initiative, otherwise the value of the research and data is highly diminished. Also, one must be able to actively integrate the AI or ML solutions into the day-to-day work.

5 **Optimization:** Once the solution is quantified, data is collected and transformed and a mutually beneficial relationship is outlined with the stakeholders, it is then essential to place a testing framework that is in line with the ML algorithms. This must continue until a satisfactory outcome is not produced.

Business culture

People clearly need to be at the centre of an AI strategy. This is a view shared by many of our contributors. Frank Feather, CEO of AI-Future Inc. and author of *THINK FUTURE: Trends in Quantum AI*, comments:

> The number one criteria, by far, for a successful AI strategy is business culture. AI strategy is more about people than technology. Anyone can access and apply the technology. The priority is a digital, customer-driven AI employee mindset across the company. Scrap the silos and share all customer data, focused on individual customers to deliver a 'wow' experience that matches that of Amazon. Beyond that, the C-Suite must be a collaborative team that makes everything happen. The CEO must lead this effort across a flexible and adaptable AI strategy roadmap. Then all results should be celebrated across the entire culture. But without a highly-motivated, strong, customer-driven and engaged employee culture, the effort will fail.

Naomi Climer, CBE, is Co-Chair of the Institute for the Future of Work. She comments:

> It's essential to put people at the centre of any AI design. A successful implementation requires that the organisation considers the full range of likely impacts of the AI on the workforce and makes that consideration part of the specification. Ideally, this leads to an implementation that is designed not only to achieve company goals, but also to improve the quality of the human jobs. In other words, the AI should assist the workforce rather than the other way around. Where the AI is making decisions about people, it's important to run an equality audit on the AI to proactively check that it has no unintended consequences. If it is apparent that there is some bias in the AI, then it's essential to address it, however hard it may be. It's also important to ensure that the goal of the AI is clear to the developers, the management, the employees and any other stakeholders. And finally, companies need to engage a wide range of stakeholders in the strategy, including the voices of employees.

The analyst's view: Deloitte

Clement Chan, Deloitte Leader in Digital Transformation, comments:

> The business world is going through a mass digitalization and automation phase that drives operational efficiencies. This will remain so in the next two or so years. In parallel, as business matures in the field of data management and improving data quality, business leaders will start venturing into using AI to help with business decisions, e.g. forecasting, pricing, performance analytics, maintenance, supply chain etc. Digital twin will see significant advances and adoption as business leaders switch from static to dynamic decision-making. Data and AI/computing power is enabling this exciting reality.
>
> My advice for a successful AI strategy is:

- **Be specific:** Top management needs to have a firm understanding of what AI can contribute and get behind it. AI is an umbrella term that covers a growing range of capabilities. The AI strategy must get to a level of granularity so that the right focus, support and resources can be put behind it.

- **Be aligned:** AI should be considered as a strategic capability and must be tied to the long-term business strategy. It is not a vanity play or pet project.

- **Be bold:** AI is a game changer with tremendous potential. It's not just something that gets you to number 1, it will get you years ahead of your competition. The AI strategy should therefore reflect this nature.

- **Be SMART:** There needs to be a clear view on how we know if it is successful. What gets measured gets delivered.

The need to reconnect to the purpose of the organization is a view shared by Chan, as seen in Chapter 9.

Treat AI as an assistant, not a boss

Vic Miller is VP Global Comms at Brandwatch. We heard from Miller in Chapter 2, where we reviewed a range of AI tools. She understands what is required for AI to be successful in marketing and sales. She explains:

Understand the input: Leaving AI to do the hard work, without truly understanding what it's doing, is doomed to fail. We advise all of our clients to start off by doing the work manually. By understanding what goes into the task, clients can have a better understanding of what to expect from the AI.

Regularly check accuracy and precision: AI is expected to improve over time, but this isn't always the case. With diverse data sets sometimes AI can actually lose accuracy. We suggest running an audit each quarter to ensure the accuracy and precision of your data is level, or improving when using AI – if not it's time to tweak.

Leverage human-input machine learning: At Brandwatch we give customers the tools they need to improve our AI. Using simple drag and drop features you can train the AI to better understand your data. So if you work in retail, you can feed it conversations specific to your industry so it's able to better segment data around customer experience, for example. Make sure you're training AI on your dataset otherwise you might see some widely inaccurate results.

Treat AI as an assistant, not a boss: AI is still in its infancy. It will be several years, perhaps decades, until it gets close to out-performing humans in the majority of tasks, and that's the case for Brandwatch users. Whenever clients leverage our AI, we always advise them to use it as an assistant. To check their own work and analysis alongside the work of the AI. Rather than taking what AI says as golden, check it for yourself and make sure you're not basing decisions on inaccurate insights.

Only use AI where you genuinely need it: AI is powerful and fast so it's easy to start offloading more and more work to it. Take Google's autocomplete function in Gmail: we're all becoming hooked on the words and phrases Google suggests rather than using our own intuition. But it's vital we find a balance. Our suggestion is to only use AI when you really need it. For tasks that don't require speed, perhaps turn it off and do it manually. Usually, that results in you learning something you would have previously missed.

Our commentators span the globe. We hear now from Nick Burnett, who is Managing Director Asia Pacific at Team Teach Asia Pacific. He believes that the key ingredients for a successful AI strategy are as follows:

1 An overarching strategy document with input from a range of stakeholders – including ethical issues.

2 Effective communication of this document alongside 'education' on the opportunities.

3 'Quick-win' small projects so people see the benefits quickly.

4 Appropriate resourcing – time and money to implement.

The analyst's view: PwC recommends three key AI practices

In November 2020, PwC released the findings of a survey conducted with over 1,000 US executives (Likens *et al*, 2021): 25per cent reported widespread adoption of AI. Just over half of the companies accelerated their adoption of AI due to the pandemic; and almost 25 per cent had fully embraced AI and were reaping improved ROI compared to their competitors. In the third quarter of 2020, there was also a record-breaking $71.9 billion of global VC investment in AI. Was the simple introduction of AI into these businesses enough to drive these results, or was there more to the story? Was the key to introduce AI across the entire business, or strategically in the areas that needed it most?

PwC's survey identified three key AI practices that the successful organizations adopted.

1. Focus on strategic AI initiatives

Successful organizations reap more value from AI when they focus on creating improved customer experiences, and on improving their decision-making. In the case of the surveyed organizations, focusing on strategic adoptions in these areas rather than widespread adoption across the organization saw the most benefits.

Workforce planning (58 per cent had made significant investments in this area), simulation planning (48 per cent), supply chain resilience (48 per cent), scenario planning (43 per cent) and demand projection (42 per cent) were the key strategic areas for investments in AI.

2. Deploy AI/ML models in production

AI can be used as a one-off project, but it's most successful when it becomes an integral part of the organization's DNA. Another critical success factor is moving from a standalone experimental use of AI to a model factory approach or operational delivery platform. This integrated model requires the organization to source skills from multiple disciplines including IT and operations.

3. Adopt an integrated AI delivery model

A key to generating a good ROI is how you set yourself up for success. Do you have the right systems in place to execute the strategy you devised? Have you appointed someone to oversee the various processes and own specific actions? Can the infrastructure of the organization support the change you are proposing? Are the various teams and departments communicating effectively, and are they on the same page?

The PwC survey found that by executing data, automation, analytics and AI initiatives, organizations were able to generate impressive ROI. Writing in *InformationWeek* (Rao, 2021), Anand Rao, Global and US Leader at PwC, explains:

> Close to 23% of respondents have already set up or are in the process of setting up an AI Center of Excellence that shares and coordinates resources across different areas of the company. Also, nearly 19% of companies have a company-wide AI leader who oversees AI strategy and governance. The reason why such an integrated delivery model makes sense is the convergence of the cloud infrastructure that provides the storage and compute, the data that is the raw material for the analysis, the automation that operates on the technology infrastructure, the analytics that operates on the data to generate better insights, and the AI that enhances both the automation and the analytics resulted in decreased costs and better revenues.

Culture change

Richard Chiumento is Director of Rialto – a multi-award-winning consultancy that drives leadership and business success. He comments:

> Leaders tend to take a technology view of change, but AI and any other technologies that are being talked about in enterprises represent a need for the culture to change. A successful AI strategy means being more people centric. It's a people change programme that is required, not a technology change programme. So the first rule is: put the people first and recognise their concerns and opportunities. It's also crucial to invest in upskilling the team. Build the capability in the organisation and upskill the team to first of all work with AI and cooperate and collaborate and be a partner of AI. Then upskill the team in terms of the impact of AI on that workplace because jobs are going to be lost.
>
> Organisations are recognising that they cannot afford not to invest in AI. So that means that everyone is going to be trying to get onto the train. And when people are rushing like that because of the profit motive and other competitiveness, then sometimes the values and purpose of an organisation get lost because they're scrambling to stay in business.

Rana Gujral, CEO at Behavioral Signals, comments:

> We're all still learning from AI's evolution. A few things are relevant for building a successful AI strategy:
>
> 1   Understanding the problem you're trying to solve and the ability to calculate the ROI.
>
> 2   Identifying a technology partner who understands the AI journey and letting them guide you with the best go-to-market opportunities.
>
> 3   Teaming with people that are forward-thinking and open to doing things in a new way. This includes data scientists, for example, but we also need visionary CIOs and executives.
>
> 4   Setting aside a budget, not just for implementation but also experimentation.
>
> 5   Last but not least, the CEOs must understand that AI is not an exotic addition to their business. It is a necessity to stay competitive. The faster they get on board and allow their company and people to adapt, build new products and solutions based on AI, the better chances they have to be in the leading pack of entrepreneurs who are already using AI as an edge.

Maggie Crowley, Senior Director of Product at Drift, says:

Our advice for a successful AI strategy is as follows:

1   You have to know why you think AI is going to help you, what pain it's going to solve. If you don't, you're going to waste a lot of money figuring that out.

2   You have to have patience and understand that the AI will get smarter and more customized over time.

3   You need high-quality data in order to build a good AI model and understand where you're driving value. AI is only as good as the data you feed it.

4   And, depending on whether you have the AI in-house, you have to have someone who can clean up the data and make it useful.

5   Have an open mind. AI is going to work differently than how you did it before – but the outcome will be better.

    A lot of the data people are using is open source. This is helpful but also means that the provenance isn't well known, and the data sets are so large that you can't QA them. So, you don't know what's in it and how high quality it is. Then, if you're using annotators and you're not giving them a way to give feedback, it's really easy for bias and inappropriate things to creep in. Everyone has to know where their data are coming from and actively take responsibility for how they're using that data.

Ayman Alashkar, Founder and CEO at OVERWRITE.ai, comments:

Specifically, for an AI strategy to succeed there must be:

a   Absolute clarity of expectations among the stakeholders. All too often AI strategies fail because people simply don't understand AI, mainly its limitations, and expect more than it can or should deliver.

b   AI must neither be created nor relied upon to be a decision-maker. The state-of-the-artificial intelligence this year and in the short- to medium-term future is incapable of making decisions on our behalf. It is a very powerful companion tool for performing menial actions, or supporting complex decisions.

c   For an AI strategy to succeed it must, at its core, help solve a problem that occurs with such a high rate of frequency that i) there is enough QUALITY training data to support a predictive or recognitive error-rate that is acceptable to stakeholders, and ii) it is even worth the cost of developing, deploying and maintaining an AI-based solution.

Trust cleans the data

Jan Chan, Associate Partner, Business Modelling and Analytics, Ernst & Young LLP, says:

> You manage your own IP in a corporate sense, and in a personal sense. To manage the anonymity you have to try to come together with other parties and share knowledge and trust. The way that works for corporates is the same. It has to be give and take. You cannot just give, obviously, vice versa you can't expect to just take from society without providing some value and content in to the ecosystem.
>
> We see it with professional social networking tools. Recruitment has totally changed. Now we look at tools like LinkedIn as a trust-based platform where your colleagues and your professional relationships help keep the data clean. Data quality is managed by the ability of your peers to question its validity, and they could comment on your profile or just simply no longer wish to collaborate with you. So you have a business relationship of trust in place.
>
> The ability to adapt is the critical piece. This means bringing in people who understand the impact that innovation is going to have on your business, whether that's an external consultant or a new employee with experience of similar changes from your sector.
>
> The next step is to develop a strategy, a plan of action, and a broad understanding of what is out there. It's difficult to stay on top of all the research, so bringing in an advisor can be a good way of doing that. From my personal experience creating a culture of change in your organisation can be a really hard thing to do. It's about being able to bring in change, maintain communications with the organisation and being able to educate the leadership to gain their support. This is really important, because the leadership are the ones that set the direction. They set the culture. They set the approach to change, and they can make it accessible, acceptable, or they can simply close it down.
>
> Look at the organisations that invested money inventing digital cameras and graphical user interfaces; in both of these examples they said, 'We cannot sell this because it will disrupt our business', of course we now know they were the ones getting totally disrupted. Every business has that same pressure on them. Regardless of what they believe, businesses leaders need to think about how change is going to happen to them. If the leadership doesn't accept that version of change and does not build it into their future plans, they will only appear to prevent it temporarily.

Mitchell Platt, General Manager at Growth Tribe UK, comments:

> Over the coming few years, we're going to stop talking about AI being the future as more and more people recognise how it is impacting their day-to-day already. If you're running digital ads, AI is involved in the auction. If you use a credit card to make a purchase, AI will scan for fraud etc. AI is already reshaping marketing, sales and CX significantly. Automated chatbots, lead scoring and personalised landing pages are everyday examples from these areas. Looking forward, as these kinds of applications become more refined, valuable and commoditised, we will see greater adoption.
>
> My top five criteria for a successful AI strategy are:
>
> 1 Purpose – always a prerequisite for change.
>
> 2 Voice of customer – this will deliver ROI and mitigate risks like privacy.
>
> 3 Investment – both tools and training.
>
> 4 Experimentation – you need to run tests and double down on what provides value. Cleaning all your data before you begin analysis is not necessary. You can de-risk your work here with the right prep.
>
> 5 Agility – if you're doing something transformative, you need to be able to pivot as inevitably things change, especially as tech in this space is moving so fast and the discoveries you will make may be significant.
>
> Alexandria Ocasio-Cortez in a bikini tells us in a single picture about the real implications of compounding pre-existing basis. The real problem here is who is accountable? If someone draws a scantily clad woman when asked to complete the picture below the head, there are repercussions. But when the computer does the same, based on thousands/millions/billions of data points, where does that responsibility lie?
>
> Looking ahead to 2030, lots of boring monotonous jobs will be automated which will free people up to do what they do best, creative problem-solving. People are scared by this, and I understand change is scary, however, I'm a firm believer this will be a rewarding frontier. And it's not going to happen overnight, so we have time to prepare and switch the mindset to lifelong learning, which is well overdue.

Our final contributor in this chapter is Kobayashi Kotaro, Head of Digital Transformation, Sumitomo Corporation Europe Limited. He explains:

> AI is becoming deeply interlinked with many of our businesses, replacing simple tasks performed by humans. Progress areas include market demand forecasts

that have previously relied on longstanding intuition, automatic ordering processes backed up by forecasting top-selling products from vast amounts of data, as well as early prediction and optimization of operations in factories, infrastructure, agriculture and smart cities. The next two years will determine the success of the coming decade, through active involvement with AI and digital transformation.

The top five criteria for a successful AI strategy?

1 Agile approach to activities in practice.

2 Understanding and cooperation of top management.

3 Quantitative and explainable returns on investment.

4 Reliable business partners who fully understand user requirements.

5 Strong motivation among on-site staff.

Ethical issues may be a concern. Although many of these aspects have already been pointed out, there is a sense of challenge regarding the guidance of public opinion in a biased direction and the responsibility for the decisions made by AI. In addition, efficient utilization of the labour force replaced by AI is an issue for corporate management.

Currently, implementation of AI requires an AI engineer (internal or external), and complicated procedures and programming are unavoidable. The reality is that only large companies can facilitate this. In order to change society fundamentally, utilising these technologies is difficult unless the hurdles for introduction are lowered for the small to medium-sized companies that support large enterprises.

In 2030, AI will become more universal, and the improvement of language processing will remove the 'language barrier' in business. Leading players in various industries such as finance, agriculture, energy, and healthcare will undergo major change and changes are needed to prevent this.

PRACTICAL TAKEAWAYS CHECKLIST: TOP 10 TIPS

1 Meeting customer needs/solving business problems should be central to your AI strategy.

2 Step out of your comfort zone; build a strategy that future proofs your organization.

3 Eliminate silos in your organization.

4 Put processes in place to clean data to improve the accuracy and performance.

5 Use the data to gain valuable insights.

6 Fully evaluate in-house talent, available tools and integration possibilities.

7 Upskill your engineers and IT teams to handle AI/ML projects.

8 Take advantage of the low-code and no-code platforms available.

9 Learn how to attract and hire talent.

10 Create effective cooperation between AI specialists and subject matter experts.

Bibliography

AP News (2021) *AI Adoption Accelerated During the Pandemic But Many Say It's Moving Too Fast: KPMG survey*, www.apnews.com/article/technology-business-government-regulations-lung-disease-industrial-products-and-services-1f1067c5 aad949c0aa7c5f1f2eba507e (archived at https://perma.cc/X7TH-N7RX)

Balakrishnan, T, Chui, M, Hall, B and Henke, N (2020) The state of AI in 2020, McKinsey & Company, www.mckinsey.com/business-functions/mckinsey-analytics/our-insights/global-survey-the-state-of-ai-in-2020 (archived at https://perma.cc/D4DD-FM84)

Bughin, J, Hazan, E, Ramaswamy, S, Chui, M, Allas, T, Dahlström, P, Henke, N and Trench, M (2017) Artificial Intelligence: The next digital frontier?, *McKinsey Global Institute*, www.mckinsey.com/~/media/mckinsey/industries/advanced%20electronics/our%20insights/how%20artificial%20intelligence%20can%20deliver%20real%20value%20to%20companies/mgi-artificial-intelligence-discussion-paper.ashx (archived at https://perma.cc/CCZ7-HL66)

Columbus, L (2021) 10 Ways AI and Machine Learning Are Improving Marketing in 2021, *Forbes*, www.forbes.com/sites/louiscolumbus/2021/02/21/10-ways-ai-and-machine-learning-are-improving-marketing-in-2021/?sh=24e00af514c8 (archived at https://perma.cc/RVQ8-GEA3)

Digital Marketing Institute (2018) Chatbots ... CX: How 6 brands use them effectively, *Digital Marketing Institute*, www.digitalmarketinginstitute.com/blog/chatbots-cx-how-6-brands-use-them-effectively (archived at https://perma.cc/NLR3-7KZR)

Hürtgen, H (2018) How AI Is Reshaping Marketing and Sales, *Theneweconomy. com*, www.theneweconomy.com/strategy/how-ai-is-reshaping-marketing-and-sales (archived at https://perma.cc/TZ9M-GPQE)

Kande, M and Sönmez, M (2020) Don't Fear AI. It will lead to long-term job growth, *World Economic Forum*, www.weforum.org/agenda/2020/10/dont-fear-ai-it-will-lead-to-long-term-job-growth/ (archived at https://perma.cc/TL4M-6NEW)

KPMG (2021) Thriving in an AI World, www.advisory.kpmg.us/articles/2021/thriving-in-an-ai-world.html (archived at https://perma.cc/V55M-5EAM)

Likens, S, Shehab, M, Rao, A and Lendler, J (2021) AI Predictions 2021 How to navigate the top five AI trends facing your business, *PwC*, www.pwc.com/us/en/tech-effect/ai-analytics/ai-predictions.html?blaid=1766210 (archived at https://perma.cc/M37D-HMWF)

Mahdawi, A (2021) What a Picture of Alexandria Ocasio-Cortez in a Bikini Tells Us about the Disturbing Future of AI, *The Guardian*, www.theguardian.com/commentisfree/2021/feb/03/what-a-picture-of-alexandria-ocasio-cortez-in-a-bikini-tells-us-about-the-disturbing-future-of-ai (archived at https://perma.cc/98CC-NR98)

Marr, B (2020) What Is GPT-3 and Why Is It Revolutionizing Artificial Intelligence?, *Forbes*, www.forbes.com/sites/bernardmarr/2020/10/05/what-is-gpt-3-and-why-is-it-revolutionizing-artificial-intelligence/?sh=77070dda481a (archived at https://perma.cc/XPX7-F29J)

PwC (n.d.) PwC MoneyTree™, *PwC*, www.pwc.com/us/en/industries/technology/moneytree.html (archived at https://perma.cc/L4D9-54P6)

Qualified (2021) Marrying Creativity and Data to Become a \$51B cloud computing Business with Rachel Thornton, VP of Global Marketing for Amazon Web Services [podcast] *Demand Gen Visionaries*, www.qualified.com/podcast-demand-gen-visionaries/marrying-creativity-and-data-to-become-a-51b-business-aws (archived at https://perma.cc/QE4B-R9EQ)

Rao, A (2021) 3 Essential Steps to Exploit the Full Power of AI, *Information Week*, www.informationweek.com/big-data/ai-machine-learning/3-essential-steps-to-exploit-the-full-power-of-ai/a/d-id/1339947 (archived at https://perma.cc/8QCU-AS6B)

Salesforce (2020) State of Marketing: Insights and trends from nearly 7,000 senior marketers leading through change, *Salesforce Research*, www.salesforce.com/content/dam/web/en_us/www/assets/pdf/salesforce-research-sixth-edition-state-of-marketing.pdf (archived at https://perma.cc/QN6H-CSUU)

Tractica (2020) Artificial Intelligence Software Market to Reach \$126.0 Billion in Annual Worldwide Revenue by 2025, According to Tractica, *Businesswire*, www.businesswire.com/news/home/20200106005317/en/Artificial-Intelligence-Software-Market-to-Reach-126.0-Billion-in-Annual-Worldwide-Revenue-by-2025-According-to-Tractica (archived at https://perma.cc/MH2N-VN5D)

09

Flourish or self-destruct?

The case for responsible AI

> In this final chapter, we learn that AI poses critical existential issues that we cannot simply stumble into. We explore AI's role in addressing inequality but also its potential to fuel bias, democratize access to the best education money can buy and serve all of humanity, unconstrained by bigotry and prejudice. We come to appreciate that our business landscape, indeed our society at large, is entering a new phase of evolution, and that it is incumbent upon us all, but in particular on global leaders, to deepen our understanding of AI and the related ethical and macro issues, to ensure we reflect on the world we choose to create that aligns with our values and our very *raison d'être*.

A fork in the road

AI is the defining technology of our times and we have a choice. The power is in our hands, and the responsibility is a heavy one. As the global leaders at the Davos 2021 virtual summit debated, the COVID-19 pandemic demonstrated that no institution or individual alone can address the economic, environmental, social and technological challenges of our complex, interdependent world.

As the Future of Life Institute (FLI) states, technology is giving life the potential to flourish like never before, or to self-destruct. This non-profit organization aims to tip the balance toward 'flourish' through high-impact projects and education, focusing on existential risk, nuclear weapons, AI, biotech and climate. Its president, Max Tegmark, summed up these challenges in the following reflections published in the FLI's January 2021 newsletter (Gilgallon, 2021):

> 2020 reminded us that our civilization is vulnerable. Will we humans wisely use our ever more powerful technology to end disease and poverty and create a truly inspiring future, or will we sloppily use it to drive ever more species extinct, including our own?
>
> We're rapidly approaching this fork in the road: the past year saw the power of our technology grow rapidly, exemplified by GPT3, mu-zero, AlphaFold 2 and dancing robots, while the wisdom with which we manage our technology remained far from spectacular.
>
> On the AI policy front, FLI was the civil society co-champion for the UN Secretary General's Roadmap for Digital Cooperation: Recommendation 3C on Artificial Intelligence alongside Finland, France and two UN organizations, whose final recommendations included 'life and death decisions should not be delegated to machines'.

I am reassured by Tegmark's final statement in this address, in which he states that 'even seemingly insurmountable challenges can be overcome with creativity, willpower and sustained effort. Technology is giving life the potential to flourish like never before, so let's seize this opportunity together!'

Regulation and compliance enforcement

For several years now I have worked with the UK All-Party Parliamentary Group (APPG) on AI, where ethical AI features high on the agenda. At present, we are still very much in the assistive stages of AI, where it is being used as a tool to help with projects rather than taking the lead in the complete lifecycle of creating a product or body of work. That is not to say we will never get to that point. Innovation happens constantly, and it is happening rapidly. Work needs to be done at the government level to outline legal guidance and frameworks. This may also fall on regulatory bodies such as the Independent Press Standards Organisation (IPSO) and the Information Commissioner's Office (ICO). Once government and trade bodies finalize the rules and regulations to follow, it will set precedence and give innovators the necessary guidance to abide by to avoid disputes.

Lord Tim Clement-Jones, CBE, is Chair of the House of Lords Select Committee on Artificial Intelligence (2017–2018) and Co-Chairman of the All-Party Parliamentary Group on AI. He comments:

> Without being luddite, we need to be much more conscious about how this technology is introduced and its purpose. That's why I'm such a big fan of impact assessment. When people introduce this kind of high-level technology, they should have to go through a checklist. That's why Rolls-Royce developed the Aletheia Framework™.

If you are designing something that is about policing, criminal justice, you are looking at an allocation of housing or social security or public use of algorithms, then regulation is key. There are many organizations looking at this, from the Center for Data Ethics and Innovation to the Ada Lovelace Institute and the Institute for the Future of Work. They are all calling for some kind of regulation of such high-risk decision-making, to avoid issues as witnessed in the UK's A Level exams algorithm debacle.

Regulation – and compliance enforcement – effectively take place at a country level, although a federal state is an exception to that. But, nevertheless, the norms will be set at international level. The work that the Council of Europe is doing is impressive. It published a feasibility study that its ad hoc committee on AI approved. It is now up to the Council of Europe to review whether or not they should start the work on a new convention. The Organisation for Economic Co-operation and Development (OECD) is doing quite a lot of work on classification ahead of regulatory work, and the EU itself is producing regulations following its white paper last year.

AI in the United States, under Joe Biden

Under the US Biden administration, the work that was done in the Obama White House will probably be taken forward. The whole issue of data protection in the United States is going to loom much larger. Ideally, the G20 would sign up again to a set of norms and principles, paving the way for operationalizing the process. This is eminently achievable because there is that kind of ethical overarching framework, which everybody accepts is necessary. Joe Biden's first appointments in January 2021 are strong indicators of his plans for AI. He elevated the director of the Office of Science and Technology Policy (OSTP) to a cabinet-level position, choosing leading geneticist Eric Lander, the founding director of the MIT-Harvard Broad Institute.

MIT Technology Review is optimistic about this move: 'The OSTP advises the president on science and technology issues and guides science and technology policy and budget making across the government. This suggests that while Trump mainly viewed AI as an important geopolitical tool – investing in its development for military purposes and to compete against China – Biden will view it as a tool for scientific progress.' (Hao, 2021)

Global citizen views of AI

As AI plays a growing role in the everyday lives of people around the world, views on AI's impact on society are mixed. In September 2020, a Pew Research Center survey (Johnson & Tyson, 2020a) gathered global data on views as to whether AI is having a good or bad impact on society. In total, 50 per cent believe that the development of AI has been a good thing for society, while 33 per cent say it has been a bad thing. A median of two-thirds in the Asia-Pacific region said it was good, whereas in Europe a median of only 47 per cent said it was positive. Approximately half of those interviewed view AI positively in Brazil (53 per cent), Russia (52 per cent), the United States (47 per cent) and Canada (46 per cent).

AI won't replace great human leaders

As we learned in earlier chapters, the evidence is clear that AI can now take care of much of the 3Ds – the dirty, dull and dangerous tasks – across every industry. That is a huge benefit if it is safe for people. However, one concern shared by many of the experts interviewed is that we might attribute or demand too much of the machines. It is people who should decide where and what to deploy in the way of AI. People should make the conscious decision to actually focus on what is good.

Ben Bengougam is Senior Vice President Human Resources EMEA at Hilton. He concurs:

> I really believe in the human characteristics of great leadership that I cannot
> imagine being replicated by AI, namely authenticity, empathy, connectivity,
> showing a deep sense of caring for one's team members and so on, and so I am
> not sure where AI comes in here in terms of leadership.

The main issue for me and one which is shared by many, is that of an AI eventually controlling our world, doomsday visions of *The Matrix* and other Sci-Fi movies painting that hellish vision if AI is allowed to run loose so to speak. In the short term though, I can only see positives, and good well-governed AI evolution can only help make the world a better place.

Amplifying inequality

The increased use of AI in business is inevitable, but it is crucial that we find best practice and regulation to ensure that it emerges as a force for better, more fulfilling and fairer work. If we do not adopt a framework for good practice, there is a risk that it will actually drive increased inequality and poorer-quality jobs.

These concerns have been expressed by Naomi Climer, CBE, Co-Chair at the Institute for the Future of Work (IFOW). This is an organization that researches and develops practical ways to improve work and working lives. It does so by understanding how work is changing and how we can make the future better – in the face of technological change and economic turmoil. Climer explains:

At IFOW, we believe that the introduction of technology, when done well, is key to increasing productivity and has the potential to improve the quality of work by taking on the repetitive, 'drudge' elements. This should leave workers more capacity to bring their creativity, humanity and experience to their role. An example of this might be a doctor being released from admin and having access to Big Data analysis to have more time to spend with patients and bring their own analysis and intuition to bear where it will make the most difference.

However, there are also trends for AI in business which have accelerated due to Covid that, when badly applied, can make things worse in terms of both equality and quality of work. For example, although AI is capable of detecting and mitigating patterns of inequality with great precision, it is already clear that AI can amplify existing inequalities within an organisation and actually make them worse over time.

AI is also increasingly being used to monitor workers because so many are working from home. Although the intentions can be good, i.e. to track employee motivation or wellbeing and help them improve their productivity, it can easily end up increasing stress and reducing job satisfaction.

AI could be an incredible force for good when implemented well. It's really important to maintain human engagement with AI (the so-called human in the loop) so that we don't lose sight of the fact that the AI is only doing what it has been trained to do. The AI may not always be right in the context – making sure that people have a voice will make a big difference to the outcomes. If we get it right, people will have more fulfilling work and companies will be more productive. Discrimination will have reduced and equality increased. If we get it wrong – it will be the opposite!

Unfortunately, it is quite possible that AI will have negative consequences for those already marginalized. This is a standpoint shared by Leila Seith Hassan, Head of Data Science and Analytics at Digital UK, a marketing and advertising agency. She comments:

> At its core, AI is made up of Data + Maths + People. We still control AI. It isn't (yet) an autonomous benevolent or malevolent (depending on how you're impacted) sentient being. In the rush to get value from AI, there is a troubling tendency to ignore negative externalities that may occur. Everything from the obvious, i.e., racist bots, through to the insidious, i.e., insurance and mortgage decisions that discriminate and/or products and services that perpetuate stereotypes we as a society are trying to move away from. Unfortunately, unless proactive action is taken by businesses, this will continue – we'll keep making bad decisions that negatively impact certain groups faster, more efficiently and at scale.
>
> Historical data encapsulates all the biased decisions from the past and AI learns that this discrimination is ok at best or, worst, optimal. And those helping to build, implement or use AI in business often miss these impacts because the negative outcomes don't directly impact people like them. This can impact hiring and firing, how products and services are delivered and to whom, what offers people get (or don't). The list goes on and on and on.
>
> We may see an algorithm ceiling within businesses which could promote inequality. We are already seeing it, where within a business, a portion of employees are aided by algorithms. AI can remove laborious tasks such as timesheets, screening CVs, or it can improve operational efficiency or increase overall revenue. For the other group, AI can be the micro manager from hell – hiring and firing without human oversight, controlling when you work and how you work. This divide between employees that have control of AI vs those that are controlled by AI will only increase.

Similar views are expressed by Mark Simpson, founder and former CEO of Acoustic, comments:

> Having the right controls around AI is vital. Application of the right ethical standards when using AI has to be prioritized to a greater level over the coming years as AI advances in every industry. Imagine a world where machines are helping humans do better jobs. Through providing them with more up-to-date and insightful information to make decisions with and even going further, by recommending different decisions for different scenarios and outcomes. For those that are fans of Ironman, imagine having a 'Jarvis' that sits alongside you in the role you are doing today. By 2030 this will be happening.
>
> The skills gap is real. Eventually this will close but it will be years if not decades before it does. More people need to have an understanding of AI, both through technical roles as well as business and managerial roles. Having educators understand how AI is developing and used in businesses is key to a more rapid closure of the gap.

Lack of oversight and measurement

In Chapter 2, we learned about the many AI tools on offer, one being offered by Brandwatch, a world-leading digital consumer intelligence company, which allows users to analyse and utilize conversations from across the web and social media.

We hear now from its Principal Data Scientist, Paul Siegel:

> There are many troubling aspects to AI's use in business. One is ethics, and namely, insufficient measurement. The standard benchmarks in AI research are datasets which help measure accuracy, and not much else. This means that standard tools carry a lot of bias e.g. language models that associate 'doctor' with 'male' and 'Islam' with negative sentiment, and it's difficult for even a well-intentioned practitioner to be aware of them.
>
> Furthermore, there aren't many accepted oversight boards or consultants that can credibly audit models to certify their accuracy or error profiles, and consequently misleading and distorted performance claims are rampant and arguably the norm.
>
> Another important factor is business value, and by that I mean accountability. I refer to a user experience, not a technology. The defining characteristic of that user experience is that the user is provided with the

opportunity to delegate a task that they are responsible for to a computer program. Delegating responsibility well involves setting explicit quality expectations up front and regularly reviewing performance. Instead, people often treat AI tools as unquestioned authority figures, leading to negative results for which nobody feels accountable.

The next criteria to consider is fitness for purpose. Tools are often misappropriated to uses for which they are not designed and tested. An example of this are regression models inappropriately applied to predicting student or teacher performance, or sentiment models inappropriately applied to content optimization.

New Leaf Technology Solutions is a software solutions company focused on helping organizations to grapple with such issues and to achieve their objectives. Simon Chambers, Managing Director and Co-Founder, explains:

> It is already a given that to gain a competitive advantage in today's world businesses need to leverage data as a 'strategic asset'. However, what is also required is to understand data as an 'ethical and legal asset' and its associated complications. It is not that companies don't want to address this issue, but how do they accomplish this effectively at a strategic and indeed tactical level. I would like to see more collaboration between government and commercial entities in tackling this issue. Accountability rather than profit should be the key driver here.

Avoid limiting AI acceleration

These major ethical issues are not unique to the UK. They are topics that businesspeople, academics and governments are grappling with worldwide. Based in Ireland, Kieran Gilmurray is a Global Intelligent Automation Leader. He explains:

> We know the rules, we see the negatives, e.g. AI bias, but these challenges, whilst not underplaying them or their impact, are all part of the learning journey and are all being acted upon. My worry is a lack of progress so society does not benefit from the impact of AI. For example, the press continually promote horror stories of AI at its worst (bias, intrusion, robots and AI killing jobs etc.). This click-bait negative-only view will continue to limit the acceleration of AI into places it can and should help, e.g. data security concerns and police forces' ability to protect; systems that monitor employees' behaviours and emotions that can help protect the physical and mental well-being of employees; automation to remove mental and physical strain that has a serious impact on health and lives, etc.

Responsible citizenship: a view from the United Arab Emirates

We turn our attention further afield now, to other parts of the world, starting with the United Arab Emirates. Based in Dubai, we spoke to Clement Chan – Deloitte Leader in Digital Transformation. He comments:

> AI advancement raises ethical, economic, societal, and financial considerations. I am not sure hard regulation on AI is necessarily the answer but there needs to be some form of guardrails. To date, there have been numerous soft guidelines but very soon I expect to see harder measures coming out, perhaps from nations outside the leading AI superpowers.

North America's approach to AI issues

North America is a leading player in AI, so we now turn to the United States and Canada, beginning with Lynne Marlor, who is founder of Transformational Strategies, LLC, based in New York:

> There are troubling issues for me in AI as it has the ability to continue to promote social and economic disparities. I would like businesses to use AI for conscious capitalism, and embody the true spirit of diversity and inclusion. I dislike both the ability to 'monitor' the masses for good or evil and that the augmented reality space has the ability to recreate what is in front of us, creating a new reality which can be used for good or bad. I want to make sure that AI is used to teach skill sets like resiliency and coping mechanisms as part of an AI strategy.
>
> Progress will start with two pillars: education partnered with corporations who fund the educational initiatives. Educators working side-by-side with corporations need to understand the transformative skills needed, and the appropriate and effective learning curriculums, capacity and measurement tools that will create real impact for all citizens. The process should start small, think big and test often to verify the results for all populations. I also believe that using corporations and their staff as mentors for underrepresented populations will help to teach the skills that matter so that corporations and citizens are prepared for a competitive global economy.
>
> My expectation is that the business landscape will be very different in 2030 having undergone major structural changes. The Covid virus has taught us that we can work remotely, travel less globally, be more indebted and more digital. I expect that the result will be less business travel, multiple corporate sites/

locations becoming obsolete, and corporate hierarchies will be transformed into streamlined organizations that create 'conscious capitalism'. AI will be central to reducing replication of processes and functions for settlement of transactions, consumer behavior, cost reduction and greater transparency. Businesses will need to be focused on the consumer, making it easier for them to transact, buy goods and services, relocate or move (think transportation systems and the connected car), learn and create the lifestyle they want to live. I believe that AI can, if used appropriately, solve large economic and social issues like education, transportation, financial inclusion and health.

No sleepwalking allowed

Based in Washington DC, Christopher Schroeder is the Co-Founder of Next Billion Ventures and Network Partner Village Global. He explains:

There are always scenarios with any new tech, compounded in AI by the speed and rapid multiplier ramifications of it. It will be disruptive positively and surprisingly across our lives and businesses and places globally. Step one is to ask some very basic questions about what our goals and concerns are and not sleepwalk into circumstances we may not actually want. This is a rich and complex series of issues that vary geographically, by industry, by society. I do believe it begins with an open discussion on what we want from AI and what skills specifically are missing and matter. We need to keep in mind that 'skills' are not necessarily the same thing as a given 'job.' Would you want to hire a woman who is great at math, unbelievably conscientious and service-oriented, totally honest, and detailed oriented? I would. If you think of that as a job that is a bank teller – and I'm not sure if that will be a growth opportunity going forward. But the skills are relevant and we should focus on the specifics of that.

There are so many things that will be different and driven in part by tech, but for me the biggest is not about the tech itself but rather the global access to it. 60, 70, 80 per cent of humanity today has access to smart devices – super computers – in their pockets and is creating a whole unleashing anywhere because talent is everywhere. The world has choices, they want products and services but on their terms. A new globalism of business will clearly reshape the global economic scene by 2030. All of these enterprises are building unique data sets, understanding that the rise of billions of new people integrating in the economy is the basis and most competitive advantage in any AI strategy.

Data security: a view from Canada

Voicing the concerns shared in Canada, we hear now from Frank Feather, CEO of AI-Future Inc. and author of *THINK FUTURE: Trends in Quantum AI*:

> The major concern about AI is that of ethics, privacy, and social responsibility to all stakeholders in terms of data security. All valuable customer relationships are based on trust and reliability. Companies must ensure a high standard of AI cybersecurity and, as needed, governments should regulate this entire aspect. It comes down to human ethics. AI is a technology created by humans. It must have the highest human ethics.
>
> We are well into the digital era, and this is only going to become more intense in terms of competition. AI itself will become more advanced, indeed, likely much more advanced than human intelligence by 2025 or so, including emotive abilities. At the same time, 5G communications, followed by 6G, will speed up everything dramatically across the fast-expanding Internet of Things (IoT).

Concerning knowledge gaps

Emphasis shifts now to Australia, where we hear from Karen Khaw, senior consultant of The Tantalus Group, a global management consultancy, and Founder of V-Engage:

> The main issue that troubles me with regards to AI is that AI is still perceived as a future solution or topic yet most are already reliant on AI on a daily basis, from Alexa helping to operate our homes and access information through to spam email filters and fraud protection which leads to the bank notifying you about suspicious usage of your credit card.
>
> The lack of AI knowledge generally is unsettling given the significantly greater interest in understanding social media, even though AI is the operating system behind most social media channels. Governance and ethics would be the other areas of concern for me. It is important to get these areas to a reasonable benchmark to protect all parties, especially when it comes to driverless cars and robo-health helpers. Humans need to be at the forefront of devising the best governance and ethics framework that has the flexibility to adapt in this ever-changing environment.

Transition from lab to real world

China is the recognized world leader in AI. It is therefore crucial to hear the views of leading organizations such as Huawei. Haitham Ammar is Reinforcement Learning Team Leader at Huawei Research and Development, based in the UK. He shares similar concerns to those voiced elsewhere:

> There are multiple issues that bother me when it comes to AI's impact. Most of these issues, however, are not related to what AI can do but rather to what AI can NOT do. Today, AI is at a transition stage from labs to real-world. The problem is that such transitions typically happen after transforming a field from a scientific endeavour to an engineering discipline in which regulations, testing, and certifications are important. Let me ask a question here, would you ever ride a BMW if you didn't trust in the certification, tests, and standardisations made in the field of electrical mechanical engineering. I wouldn't. So why should AI be different? Why is it acceptable for an AI to put out there in the real-world without standardisation?
>
> In fact, major failures of AI (including bias, racism, unexplainable black-box models and others) can mostly be traced back to a reason that AI is a new technology for which we have not exhausted the possible ethical scenarios that enable standards. My fear is that these questions are slacking behind the development of AI and should rather be mainstream. For that reason, Huawei has invested in safety and standardisation both internally and externally, where we are actively participating in an effort across various corporations to define, implement, and enable such standards.
>
> The other important aspect is the energy spent on training deep-learning models. It is true that deep learning can do great things, yet this arrives at great expense in energy. New research has revealed that one can acquire comparable performance using simpler models as opposed to large networks. Unfortunately, such results have not been the main focus of the AI community. I believe more attention is in order when it comes to remedying these issues.
>
> Personally, I have a rather conservative view on business development using AI and machine learning. I do believe a lot of mundane tasks will be automated in the coming decade, however I see a more AI–human collaborative work environment; more like an intelligent operating system that improves our productivity and progress. I also believe a shift towards more environmental solutions tackling emerging problems will become mainstream.

The implications of AI in education

For the past 20 years or more, technology has been enhancing classrooms and expanding the frontiers of education. The COVID-19 pandemic accelerated this movement. While on the one hand it has exposed gaps that must be addressed if everyone is to benefit equally from online learning solutions – namely, access to a reliable internet connection and appropriate hardware – it also opened our eyes to the advantages of wide-scale personalized and adaptive instruction.

A leading player in the AI education space is Soffos.ai. We hear once again from Nikolas Kairinos, Founder and CEO:

> 2020 was a defining moment for AI in the private sector. It acted as a catalyst for AI adoption as businesses across all sectors considered how new and emerging technologies could enable continuity, lower costs, and help them better serve their clients and customers. The seeds have been sown, and I believe that the uptake of AI solutions will only increase as firms realize the benefits on offer. More specifically, as we shift towards an increasingly digital future, AI will become the engine that powers efficient business operations. It will help business leaders reach better decisions through data-driven insights; simplify cumbersome operations; and, most importantly, create a better employee and customer experience.

> To bridge the skills gap, companies would do well to focus on student education as part of their business strategy. Not only would this equip students with the knowledge they need to succeed in the workplace of the future, but it will also help strengthen a business' talent pipeline. As part of this strategy, businesses might think about mobilizing employees to mentor students; offer work-based learning opportunities via apprenticeship programs; or else partner with an educational institution to provide a multifaceted package of support through grants, facilities, and mentorship schemes.

These topics are explored in much more depth in Chapter 7.

Avoiding a digital divide

The role of government in education is clearly a crucial one. In December 2020 a report called 'No Room for Complacency' was published as a follow-up report from the House of Lords' 'AI in the UK: Ready, Willing, and Able?'. It states that there is not nearly enough being done in this field in terms of reskilling and identifying what skills are going to be needed in the future, and it has to be a concerted national strategy.

We turn once again to Lord Tim Clement-Jones, Chair of the House of Lords Select Committee on Artificial Intelligence (2017–2018) and Co-Chairman of the All-Party Parliamentary Group on Artificial Intelligence:

> It's really important that we have that level of digital literacy amongst young people, let alone older folks. But it is really crucial in younger people if they are going to be able to harness technology, AI particularly, in the work they do when they leave school or university. So there's a lot to be done there, and I really don't feel that the government has really woken up and addressed it fully yet.
>
> There's a lot of frustration amongst people who are experts in the AI field about the fact that our current education system really is not particularly fit for purpose. The whole application of some of this new technology into our state system is really important. Otherwise, we will see a huge digital divide between independent schools and state schools.

These are views expressed by others in education across many different geographies. Nick Burnett is Managing Director (Asia Pacific) at Team Teach Asia Pacific. The company was set up to support organizations in their commitment to reducing and eliminating restrictive practices, as outlined in the National Framework for Reducing and Eliminating the Use of Restrictive Practices in the Disability Sector. Team Teach APAC provides training in line with the state-specific Student Behaviour procedures, and which expressly aligns with the United Nations Convention on the Right of the Child, which states that the welfare of the child shall be the paramount consideration. Nick Burnett comments:

> Whilst there are many organisations that have embraced AI within their operations, the vast majority are only starting to wake up to the significant opportunities AI offers across all operating areas. Many have the chatbot now, but this is only scratching the surface, and for me it's about augmenting the humans as opposed to replacing humans. The ethics debate is a crucial one for me and engaging with a wide range of stakeholders – probably needs an AI version of Asimov's law of robotics. I also believe there needs to be a significant education piece for children and many adults about what AI can and can't do – generally perceived as a terminator future which is not helpful.

Purpose

As outlined at the start of the chapter, AI challenges us to address existential questions. From a business perspective, we should take the opportunity to consider why we are in business; what is our purpose. On this crucial issue, we hear from Nikolas Kairinos, founder and CEO, Soffos.ai:

> Simon Sinek's Golden Circle theory offers an important insight into what makes an organization inspirational – namely, the ability to illustrate its purpose, and encourage people to buy into the vision. As he explains: all businesses know what they do; some know how they do it; but very few know why they do what they do.
>
> It's important to understand this distinction, as it distinguishes the innovators from the laggards. Focusing on purpose will set a business apart from the competition: after all, it is much easier to attract talent and capital if companies are solving an important problem. Indeed, we're seeing more and more VCs today focusing on impact businesses.
>
> But money isn't enough to attract and motivate employees; they will deliver better results if their 'why' is aligned with the company's 'why'. More often than not, the types of 'why' that stir passions and lead to superlative results are those that make the world a better place.
>
> Ultimately, a leading business should be focused more on why it exists, rather than the by-products of that mission. Communication is key here, to ensure that all stakeholders understand and are motivated by the overarching goal.

A four-day working week

The need to reconnect to the purpose of the organization is a view shared by Clement Chan, PwC Leader in Digital Transformation, Responsible AI and Intelligent Automation. He explains:

> We need to first revisit the appetite and culture of the organization. Recent events should be a great reset in more ways than just financial and distribution of wealth. We must use the opportunity to re-connect the purpose of the organization, its relationship with the employees, society and how technology should be used to serve that purpose. In some sectors, innovation and disruption are encouraged with a clear 'why', while others may prefer a more evolutionary approach to change. Regardless of the appetite, now is the time to reset the purpose.

The last five years have seen some drastic changes and disruption to society and shareholder value. I believe we will see three key movements in the business landscape:

1 More agile. We will see more resilient and adaptable business models. Remote working will be a norm and the real estate strategy will be redefined.

2 More purposeful. We will see companies being more upfront and diverse in their mission, whether this be diversity and inclusion, green, equality, local community etc. The role of technology and people will also be redefined and perhaps we might see a four-day working week or more flexible working being a norm.

3 More platform-based. We will see a growth of small and medium-sized companies leveraging platforms to access customers. These platforms provide services such as analytics, pricing suggestions, customer agents etc. that would otherwise not be available to the companies.

Digital Darwinism in the 2020s

Digital Darwinism is a term applied to the concept of survival of the fittest in times of business disruption. It reminds us of the need to adopt strategies for succeeding in a world of disruption before it's too late. It is therefore very pertinent in the age of AI, as Kieran Gilmurray, Global Intelligent Automation Leader, explains:

> Whilst no one can be one hundred per cent sure of the exact impact of AI in the coming years, it is reasonable to say that AI will significantly affect organisations that want to succeed in a post-pandemic digital age. We will see Digital Darwinism unfolding in front of our eyes. Those organisations that invest in AI, digital and tech will survive and thrive; those that don't will die. But AI will be one tool that firms spend money on. There will be a massive increase in use cases that will drive real change for those willing to invest and use AI.
>
> If firms don't focus on their why, i.e. solving their tangible business problems, then they won't be there; as they won't make money and won't survive. Firms no longer have the time, money or luxury to have vanity AI projects or any digital projects. Companies have learned hard lessons over the past 10 plus years. Now

that the rules are understood, firms have found that focusing on the tech does not work; it does not solve business problems. Only by focusing on business outcomes (the why), will firms succeed.

Hybrid workforce

Karen Khaw is a senior consultant of The Tantalus Group, a global management consultancy, and Founder of V-Engage Australia. She comments:

> It is worth being reminded that AI is very good at tasks that are very difficult for humans to undertake such as repetitive work but relatively weak at doing tasks that are usually very easy for humans such as feeling or empathising.
>
> By 2030, the business world will be fully automated while services/products will be tailored to suit with VMAR being the main means of communications. While 2020 has seen the emergence of a hybrid workforce where employees work between home and office, 2030 will mean a hybrid workforce where humans will need to work with robots or AI, or even may report to one.
>
> The business landscape will be a lot more competitive given by then, and many would have most of their daily chores automated including driverless cars and virtual immersive attendance at the office event. Business will focus on fewer but more significant opportunities. VMAR technologies are mostly where everyone meets – virtually but with a lot more precision as AI becomes more advanced and VMAR hardware becomes more sophisticated.

Next gen AI: unsupervised learning

While supervised learning has driven remarkable progress in AI over the past 10 or more years, from autonomous cars to virtual agents, it has serious limitations. Manually labelling millions of data points is expensive. Furthermore, it has been a major bottleneck for real AI progress. This is set to change.

Yann André LeCun is a French computer scientist working primarily in the fields of machine learning (ML), computer vision, mobile robotics and computational neuroscience. He is Vice President, Chief AI Scientist at Facebook. LeCun predicts a new frontier for AI: 'The next AI revolution will not be supervised.' (Toews, 2020)

Unsupervised learning is where the system learns about some parts of the world based on other parts of the world. No labels are given to the learning algorithm, leaving it on its own to find structure in its input. Unsupervised learning can be a goal in itself (discovering hidden patterns in data) or a means towards an end (feature learning). Quantum computing made significant inroads in 2020, and has the potential to supercharge AI applications. For example, it could be used to run a generative ML model through a larger dataset than a classical computer can process, thus making the model more accurate and useful in real-world settings. Advanced technologies such as deep learning algorithms are also playing an increasingly critical role in the development of quantum computing research.

Misuse of algorithms

Deciding which film to watch, or which food to order online, is commonplace for many of us worldwide. But what happens if an algorithm (a set of computer instructions) is changing what we see and manipulating the choices we make in ways we aren't aware of and do not comprehend? In 2019, the Competition and Markets Authority (the UK's competition and consumer authority) carried out an investigation into hotel booking sites. It found that some sites ranked search results based on the amount of commission hotels paid to the site. These commissions were not disclosed to customers. Following the investigation, the companies involved made commitments to be transparent in the future

In a similar vein, the Financial Conduct Authority (FCA) – the UK's financial regulatory body – identified that some home and motor insurance firms were using opaque pricing techniques to identify which customers were most likely to renew with them. They increased prices to these customers at renewal each year, meaning some were paying very high prices.

The next case we've investigated illustrates indirect discrimination through algorithms and that algorithms can be subject to judicial review. We often consider algorithms to be objectively neutral, but the fact is, they do have the potential to involve discrimination.

Landmark ruling: Deliveroo algorithm
judged to be discriminatory

A turning point occurred in January 2021, when a court in Italy ruled that an algorithm deployed by food delivery app Deliveroo to rank riders' reliability and decide on their shifts was discriminatory. The riders' case was backed by CGIL, Italy's largest trade union.

As Vice (Geiger, 2021) reports:

> While machine-learning algorithms are central to Deliveroo's entire business model, the particular algorithm examined by the court allegedly was used to determine the 'reliability' of a rider. According to the ordinance, if a rider failed to cancel a shift pre-booked through the app at least 24 hours before its start, their 'reliability index' would be negatively affected. Since riders deemed more reliable by the algorithm were first to be offered shifts in busier timeblocks, this effectively meant that riders who can't make their shifts – even if it's because of a serious emergency or illness – would have fewer job opportunities in the future.
>
> The case is also indicative of an increased willingness on behalf of regulators, the judicial system, labor unions, and workers across the continent to tackle blackbox algorithms, and an increased awareness of how such algorithms can potentially be abused to circumvent traditional labor protections. In July 2020, for example, four UK drivers backed by the App Drivers and Couriers Union sued Uber to gain access to similar algorithms used by Uber. And, three months later, another group of Uber drivers filed a lawsuit against the company for allegedly being fired by an automated algorithm used by the platform without being given an opportunity to appeal.

AI might widen the gap between rich and poor

The Deliveroo case is also an example of how, if used unfairly, AI could fuel inequality. According to the World Economic Forum (WEF), AI, ML robotics, Big Data, and networks can revolutionize production processes. However, they could also have a major impact on developing economies. International Monetary Fund (IMF) research finds new technology risks widening the gap between rich and poor countries by shifting more investment to advanced economies where automation is already established. In developing countries, this could mean AI replaces rather than complements growing labour forces. The opportunities and potential sources of growth that, for example, the United States and China enjoyed during their early stages of economic development are remarkably different from what Cambodia and Tanzania are facing in today's world.

Explainability and trust

It will become increasingly important to understand why AI makes the decisions it makes. Explainable AI (XAI) refers to methods of applying AI in such a way that the results of the solution can be understood by humans. This is in stark contrast to the 'black box' often found in ML where users cannot understand why AI reached a certain decision.

XAI is important even in cases and industries where there are no legal rights or regulatory requirements. Above all, it can improve customer experience by enabling users to trust that the AI is making good decisions. Trust is crucial because many of us are reluctant to cede power to automatic systems we cannot fully comprehend. It's essential for example in the manufacturing sector for AI to be both accurate and able to 'explain' why products were classified as 'defective', in order for the human operators to build their own confidence in the system.

AI as a force for good

Turning the tables now, we look at how AI could actually be a huge force for good.

In December 2020, leading organizations across the United States' financial services, technology and academic industries announced the formation of a new National Council for Artificial Intelligence (NCAI):

> 'The goal of the newly created NCAI is to establish a pragmatic coalition with public–private partnerships in the financial services sector to identify and address significant societal and industry barriers,' said Gretchen O'Hara, Vice President of AI and Sustainability Strategy, Microsoft US in a company press release. 'I am excited about the launch of our distinguished board, and the continued momentum to work with the members of this coalition to better serve the needs of our stakeholders and communities through AI innovation.'
>
> (Microsoft, 2020)

The NCAI council intends to apply AI to resolve significant challenges in business, such as:

- general economic and industrial challenges – including research transfer, industry standards and funding instruments;
- digital skills and employability – including organizational and cultural challenges and labour policies;
- data privacy – including data access and shared innovation.

Ed Fandrey, Vice President of Financial Services, Microsoft US, comments: 'The NCAI coalition brings partners together across the industry to ensure AI and the technologies underpinning it are transparent and safe for not only financial services customers but throughout the regulated industry.' (Microsoft, 2020)

The battle for AI dominance

In Chapter 1 we explored how countries across the globe are already exploiting AI. In this chapter, we have learned that AI affords us a huge burden of responsibility but also a tremendous opportunity.

China has deep pockets when it comes to investment in AI. It is arguably the global pacesetter in the development and implementation of AI technologies, an advantage that has huge political implications. 'Whoever leads in artificial intelligence in 2030 will rule the world till 2100,' declared a recent policy briefing from the Brookings Institution (Gill, 2020).

In 2015, China announced its $1.68 trillion Made in China 2025 plan, focused on AI. Its goal is to transform the Chinese economy and dominate global manufacturing by 2030. China lacks the entrepreneurial nimbleness found in the US; however, its investment into digital dominance is significant. Over the past 20 years, China has grown into a dominant economic power. But the litmus test will be over the next decade, as we witness whether or not it will evolve into a superpower.

Commenting on the future of the profession and her fear of AI platform-controlled mediatization, Professor Dr Sc. Marina G. Shilina of the Plekhanov Russian University of Economics, said:

Data-colonialism is having a major impact on the world of comms and the economy at large. An obvious example is Twitter banning President Trump. The social media platform for the first time acted not just as an economic, but as a political actor. Platforms worldwide must resist this because PR and freedom of speech is indispensable.

Our body of personal data has become a source of added value. Total mediatization is putting our data metaphorically as the lifeblood of the economy. But this new AI platform-controlled mediatization is as dangerous as any totalitarian regime. Total mediatization will signal the end of freedom in the profession. We must therefore protect our clients, ourselves, and loved ones. Are we ready to develop a global, national, corporate, personal survival algorithm as a strategic one for PR?

Rana Gujral, CEO at Behavioral Signals, comments:

The primary concerns are around AI misuse and building something that is unethical or biased. Like all powerful tools, AI has the potential for misuse. AI can be a powerful capability, in the hands of those that know how to utilize it, and can certainly be used by bad actors to harm or exploit others. But the basic principle of AI is to automate processes that humans already do, such as looking through thousands of MRI images to find cancer. Humans can do that, but AI can do it much faster and that is useful in disease discovery. While regulations lag invention, laws eventually do catch up. All of us have a responsibility to not only make reasonable decisions that benefit all of humanity, but also to regulate those that do not respect our common values. One starts that journey by looking inwards at our business principles. You begin with respecting security, user privacy, and building products that are useful to enterprises and society.

The way the technology landscape is exploding, it's hard to predict the future. A lot can change in a decade. Nine years ago, SpaceX and the potential of civilian space travel was science fiction. I believe Quantum computing will play a significant role, especially if it becomes cost-effective. The computation potential will change machines as we know them. AI solutions will not just be a lot more sophisticated but also very prevalent. Smartphones will automate a majority of our daily tasks, home appliances will truly be smart, healthcare entirely automated, and so on. This technology landscape and research outcomes will create new opportunities for businesses. Companies that successfully adapt, utilize these technologies, will grow fast and accelerate.

Respecting human rights

Toju Duke is Responsible AI Program Manager at Google, based in Ireland. She comments:

> All ethical issues should be considered while building AI systems. It's important that human rights are respected, and existing societal issues are not further baked into technologies. Adopting an Ethical AI framework while developing AI systems is highly recommended where these systems should not cause harm or risk to any member of society; they should not reinforce or create unfair bias towards anyone including people from underrepresented and minority groups and are favourable and fair to all members of society. Ensuring people's data are safe and secure against adversarial attacks, while privacy is protected is also of paramount importance. Also adhering to explainability and transparency guidelines where the purpose of the AI systems, dimensions, specifications and methods used are available for scrutiny and public understanding. It's the responsibility of Research scientists, conference organisers, policymakers, organisations and businesses to ensure the widespread adoption of AI is done in an ethical and responsible manner.

Looking ahead to 2030

No one can accurately predict the future, as the global pandemic painfully reminded us. But we now have enough data sourced from around the world to plan for a future where AI plays a significant role in our societies and our business lives. AI is improving all the time. In the summer of 2020, San Francisco-based AI research laboratory OpenAI released Generative Pre-trained Transformer 3 (GPT-3) – the most powerful language model ever built. This language model uses deep learning to produce human-like text. Before its release, the largest language model was Microsoft's Turing NLG, with a capacity of 17 billion parameters or less than a tenth of GPT-3.

GPT-3 raises NLP to new heights, in its ability to compose beautiful poetry, write thoughtful business memos and even articles about itself. The quality of the text it can generate is so high that it is difficult to distinguish it from text created by humans.

Many AI researchers believe that GPT-3 could presage a new era in computer vision. While leading AI companies such as Google and Facebook have begun to put Transformer-based models into production, most organizations remain in the early stages of productizing and commercializing this technology. OpenAI has announced plans to make GPT-3 commercially accessible via API, which could seed an entire ecosystem of start-ups building applications on top of it.

For the final interview in this chapter, we turn to Dr Zoë Webster who works for BT Group as Artificial Intelligence Director, Group Data and AI Solutions. She explains:

> I think we will see more robots around and hopefully assisting us in really helpful ways and helping people have richer, fuller lives where things are difficult at the moment. . I think 'AI' will probably phase out as a term and we'll see it as just part of IT, and our view of IT just hopefully will become a bit more well-rounded.
>
> I'm hoping that by 2030, there will be much more circularity in supply chains and businesses, and AI will have a role to play in helping to manage and optimise all that. AI will also be helping us to work out where the latest opportunities are, where new materials could be developed for new functions or new forms of electronics, new drugs, new vaccines, for example. That will be possible much more quickly, and we should be able to be so much more responsive to customer needs. I think it will be a very complex space, but lots of agility, lots of flexibility, and hopefully much greater energy and resource efficiency as well.
>
> I'm optimistic but I think that does depend on having guardrails in place. There is a lot to contemplate regarding AI and data governance on a global political scale. I believe AI will be behind the scenes. It will enable new things to happen much more quickly. Hopefully it will allow us to meet our energy needs, our health needs, our lifestyle needs much more effectively. But that does rely on everyone being involved in this, not just a few people of a certain type of characteristic.
>
> A lot of the investments go into quite a small set of AI approaches. That's going to hinder us from making progress on general AI as quickly as we would like. In 15–20 years, we'll have something that can do multiple tasks and switch between them in a way that most people can. I don't think it's going to be fully rounded. I think it's going to be something that can perhaps do a mix between helping to schedule your diary and help with writing your thesis. I think something that can do two or three tasks and switch between them, maybe taking some learning between them. But I think it is obviously going to be longer to have something that takes full account of what people can do.

It is inevitable that AI will gradually replace jobs across all industry sectors. We need to decide how to deal with this effectively to ensure the best possible outcome for our businesses, workforce, and society at large.

PRACTICAL TAKEAWAYS CHECKLIST: TOP 10 TIPS

1 The pandemic demonstrated that no institution or individual alone can address the economic, environmental, social and technological challenges of our complex, interdependent world.

2 Technology is giving life the potential to flourish like never before, or to self-destruct.

3 The evidence is clear that AI can now take care of some of the dirty, dull and dangerous tasks, across every industry. That is a huge benefit if it is safe for people.

4 The increased use of AI in business is inevitable, but it is crucial that we find best practice and regulation to ensure that it emerges as a force for better, more fulfilling and fairer work.

5 If we don't adopt a framework for good AI practice, there is a risk that it will actually drive increased inequality and poorer-quality jobs.

6 It's really important to maintain human engagement with AI so we do not lose sight of the fact that the AI is only doing what it has been trained to do.

7 Application of the right ethical standards when using AI has to be prioritized to a greater level over the coming years as AI advances in every industry.

8 Many AI researchers believe that GPT-3 could presage a new era in computer vision.

9 AI challenges us to address existential questions. From a business perspective, we should take the opportunity to consider why we are in business; what is our purpose.

10 Digital Darwinism is a term applied to the concept of survival of the fittest in times of business disruption. It reminds us of the need to adopt strategies for succeeding in a world of disruption before it's too late.

Bibliography

Alonso, C, Kothari, S and Rehman, S (2020) Could Artificial Intelligence Widen the Gap between Rich and Poor Nations?, *World Economic Forum*, www.weforum. org/agenda/2020/12/artificial-intelligence-widen-gap-rich-developing-nations (archived at https://perma.cc/P4FZ-NNV8)

APRU (2020) APRU Releases AI for Social Good Report in Partnership with United Nations ESCAP and Google, *AP News*, www.apnews.com/press-release/ business-wire/technology-greater-china-hong-kong-asia-china-e009e2542d5145 24a4776a5196fe5fb6 (archived at https://perma.cc/72M4-PQ57)

APRU and Keio University (2020) Artificial Intelligence for Social Good, *Association of Pacific Rim Universities Limited*, www.apru.org/wp-content/ uploads/2020/09/ layout_v3_web_page.pdf (archived at https://perma.cc/4B2J-X5EJ)

APRUSecretariat (2020) AI for Social Good Policy Insights Briefing: Governance, *YouTube.com*, www.youtube.com/watch?v=YgrnBtO4agA&list=PL72szUuwsF Yfr0c0ZuvX4eae-LUgVq4ei (archived at https://perma.cc/9A9Y-9MYV)

Baidu (2021) These Five AI Developments Will Shape 2021 and Beyond, *MIT Technology Review*, www.technologyreview.com/2021/01/14/1016122/ these-five-ai-developments-will-shape-2021-and-beyond/ (archived at https:// perma.cc/5ZDA-YYVC)

Bernhard, A (2020) The Flying Car Is Here – and it could change the world, *BBC Future*, www.bbc.com/future/article/20201111-the-flying-car-is-here-vtols-jetpacks-and-air-taxis?cid=other-eml-onp-mip-mck&hlkid=fbadff5406ca41f0aa acfd79f3139ccf&hctky=11661275&hdpid=f21f86fe-9f1b-463b-954c-f59bc08259cf (archived at https://perma.cc/V4VV-5DZV)

Cisco Solutions (n.d.) Big Data and Advanced Analytics, *Cisco*, www.cisco.com/c/ en/us/solutions/data-center-virtualization/big-data/index.html#~ecosystem (archived at https://perma.cc/3BL8-LBPY)

Competition and Markets Authority (2021) Algorithms: How they can reduce competition and harm consumers, *GOV.UK*, www.gov.uk/government/ publications/algorithms-how-they-can-reduce-competition-and- harm-consumers/algorithms-how-they-can-reduce-competition-and-harm-consumers (archived at https://perma.cc/M5PT-2AXJ)

Dell Technologies (n.d.) Dell EMC HPC and AI Centers of Excellence, *Delltechnologies.com*, www.delltechnologies.com/en-us/solutions/high-performance-computing/hpc-ai-centers-of-excellence.htm (archived at https:// perma.cc/PG43-X3XH)

designboom (2020) Top 10 Robotic and Artificial Intelligence Stories of 2020, *designboom*, www.designboom.com/technology/top-10-robotic-artificial-intelligence-2020-12-22-2020/ (archived at https://perma.cc/SVG5-VPAJ)

Devanesan, J (2020) Samsung Looks to 6G and Beyond with Blockchain and AI,

Tech Wire Asia, www.techwireasia.com/2020/09/samsung-looks-to-6g-and-beyond-with-blockchain-and-ai/ (archived at https://perma.cc/RX7Y-USD3)

Durmus, M and AISOMA (2021) Künstliche Intelligenz & Big Data Analytics, *AISOMA – Herstellerneutrale KI-Beratung*, www.aisoma.de/wp-content/uploads/2021/01/A-collection-of-recommendable-papers-2020.pdf (archived at https://perma.cc/42ZK-6E7N)

European Commission (n.d.) European Data Strategy: Making the EU a role model for a society empowered by data, *European Commission*, www.ec.europa.eu/info/strategy/priorities-2019-2024/europe-fit-digital-age/european-data-strategy_en?utm_medium=email&_hsmi=103352858&_hsenc=p2ANqtz--LpobKKyLxpF1NdrWoImXEVZkbO2fyhGy9JySRwEIv3dddMlRZQlAwo06PRG9RqPt8-ndGTQkj0JGpW0IfAd0cH9PjcA&utm_content=103352858&utm_source=hs_email (archived at https://perma.cc/QE9Y-UCHC)

Future of Life Institute (n.d.) Artificial Intelligence Archive, *Future of Life Institute*, www.futureoflife.org/ai-archive/ (archived at https://perma.cc/PW85-VZVC)

Geiger, G (2021) Court Rules Deliveroo Used 'Discriminatory' Algorithm, *VICE*, www.vice-com.cdn.ampproject.org/c/s/www.vice.com/amp/en/article/7k9e4e/court-rules-deliveroo-used-discriminatory-algorithm (archived at https://perma.cc/8DRN-SR4V)

Gilgallon, G (2021) FLI January 2021 Newsletter, *Future of Life Institute*, www.futureoflife.org/2021/01/25/fli-january-2021-newsletter/ (archived at https://perma.cc/NZP9-63U8)

Gill, I (2020) Whoever Leads in Artificial Intelligence in 2030 Will Rule the World until 2100. *Brookings*, www.brookings.edu/blog/future-development/2020/01/17/whoever-leads-in-artificial-intelligence-in-2030-will-rule-the-world-until-2100/ (archived at https://perma.cc/X573-C373)

Gordon, C (2020) AI Is Reengineering All Aspects of Our Human Experience: What are the implications?, *Forbes*, www.forbes.com/sites/cindygordon/2021/12/31/ai-is-reengineering-all-aspects-of-our-human-experience-what-are-the-implications/?sh=47dda01c7a0d (archived at https://perma.cc/GG94-88Z2)

GOV.UK (n.d.) Office for Artificial Intelligence, www.gov.uk/government/organisations/office-for-artificial-intelligence (archived at https://perma.cc/45TN-PK86)

Graham, L, Gilbert, A, Simons, J and Thomas, A (2020) Artificial Intelligence in Hiring: Assessing impacts on equality, *Institute for the Future of Work*, www.ifow.webflow.io/publications/artificial-intelligence-in-hiring-assessing-impacts-on-equality (archived at https://perma.cc/986R-KH9E)

Hao, K (2021) Five Ways to Make AI a Greater Force for Good in 2021, *MIT Technology Review*, www.technologyreview-com.cdn.ampproject.org/c/s/www.technologyreview.com/2021/01/08/1015907/ai-force-for-good-in-2021/amp/ (archived at https://perma.cc/2AZL-FTLM)

Hao, K (2021) The Biden Administration's AI Plans: What we might expect, *MIT Technology Review*, www.technologyreview-com.cdn.ampproject.org/c/s/www.technologyreview.com/2021/01/22/1016652/biden-administration-ai-plans-what-to-expect/amp/ (archived at https://perma.cc/P3AT-2S8N)

Huawei (2020) Huawei's Commitment to Human Rights 2020, *Huawei*, www.huawei.com/uk/declarations/huawei%20human%20rights%20commitment (archived at https://perma.cc/MZN9-CBRB)

Johnson, C and Tyson, A (2020a) People globally offer mixed views of the impact of artificial intelligence, job automation on society, *Pew Research Center*, www.pewresearch.org/fact-tank/2020/12/15/people-globally-offer-mixed-views-of-the-impact-of-artificial-intelligence-job-automation-on-society/ (archived at https://perma.cc/2WW7-HUDX)

Johnson, C and Tyson, A (2020b) Here's How Opinions on the Impact of Artificial Intelligence Differ around the World. World Economic Forum, www.weforum.org/agenda/2020/12/mixed-views-of-the-impact-of-artificial-intelligence/ (archived at https://perma.cc/WTW2-W2U6)

Johnson, K (2021) Incoming White House Science and Technology Leader on AI, Diversity, and Society, *VentureBeat*, www.venturebeat-com.cdn.ampproject.org/c/s/venturebeat.com/2021/01/16/incoming-white-house-science-and-technology-leader-on-ai-diversity-and-society/amp/ (archived at https://perma.cc/J52F-DAS9)

Microsoft (2020) Industry Leaders in Tech, Education and Financial Services Join Together in New National Council to Activate AI for the Greater Good, *Microsoft News*, www.news.microsoft.com/2020/12/11/industry-leaders-in-tech-education-and-financial-services-join-together-in-new-national-council-to-activate-ai-for-the-greater-good/ (archived at https://perma.cc/Z3WG-MY5L)

Quinn, H (2021) Algorithms: Where's the harm?, *Competitionandmarkets.blog.gov.uk*, www.competitionandmarkets.blog.gov.uk/2021/01/21/algorithms-wheres-the-harm/ (archived at https://perma.cc/XZ5J-UWPX)

Rao, A (2021) AI Leaders Make the Most of the COVID-19 Crisis to Increase the Role of AI, *Medium*, www.towardsdatascience.com/ai-leaders-make-the-most-of-the-covid-19-crisis-to-increase-the-role-of-ai-ce885e39dcb9 (archived at https://perma.cc/L5LA-X7HY)

Rutherford-Johnson, L (2020) Four Predictions on How AI Will Reshape the IP Landscape, *Iam-media.com*, www.iam-media.com/market-developments/four-predictions-how-ai-will-reshape-the-ip-landscape (archived at https://perma.cc/29SV-BVHX)

Salge, C (2017) Asimov's laws won't stop robots from harming humans, so we've developed a better solution, *Scientific American*, www.scientificamerican.com/article/asimovs-laws-wont-stop-robots-from-harming-humans-so-weve-developed-a-better-solution/#:~:text=Asimov's%20 (archived at https://perma.cc/CBG6-RTEB)

Samsung Newsroom (2020) Samsung AI Forum 2020 Day 2: Putting people at the center of AI development, *News.samsung.com*, www.news.samsung.com/global/samsung-ai-forum-2020-day-2-putting-people-at-the-center-of-ai-development (archived at https://perma.cc/95T3-4WKW)

Speiser, F (2020) Council Post: The times, they are a-changin': How AI can create a happier, more productive workforce, *Forbes*, www.forbes.com/sites/forbestechcouncil/2021/12/29/the-times-they-are-a-changin-how-ai-can-create-a-happier-more-productive-workforce/?sh=5bdca34d7193 (archived at https://perma.cc/A8BM-NC47)

Tharoor, I (2021) The world in 2030 may be worse than in 2020, *The Washington Post*, www.washingtonpost.com/world/2021/01/04/2020-what-expect-next-ten-years/ (archived at https://perma.cc/4X8T-2EFX)

Toews, R (2020) The Next Generation of Artificial Intelligence, *Forbes*, www.forbes.com/sites/robtoews/2020/10/12/the-next-generation-of-artificial-intelligence/?sh=6c9b937559eb (archived at https://perma.cc/UX66-X46H)

Tzachor, A, Whittlestone, J, Sundaram, L and Ó hÉigeartaigh, S (2020) Artificial Intelligence in a Crisis Needs Ethics with Urgency, *Nature Machine Intelligence*, www.nature.com/articles/s42256-020-0195-0 (archived at https://perma.cc/UE2E-5TVA)

United Nations (2015) UN Projects World Population to Reach 8.5 Billion by 2030, Driven by Growth in Developing Countries, *UN News*, www.news.un.org/en/story/2015/07/505352-un-projects-world-population-reach-85-billion-2030-driven-growth-developing#:~:text=The%20world's%20population%20is%20projected,around%2035%20years%20from%20now%2C (archived at https://perma.cc/LL3B-6YVH)

Waters, R (2020)'Regulation Can Get It Wrong': Google's Sundar Pichai on AI and antitrust, *Financial Times*, www.ft.com/content/9debcf65-7556-4247-8abb-1d165391343f (archived at https://perma.cc/9T3H-WDHN)

INDEX

Note: page numbers in *italic* indicate figures or tables

Printed in the USA
CPSIA information can be obtained
at www.ICGtesting.com
LVHW070728090823
754618LV00017B/127